DAY LOAN

KEY TEXT

REFERENCE

VARIETIES

OF

ENGLISH

Studies in English Language

VARIETIES OF ENGLISH

AN INTRODUCTION TO THE STUDY OF LANGUAGE
Second Edition

Dennis Freeborn

with Peter French and David Langford

palgrave

First edition 1986
Reprinted 1986 (with corrections), 1987, 1988, 1989, 1990, 1991
Second edition 1993

Published by
PALGRAVE
Houndmills, Basingstoke, Hampshire RG21 6XS and
175 Fifth Avenue, New York, N.Y. 10010
Companies and representatives throughout the world

PALGRAVE is the new global academic imprint of
St. Martin's Press LLC Scholarly and Reference Division and
Palgrave Publishers Ltd (formerly Macmillan Press Ltd).

ISBN 13: 978–0–333–58917–5 paperback
ISBN 10: 0–333–58917–3 paperback
ISBN 13: 978–0–333–58916–8 hardback
ISBN 10: 0-333-58916-5 hardback

This book is printed on paper suitable for recycling and
made from fully managed and sustained forest sources.

A catalogue record for this book is available
from the British Library.

12 11 10
06 05

Printed and bound in Great Britain by
Creative Print & Design (Wales), Ebbw Vale

Contents

Contents of the cassette tape

The *Varieties of English* cassette tape is essential for a proper study of the transcriptions of spoken English. The following list of contents provides reference to the first and second editions of this book. (The cassette tape is available from your bookseller: ISBN 0–333–40670–2.)

Symbols

Words or phrases quoted as linguistic examples are printed in *italics*.

Written English

A symbol in caret brackets, e.g. <d>, refers to its use as a letter in written English. The symbol ∅ indicates a deleted element.

Transcribing spoken English

The symbols of the International Phonetic Alphabet (IPA) are used to refer to the spoken sounds of English (see chapter 4, section 4.4.1).

(i)   A symbol in **diagonal brackets**, e.g. /œ/, /ŋ/, /ʤ/, refers to a member of the set of contrastive vowel or consonant sounds (**phonemes**) in spoken English, but without specifying its pronunciation in any particular context.

For example, there are references to 'the sound /r/' in chapters 4 and 5 , but this 'sound' is pronounced, or 'realised', differently in the various dialectal accents of English – as [ɹ] in RP and other accents, as [r] in parts of Scotland, and as [ʀ] in parts of Northumberland. Clearly, it is necessary to have heard and to know these pronunciations of 'the sound /r/' if the IPA symbols are to make sense.

(ii)   A symbol in **square brackets,** therefore, eg [ɔ], [ð], [ɹ], refers to the actual pronunciation of sounds (**phones**).

Note to teachers and lecturers

This book does not use the word *phoneme* in discussing spoken English, although the term is fundamental in the study of phonology in linguistics. Many students do not find the theory of the phoneme easy to grasp at first, and in the brief introductory survey of aspects of spoken English in chapters 4–6, it was thought better to establish an uncomplicated approach to pronunciation, even though it avoids some problems. The word *phoneme* refers to an abstract concept, not to an actual sound.

This should not deter teachers from introducing the concept and using the term *phoneme* if they wish, especially if they are teaching the phonology of English as part of a wider syllabus in the study of the language.

Transcribing conversation

For the conventional symbols used in conversation analysis, see chapter 5, section 5.2: Making a transcription.

Acknowledgements

The author and publishers wish to thank the following for permission to use copyright material:

The British Broadcasting Corporation for extracts from an interview between Margaret Thatcher and David Dimbleby, *Panorama*, 17 February 1986;

Carcanet Press Ltd. for 'Poem' from *Collected Poems* by William Carlos Williams;

David L. Cordiner, Dr E. S. Leedham-Green and L. B. Wheatley for letters to *The Times*, June 1978;

Faber and Faber Ltd. for 'Cut Grass' from *High Windows* by Philip Larkin;

The Guardian for material from their 15 July 1991 and 5 August 1986 issues;

The Independent for extracts from 'I couldn't be a racist, could I?' by Angela Lambert, 30 November 1991, 'Faith and reason' by Revd Dr Brian Castle, 30 November 1991, and 'Inner city task force get black leaders', 3 July 1987;

John Mitchell, Jim Sandhu, L. A. Walters for letters to *The Guardian*, April 1986, Ged Taylor, June 1988, and Deborah Turner, 15 July 1991;

NALGO for extracts from the leaflet *Watch your Language! Non-sexist Language: a Guide for NALGO members*, 1987;

Pravda for 'Police "victory" over hippies', 19 June 1986;

The Spastics Society for *What the Papers Say and Don't Say about Disability* by Steve Smith and Antoinette Jordon;

Syndication International Ltd. for 'So where does he go now?', *Daily Mirror*, 10 June 1986 and 'No hippy ending then' by George Gale, *Sunday Mirror*, 8 June 1986;

Times Newspapers Ltd. for Times Diary article, 'Heresy', June 1978, and extracts from 'Jury clear man who used word "nigger"', *The Times*, 7 January 1978;

Volkswagen for advertisement, *Guardian*, 10 March 1992.

Every effort has been made to trace all the copyright holders, but if any have been inadvertently overlooked the publishers will be pleased to make the necessary arrangement at the first opportunity.

Introduction to the second edition

This second edition is a complete revision and enlargement of the first, with additional texts, commentaries and chapters. Since the publication of the first edition in 1986, two significant developments have taken place in schools in the field of English Language teaching – firstly the growing popularity of two English Language A-level syllabuses, and secondly the introduction of the National Curriculum, in which the study of the English language is an essential part of the curriculum for English, based on the *Report of the Committee of Enquiry into the Teaching of English Language* 1988 (the Kingman Report). The contents of this book are relevant to both developments.

The purpose of *Varieties of English* is to demonstrate how the formal academic study of language, linguistics and its associated disciplines, can be applied to written and spoken English in order to describe styles and varieties of language use precisely and accurately. The approach is **empirical**, that is, 'based or acting upon observation or experiment'.

Each text provides a distinctive sample of English in use. The descriptive commentaries show how a linguistic study can help to identify those features of a text that make it distinctive. The studies are not primarily concerned with evaluating the texts, to say whether they are good or bad of their kind, but will form a sound basis for critical discrimination where this is appropriate.

Chapter 1 looks at people's beliefs about, and attitudes to, good or correct English. Chapters 2–4 discuss how English has changed in time over 1000 years and more, and how its vocabulary, structure and pronunciation vary according to geographical region and social class. Chapter 5 examines the differences between spoken and written English – that is, variations in the medium which we use to communicate with other people in the English language. Chapter 6 gives examples of the successive varieties of children's speech before they use, more or less, the English of their parents and other adults.

Chapters 7 and 8 (expanded from chapter 7 in the first edition) present some familiar varieties of spoken English. Chapters 9 and 10 (from former chapter 8) contain examples of written English that are associated with specific functions, 'the language of ...'. Chapter 9 focuses exclusively on news reporting in the press, and shows that an explicit understanding of how choices of vocabulary and grammar contribute to the making of meanings can more readily detect 'selective perception' and biased reporting. Chapter 10 is concerned with style in both literary and non-literary texts. Styles of speech or writing change to suit the occasion, the people addressed and the topic under discussion; studying these examples of different styles of written English should help you to be much more aware of how you adopt an appropriate one.

Chapter 11 (formerly part of chapter 9 in the first edition) applies some linguistic concepts to the study and appreciation of verse. Chapter 12 is new, and provides near-contemporary data on 'politically correct language', a controversial issue but one which any serious student of language must consider.

In order to demonstrate this methodical approach to the description of style in sufficient detail, the number of topics has had to be restricted. There are many more varieties of English than those discussed in this book, but a similar process of analysis and description to that demonstrated here can be used on any other variety.

How to use the book

The chapters are subdivided into topics, and give activities which should be discussed and worked before going on to examine the descriptive commentaries that follow. The commentaries are sometimes detailed, and are intended to teach important basic concepts about the language.

Some topics include further texts and activities without commentary, but in the restricted space of a single textbook, it is not possible to include many texts for additional study. Teachers and lecturers will be able to provide their own follow-up work, or make use of other books in this series.

It is not essential to follow the order of the chapters consecutively. Some teachers may prefer to select or to begin, for example, with chapter 5 on spoken and written English, rather than with chapter 1 on attitudes to good English.

The linguistic features that are described arise in an *ad hoc* way from the nature and style of each individual text. The book does not, therefore, cover all aspects of the sound and sentence patterns of English, since some may not appear in the selected texts and others, on the other hand, occur more than once. When the linguistic features are identified, they are related to the meaning and function of the texts. It is hoped that teachers and lecturers will find the texts useful for other topics in English teaching which are either not mentioned in the commentaries, or only referred to in passing.

Teachers and lecturers must decide for themselves how to relate this study of varieties of English to the necessary understanding of the phonology and grammar of the language which makes it possible. Theory and practice may be taught concurrently, with the teacher using the texts to demonstrate in greater detail those aspects of the sound or sentence structure that arise from them. Alternatively, the texts may be studied after an introduction to the phonology and grammar of English has begun.

In chapters 4–6, students will need help from their teachers or lecturers in learning to transcribe the sounds of speech and to distinguish the features of dialectal accent and children's language. The activities provided are minimal, and limitations of space make it impossible to provide a more detailed, step by step approach to transcription. Chapter 4 is not in itself a complete introduction to the sound patterns of English, and presupposes additional teaching.

It is certain that only a limited understanding will be possible if the texts are studied without some model of language and its appropriate terminology being available to the student. The terminology used in this book is largely traditional and well established. Only those terms that are necessary for a satisfactory analysis or description are introduced.

Dennis Freeborn

1. Variety, change and the idea of correct English

1.1 Good English

You are reminded of the necessity for good English and orderly presentation in your answers.

This sentence appears on the front page of all the question papers of an A Level Examining Board. It presumes that you know what good English is, and that you could choose not to use it.

The same word *good* is applied to spoken English also. The following description of a man wanted by the police appeared in a provincial newspaper:

> A man with a cultured accent is being sought by police ... He wore a tattered brown trilby, grey shabby trousers, crepe-soled shoes and a dark coloured anorak. He carried a walking stick and spoke with a good accent, the police say.

Activity 1.1

(i)   Discuss what you think the examining board means by *good English*.

(ii) The *cultured, good accent* doesn't seem to fit with the rest of the description of the wanted man. Why is this? What would a reader of the newspaper understand by it, and how would he or she recognise it?

Commentary

The *good English* demanded by the examining board is a style of written English that is thought to be suitable for a formal occasion like an examination, but which is not easy to define except by saying what you must not do. We can take it for granted that legible **handwriting** is necessary, otherwise communication between writer and examiner would be difficult. Accurate **spelling** is also required – that is, conformity

1

to the conventional standard spellings which can be found in dictionaries, together with the acceptable **punctuation** of sentences, which is closely linked to correct **grammar** – the right order and relationship of words, phrases and clauses in sentences. In choosing your words, you have to avoid **slang** and **colloquial phrases,** which are considered to be appropriate in spoken conversation and informal settings only, otherwise your writing will be called *bad English*.

Here is some evidence of what is thought to be *bad English*, taken from a newspaper report in February 1992. The headline was:

Bad English could cost pupils 5% of GCSE marks

The report then referred to writing in A level examinations also as 'increasingly shoddy', 'sloppy', and that 'candidates write very badly' and added, 'other exam boards are lamenting illegible and untidy handwriting, bad grammar, and inappropriate slang'.

These evaluative terms are impressionistic and subjective. The evidence for *bad English* quoted from an examiners' report was:

(i)   colloquialisms such as *up-front, laid-back, over the top, bullshit* and *stuck up and posh*;
(ii)   inability to spell *accommodation*;
(iii) use of *would of* and *could of* instead of *would have* and *could have*.

The *good accent* of the wanted man is even more difficult to define in linguistic terms. It is the accent which has in the past been called *the Queen's English, public school English, upper-class English, educated English* or *BBC English,* The wanted man's accent was described in the newspaper as *cultured*. Informally, those who don't speak it might have called it *posh*. It is associated with a particular social class in England (not Scotland, Wales or any other English-speaking nation). We do not normally associate this class with *tattered, shabby* clothing.

Our use of English always varies according to a number of factors, and has to be appropriate to the **occasion**, the **audience** and the **topic**. In speaking or writing English therefore, we have to make choices from:

(i)   our **vocabulary**, or store of words, (sometimes called **lexis**, so that we are said to make lexical choices);
(ii)   **grammar**, that is, the form that words take (word-structure or **morphology**), and how words are ordered into sentences, (sometimes called **syntax**);
(iii) **pronunciation** in speech.

We have practically no choice in spelling in writing, because there is an accepted spelling recorded in dictionaries for every English word, without regard to variations in pronunciation.

The variety of English that people usually have in mind when they talk about *good English* is called **Standard English**, and is discussed in chapter 2. It has been accepted as the variety of written English against which other varieties are assessed. Some people speak Standard English as their normal dialect, and it is the variety you expect to hear on radio and television news, for example, and which you are expected to speak in school. You may hear people use the term *Standard English* when they are talking about the kind of pronunciation just described as a *good accent*, but it is better to use the term **Received Pronunciation** (RP) for this, and to distinguish pronunciation from the vocabulary and grammar of dialects and varieties. (This is explained in chapter 4.)

1.2   A Letter to the Editor

The following text introduces you to a point of view towards English and its use that is typical of men and women who are certain in their minds that they know what *good English* is. All newspapers publish letters to the editor, written by readers who have something they want to say and would like to see in print. Sometimes a letter will start off a series of other letters in reply, and public debate then takes place. The subject may be a serious contemporary political or social topic, or a not so serious comment on something that has caught the reader's fancy. One subject has always been good for a lot of heated argument – the English language and how it is written or spoken. The letter to *The Times* that is printed below began a series in which twenty-one other letters in reply were printed, some supporting and some attacking the original by J. R. Colville (later Lord Colville).

Activity 1.2

Read the letter and make your own response to what it says, either agreeing or disagreeing. Examine the argument carefully. Do this before you go on to read the detailed commentary which follows.

The Times
LETTERS TO THE EDITOR

Correct English

From Mr J. R. Colville
Sir, I hope you will lead a crusade, before it is too late, to stop what Professor Henry Higgins calls "the cold blooded murder of the English tongue". 5
It is not merely a question of pronunciation, which is to some extent regional and which changes with every generation, painful though it be to hear 10 BBC speakers describe things as formídable, compárable, laméntable, or even, the other day, memorable. Contróversy and primárily are particularly vile. 15 However, the Professor's and my main objection is to the mushroom growth of trans-atlantic grammatical errors and, in particular, to the misuse of 20 transitive verbs.

It would be a pleasure to meet you and, no doubt, profitable to consult you on a number of matters. On the other hand to 25 meet with you, or to consult with you, would be distasteful to us. The newspapers, including The Times, are increasingly guilty of these enormities, and 30 on June 12 a formal motion in the House of Commons about Maplin descended to the depth of demanding that there should be a "duty to consult with 35 certain statutory bodies".

Professor Higgins and I also deprecate the infiltration of

German constructions into our language. This is doubtless due 40 to too literal translation of German into English by the early inhabitants of Illinois. "Hopefully it is going to be a fine day" translates back well 45 into German; but it is lámentable English. Amongst the other adverbial aberrations threatening us, the Professor and I, who were brought up to 50 believe that short words of Anglo-Saxon origin are (except when obscene) preferable to long words of Latin origin, strongly object to the sub- 55 stitution of "presently" (which used to mean "soon") for "now". All this, Sir, is but the tip of a large German-American iceberg which, we fear, will presently 60 become uncontrollable.

I am, Sir, your obedient servant,

J. R. COLVILLE

Notes

Professor Henry Higgins is a character in Bernard Shaw's *Pygmalion*, which was adapted as the musical *My Fair Lady*. He is a professor of phonetics.

Maplin refers to a place which was the subject of an enquiry into the siting of another airport for London.

Commentary

First, identify accurately what Lord Colville objects to in other people's English usage:

(i) *Pronunciation*
He finds the placing of **primary stress** on the second syllable of four-syllable words painful, that is, he doesn't like to hear:

formídable	compárable	laméntable
memórable	contróversy	primárily

You can infer that stress on the first syllable is his own choice, as he later writes *lámentable*.

fórmidable	cómparable	lámentable
mémorable	cóntroversy	prímarily

Try saying them aloud and decide which patterns of stress you usually use. Do different pronunciations cause confusion or loss of meaning?

(ii) *'Transatlantic grammatical errors'*
That is, features of English grammar which are thought to be typical of American usage.
(a) *'the misuse of transitive verbs'*   Verbs (V) are **transitive** when they are followed by a **direct object** (DO):

	V	DO
It would be a pleasure to	meet	you.

4

<table>
<tr><td></td><td>V</td><td>DO</td></tr>
<tr><td>It would be profitable to</td><td>consult</td><td>you</td></tr>
</table>

Lord Colville finds distasteful the form *meet with you* and *consult with you*.

Meet with and *consult with* are two examples only from a very large number of similar constructions which have been used for centuries, especially in informal spoken English, and which are still growing in number. They consist of a verb with an adverb and/or a preposition (sometimes called *phrasal verbs* and *prepositional verbs*) which together make a single lexical unit in meaning. For example:

I'll **come over** tomorrow.	verb + adverb
She **caught up** the child and ran.	verb + adverb (+ object)
The dog **came at** me viciously.	verb + preposition
The accident **put** him **off** driving.	verb + preposition (+ object)
The water **came up to** her waist.	verb + adverb + prepostion
Don't **take** it **out on** me!	verb + adverb + prepositiom (+ object)

Many new forms do come from across the Atlantic, but the term *Americanism* tends to be used against many other things and ideas that originate over there, and which people dislike or distrust.

Such new combinations of common, ordinary verbs and adverbs or prepositions often supply new meanings. Try discussing with others what *to consult with* means. Is it different from *to consult*? If so, is it a useful distinction and therefore good English?

A look into the *Oxford English Dictionary* confirms that the form *meet with* is recorded at least as early as 1275, and so has a good pedigree. The verb *consult with* had appeared by 1548.

(b) *'the infiltration of German constructions'*   Lord Colville's case is that the German immigrants to the USA who settled in Illinois have introduced a German construction into English by translating word for word from a German sentence beginning *Hoffentlich...*, *Hopefully....* This use of *hopefully* is similar to our use of a large set of words which are a type of **sentence adverbial** called **disjuncts**. They function like compressed sentences, and express a speaker's attitude to what he or she is saying:

Naturally I'll take you to the station.	Basically it's a matter of prejudice.
Obviously she can't come.	Inevitably they take a lot of persuading.
Possibly he'll make it tomorrow.	Fortunately, no one else bothers.

It is possible, if unusual, to use the same adverb twice in the same sentence, as in *Clearly, she speaks very clearly for a young child*, meaning *It is clear to me that...* So the use of *hopefully* to mean something like *I hope that...* may be a relatively recent usage, but it conforms to a well-established use of adverbs, and it is difficult to understand what objection there can be to it.

The most amusing letter published in the series that followed was from a correspondent in Germany, who questioned the argument about the infiltration of German constructions into English simply by writing a letter which was a literal word-for-word translation of the German:

Sir, It was me a small Bite surprising, the Letter of the Lord J. R. Colville, in your Edition of the 27. June this Year's to read, in which it says, that the english Speech to the "Infiltration of german Constructions", owing to the "too literal Translation" out of German onto English from "the early Inhabitants of Illinois", succumbs.

Although it me unknown is, how these Persons of the Past spake, can i, as Resident the modern Germany's, thereto attest, that the english Speech most chiefly the littlest Resemblance with the Structure of the German Speech of the present has. Hopefully attests this Letter self that fact.

I might thereto also say, the Meaning of the Lord Colville, that there the Danger gives, socalled "german Constructions" onto the English make "the Tip of a german-american Iceberg, which ... presently ... uncontrollable" be-come will, a great Unsense is. Since when, so how my german Friends say would, is an Iceberg controllable? Perhaps means he that, the Growth the Iceberg's uncontrollable become would, if we not foresighted are. That can i also not believe, if i it to say dare.

With the best Compliments,
DAN VAN DER VAT
Bonn

English and German are **cognate** languages, that is, they both originally developed from a common source, which linguists call West Germanic, but their development over the past 1000 years and more shows them changing in different ways under different historical circumstances. Is Lord Colville's argument from the use of *hopefully* sufficient to support his claim about the influence of German-American?

(c) *'other adverbial aberrations'*   Lord Colville states that the adverb *now* (a short word of Anglo-Saxon origin), is preferable to the recent substitution of *presently* (a longer word of Latin origin), which used to mean *soon*.

To refer to a dictionary to discover a present-day meaning of a word cannot be conclusive. Dictionaries are out of date as soon as they are printed, because language is in a constant state of change. You can, however, rely on dictionaries for past meanings, and for the origins of words. The *Concise Oxford Dictionary* of 1976 gives the origin of *presently* as from *present* + *-ly*, and of *present* as from Middle English, which took it from Old French, a language directly descended from Latin. The Old English (Anglo-Saxon) word *nu*, meaning *now*, itself came originally from the Latin *nunc*. So to prefer *now* to *presently* on the grounds of its origins is not convincing if you take the word's source back far enough.

But is the meaning of *presently* for *now* a new sense? The *Oxford English Dictionary* tells us that it has had this meaning since the fifteenth century, and has retained it in dialects and in Scottish English continuously since that time. It came to mean *soon* in literary English only in the seventeenth century. If its use to mean *now* has come from the United States, then it appears to be re-establishing its *original* meaning.

In addition, if you look up the meaning of the Old English word *sona*, from which *soon* has derived, you find that it formerly meant *at once, immediately*. So clearly there is no absolute 'correct meaning' of this set of words, *now, soon, presently* except the one agreed on by speakers of English in a particular place, and at a particular time. *Soon* and *presently* in particular have fluctuated in meaning continuously. Changes of meaning overlap in time, so you will often find older people disagreeing with the younger generation over the meaning and use of words.

It is always something of a shock to hear words used in an unfamiliar way, but we should not assume that the speaker or writer is wrong and that we are right, or even that the usage is new.

Activity 1.3

A variety of opinions about language use are put forward in the following extracts from letters published in *The Times* in response to Lord Colville's first letter.

(i)   Discuss the particular feature of language use which is raised in each letter, and say whether the writer supports or opposes Lord Colville's point of view. (Remember that a writer may be ironic – that is, she/he may give an opinion whose literal meaning the reader is intended to interpret differently.)

(ii) What is your opinion about the points put forward?

1   Sir, Mr Colville's letter is welcome, and the spirit which inspired it praiseworthy. The examples which he deplores are, almost without exception, illustrative of what is "too long and melancholy a Mischance to relate presently" (OED 1697).

It is, however, a recognized fact that a number of linguistic imports – notably from America – are healthily corrective. Mr Colville would have done well, before putting stamp to envelope, to reflect upon Locke's warning that "it should not be done presently, lest Passion [and inaccuracy] mingle with it".

2   Sir, I have much sympathy with Mr Colville in his objection to the use of the expression "meet with", which is both clumsy and un-necessary, but it can hardly be described as a modern usage, because it has the respectable authority of Jane Austen, who uses it fairly often.

3   Sir, It is a pity that Mr J R Colville in his excellent letter on correct English said of the infiltration of German constructions that it was "doubtless due to too literal translation of German into English". Nothing, it seems to me, was due or owed or required. Was it not *because of*?

4   Sir, "The captain advises that we shall be airborne momentarily" is a new piece of frightening illiteracy which now attends preparations for take-off. Hopefully the captain does not mean what he says.

5   Sir, There is ample room in English for the construction *consult with*, especially in Government statements. *Consult + NOUN PHRASE* has an unwanted implication of def-

erence to authority; and *confer with* (apart from being a lamentable borrowing from trans-Channel Latin) does not make it clear that specialist information and opinion is being sought.

As for the poor Americans: according to the OED, *consult with*, meaning "to take counsel with, to seek advice from" is recorded in 1548. In those days, you could even consult with *books* (1618). This is but one example of an "Americanism" which is in fact the older form; another is that American English retains the seventeenth century English necessáry, adversáry, and monetáry, which we British have since changed.

6   Sir, I sympathize with Mr Colville's concern over the import of some American pronunciations (I detest harássment), but more worrying is the tendency to use "anticipate" as a synonym for "expect" and to use "infer" to mean both "infer" and "imply". In each case there is a danger of misunderstanding. ...

Finally, I was sorry to note in the first sentence of the penultimate paragraph of Mr Colville's letter the implication that he and Professor Higgins are adverbial aberrations! Clearly mistakes in sentence construction and usage of words are more dangerous since they may lead to a breakdown in communication.

The correspondence ended with a statement by one of the newspaper's regular columnists:

I can no longer restrain myself from commenting on the correspondence in our columns about correct English. The very term "correct English" seems to me incorrect. Language is not static but a pliable tool for communication. English which communicates well and is easily understood is good English, that which does not is bad English.

Grammatical precedents (they are not rules) should be followed when they aid clear communication, as they usually do. There is no harm in ignoring them if there is no resulting loss of clarity. I know those inquisitorial folk who write testily about my own departures from Fowler will regard that as a heresy, but there it is.

Activity 1.4

Write your own Letter to the Editor, either in reply to Lord Colville's letter, or raising other matters concerning the use of English.

Activity 1.5

Consult (or consult with?) a dictionary and find out how the following words have changed meaning since they were first recorded in written English:

meat	deer	lord	lady	manufacture
sad	prove	starve	fowl	spill

Here are quotations of older English sentences containing some of the words, taken from the *Oxford English Dictionary*:

(i)   Thy *mete* shall be mylke, honye, & wyne. (1440)
(ii)   Lamb iss soffte and stille *deor*. (c. 1200)
(iii) Settl'd in his face I see *Sad* resolution and secure. (1667 Milton)
(iv)   *Prove* all things: hold fast that which is good. (1611 Bible)
(v)   Here children *sterven* for cold. (1381)
(vi)   To defend them from Eagles and other ravening *Fowls*. (1607)

Activity 1.6

Read the following letter to a newspaper editor about language use, and discuss how you would answer it.

Dear Sir,

What is (or perhaps is it now to be "are"?) the BBC coming to when one of "their" announcers makes the amazing statement: "Here are the Brodsky Quartet".

How can we mere mortals speak Queen's English if the BBC acclimatises us to such bad grammar made truly ludicrous by being spoken with such refinement and articulation?

1.3   An Acceptability Test

1.3.1   *Attitudes to English usage in the past*

About a hundred years ago, a book was published for 'pupil teachers' called *A Manual of Our Mother Tongue*, written by H. Marmaduke Hewitt, MA, LL.M. The subject called 'English' was taught differently at that time, and it included the study of grammar, which was intended to teach the *correct* way to speak and write. This is called a **prescriptive grammar**. The English that was taught was Standard English, though it was not usually referred to by that name, because other forms of English were regarded as incorrect or corrupt variants of proper English.

A favourite way of trying to teach good English was to list the things that you should *not* write or say. This way of trying to teach good English is called **proscriptive**, because it *proscribes* or forbids you to say or write certain expressions. *A Manual of Our Mother Tongue* contains a list called 'A Collection of Examples of Bad Grammar', and claims,

> *The correction of errors is a useful exercise. It awakens and keeps alive the critical faculty, and serves to impress the rules of grammar more firmly upon the memory. All, or nearly all, the principal points in regard to which it is possible to go wrong are exemplified in this collection.*

A modern reference grammar, like *A Comprehensive Grammar of the English Language* (1985), is a **descriptive grammar**, not a prescriptive grammar, and takes its examples from authentic speech and writing which was tape-recorded and collected in the 1960s. *A Manual of Our Mother Tongue* is partly descriptive, but at the same time prescriptive and proscriptive in its claim to show its readers what 'Bad Grammar' is like. It assumes that there is one correct form of the English language. A few of the examples of Bad Grammar are taken from literature, and include quotations from Dickens, Shakespeare and Milton. Here are some of the 173 examples from the collection.

1. Leave Nell and I to toil and work. (Dickens)
2. How sweet the moonlight sleeps upon this bank! (Shakespeare)
3. He would have spoke. (Milton)
4. He parts his hair in the centre.
5. Homer is remarkably concise, which renders him lively and agreeable.
6. Who are you speaking of?
7. This is quite different to that.
8. What sort of a writer is he?
9. I have business in London, and will not be back for a fortnight.
10. 'The boy stood on the burning deck,
    Whence all but he had fled.' (Hemans)

Activity 1.7

Say what you think the correct version of these ten sentences was supposed to be.

The belief that we should all speak and write good English, but that many of us don't or can't or won't, is still widespread. There is a lot of prejudice about forms of speech, which is related to social class distinctions as much as to regional variation. The attitude of the late nineteenth century can be seen in this passage from *A Manual of Our Mother Tongue*:

> *There are in Great Britain five principal dialects. Distinct and separate errors of pronunciation are peculiar to each dialect, beside which one dialect often contains some of the peculiarities of another.*

The author then asks the reader's pardon for 'the insertion of an anecdote'. He refers to a railway porter's pronunciation of 'Change here for Selby an Ool', and says:

> *It created some little amusement among the passengers from the South. One little man, looking around the carriage with a complacent smile and an air of benevolent superiority, explained to his fellow-travellers, "'E means 'Ull."*

The implied superiority of the author and passengers from the South is clear. Everybody knew that it was wrong to drop your aitches, and that the pronunciation of *Hull* in the North was an amusing peculiarity of the natives, and not good English.

1.3.2 *Attitudes to English usage today*

It is an interesting project to test people's reactions to different forms of language, and to see whether Marmaduke Hewitt's proscriptive attitudes to usage are still held, and what they are.

The following sentences contain a miscellaneous collection of forms that are used, most of them being *authentic*, that is, they can be heard or read in present-day English. A few of them exemplify the 'bad grammar' that we are still told to avoid by some people.

Activity 1.8 ───────────────────────

Test your own reaction to the sentences as honestly as you can, before going on to read the commentary. If you find one wrong, unacceptable, awkward or otherwise odd, try to say why, as precisely as you can. If you think a sentence to be normal or acceptable, don't try to find something wrong with it.

Remember that what you say, what you think you say, and what you think you ought to say, may be different. When you have thought about the sentences, or discussed them, you can try them out on others as a piece of linguistic field work (see Activity 1.9).

Acceptability Test

1. I aren't/an't bothered. *[nb The spelling* aren't *is misleading, because the negative form derives from* I am, *not* I are.]
   or I ain't bothered.
   or I amn't bothered etc. *or any other spoken variant that is **not** I'm not bothered*
2. I'm right, aren't I?
3. We've got to finish the job by next week or we'll be getting a bad reputation.
4. Jane met up with Bill in London.
5. He failed to completely finish the examination but got good marks in spite of that.
6. He's older than me, but I'm a good three inches taller.
7. Don't you bother yourself. Let he and I do it – we can manage between us.
8. That window's been broken for six weeks, but he won't do nothing about it.
9. That's a funny looking gadget! What's it for?
10. He didn't turn up on time and I was sat there waiting for half an hour. I felt a right fool.

11.   Mary was elected chairperson of the Parish Council.
12.   I can't see you while four o'clock this afternoon.
13.   He omitted to lock his car door and found his radio and briefcase were missing when he got back.
14.   The two sisters are dead alike! You can't tell one from the other.
15.   Hopefully it's going to be a fine day, so let's take a picnic and go to the park.

Commentary

(*an explanation of the language features that the test is intended to question, with detailed analysis where appropriate*)

1   *I aren't/an't bothered. I ain't bothered. I amn't bothered*, etc.

One of the forms of the **contracted negative, present tense**, of the verb *be* is often taken as a **marker** of social class, and parents and teachers may tell you not to use *I aren't/ain't/amn't*. They are dialectal pronunciations, not normally used by Standard English speakers whose accent is RP. An explanation is interesting:

(a)   The full present tense, negative, of the verb *be* is:

   I am not/you are not/she is not/we are not/they are not

which is usually **reduced** in speech by either contracting the verb *am/are/is*:

   I'm not/you're not/he's not/we're not/they're not

or by contracting the word *not*:

   I ?/you aren't/it isn't/we aren't/they aren't

What form is used with *I am* (**first-person singular**), when the word *not* is reduced to *n't*? For RP and some other dialect speakers, there is a blank – they use *I'm not* only. Why? Probably because *I aren't/I ain't* is associated with 'vulgar' speech. If you want to talk correctly, you don't speak like common people. *I amn't* is commonly used in parts of Scotland, *I aren't* in parts of the Midlands and North, and *I ain't* in the South. There are many variant pronunciations. Some speakers also use *ain't* as a contraction of *have not*.

(b)   There is a change in the pronunciation of the vowel [æ] in some other verbs. The reduced negative of *cannot* is *can't*, [kæn] → [kɑnt]; similarly, *shall not* becomes *shan't* , [ʃæl] → [ʃɑnt]. By a similar rule of sound change, *am not* becomes *aren't*, [æm] → [ɑnt]. In each *verb + n't* the vowel [æ] becomes [ɑ]. But nobody regards *can't* and *shan't* as incorrect pronunciations, so why object to *an't*?

(c)   A third observation on the use of *I aren't/an't* is in the following comment on sentence 2.

2   *I'm right, aren't I?*

If *aren't I* in *I'm right, aren't I?* is generally acceptable, can there be any convincing reason for not using *I aren't*? It is often a shock for people who have just said that you mustn't use *I aren't*, to realise that this form of **tag question**, *aren't I?*, is the same phrase in question form. The explanation must be that it is a matter of familiarity and social judgement. *I ain't* and *I aren't* are associated with dialectal or lower-class speech by some people, while *aren't I?* is not.

3 *We've got to finish the job by next week or we'll be getting a bad reputation.*
Some say that you should avoid using the useful little words *get* or *have got to*, but everyone uses them, especially in informal speech and writing. It's a matter of style, not grammar.

4 *Jane met up with Bill in London.*
Some don't like verb constructions like *meet up with* – verb + adverb + preposition. Examples have been discussed in section 1.2. Try asking yourself and others whether *to meet up with* means (a) to meet by arrangement, or (b) to meet by chance. It is likely that you will get both answers, which suggests that the meaning hasn't yet been agreed and therefore that the combination is still new.

5 *He failed to completely finish the examination but got good marks in spite of that.*
The **'split infinitive'**. *To finish* is regarded as an indivisible lexical item, and is said to be 'split' by the adverb *completely*. Ask where *completely* ought to go if the sentence is not liked. If you put it after *failed*, the meaning is changed. The split infinitive was an invention of prescriptive grammarians, and continues to be the subject of argument. Some regard it as a marker of educated style, but it is a very dubious rule, for the following reasons:

(a) The **infinitive** of a verb is the **base form**, e.g. *see, run, write, be, laugh.*

(b) Sometimes it occurs in a sentence preceded by *to*, as in *She wants **to come,*** in which *to come* forms an **infinitive phrase**.

(c) Often the infinitive occurs on its own, without *to*, as in *She let him come, He can come.*

(d) The use of the single infinitive *come* or the infinitive phrase *to come* depends upon the preceding part of the construction, e.g. in conversation we would say, *Let him come, he wants to badly.*

(e) The words which are said to 'split' a to-infinitive are **adverbs**, e.g. *to **really** mean, to **totally** deny, to **vigorously** resist.* It is quite normal for this kind of adverb to precede a verb, for emphasis, e.g. *If you **really** mean it, He will **totally** deny it if you ask him, They will **vigorously** resist any opposition.* There seems little logic in denying this use in an infinitive phrase.

(f) The following sentence, in which the adverb *deliberately* precedes a verb, was adapted from a newspaper report. The construction uses the preposition *by*, and so the *-ing*-participle of the verb must be used – *by exposing*. No one would regard the construction as ungrammatical or unacceptable, even though the verb phrase is split by the adverb:

> They have breached the Geneva Convention **by deliberately exposing** prisoners of war to danger

(g) If the sentence is slightly altered so that the the infinitive phrase *to expose* must be used, the 'split infinitive' is produced:

> It was a breach of the Geneva Convention **to deliberately expose** prisoners of war to danger.

(h) Avoiding the 'split infinitive' produces the form actually used in the newspaper, in which the adverb precedes *to*:

> It was a breach of the Geneva Convention **deliberately to expose** prisoners of war to danger.

(i) Unfortunately, this form can sometimes produce **ambiguity** or double meaning in a sequence *verb + adverb + to + verb*. The following sentence is probably not ambiguous:

> The scheme **has failed conspicuously to meet** its targets.

because the sense makes it likely that *conspicuously* is intended to modify *failed*, not *meet*. The adverb *conspicuously* is in its normal position in a clause, following its verb – *The scheme has failed conspicuously*. But in the next sentence,

> My colleagues **try slowly to improve** this situation.

the meaning is not clear, because the colleagues could have been *trying slowly*, or else wanting the situation *to improve slowly*. In these examples, all from newspaper reporting in the early 1990s, the journalists are obeying their editors' rule not to 'split the infinitive', but with often unhappy results, for example:

> The poll tax **continues malevolently to distort** domestic politics.
> He faces action by his party for **failing publicly to support** the official candidate.
> And yet, when they seem **momentarily to fail** ...
> He **planned immediately to up** his control of the world's oil reserves.

This is a controversial topic, but if you understand the grammar of the 'split infinitive', then you can choose to observe the convention or not in your own writing. Everybody 'splits the infinitive' in speech.

6 *He's older than me, but I'm a good three inches taller.*
Should it be *than me* or *than I*? Some say that the phrase is a shortened form of *than I am*, so we should use *than I*. But *than*, part of the **comparative** construction *more/ -er ... than*, functions very much like a **preposition**, and prepositions in Standard English are followed by the object form of pronouns:

	give it to me	she sat by him	we looked at them
not	give it to I	she sat by he	we looked at they

7 *Don't you bother yourself. Let he and I do it – we can manage between us.*
The problem is the **coordinated** phrase *he and I*, which seems to function differently from its separate parts *he, I*.

Let him do it	*not*	Let he do it
Let me do it	*not*	Let I do it

therefore *Let him and me do it*. This is the grammatical explanation. Nevertheless, people say *Let he and I...* Does it sound politer than *him and me* or *me and him*?

8 *That window's been broken for six weeks, but he won't do nothing about it.*
The **double** or **multiple negative**, very common in almost every English dialect except Standard English, is discussed in chapter 3.

9 *That's a funny looking gadget! What's it for?*
At the end of the seventeenth century, a prescriptive grammatical rule was invented for written English that you should not end a sentence with a **preposition**, which in this sentence is *for*. This is an example of a wholly artificial prescription, which attempts to counter a common feature of English with a rule based upon Latin usage (the Latin *pre-* means *before, in front of*). The dilemma for anyone who wishes to conform to this rule is shown in sentence 9. Is it English to say, *'For what is it?'*

10 *He didn't turn up on time and I was sat there waiting for half an hour. I felt a right fool.*
Some will object to *I was sat*, claiming that this is the **passive** form of the **active** form *(Someone) sat me there*. It could be so, but not in this example, because the common sense interpretation is the same as the Standard English *I was sitting*. *I was sat*, and *I was stood*, (also *I were sat/ stood)* are dialectal forms, certainly Northern, in which *sat* and *stood* may be analysed as **adjectives**.

11 *Mary was elected chairperson of the Parish Council.*
Chairperson, Chairman, Chairwoman or *Chair*? The word *man* has traditionally been assigned two meanings: (a) *a human being,* or *the human race*, and (b) *an adult human male*. Meaning (a) includes male and female, and the argument for the retention of words like *chairman, postman, milkman*, is that the word functions like a **suffix**, *-man*, and is neutral in its assignment of **gender**.

The argument against is that the word/suffix *-man* inevitably implies male. The older word for someone who scrubbed floors and cleaned rooms was *charwoman*, because in English society men did not do that sort of work. Therefore the word *charman* does not appear in the *Oxford English Dictionary* (see further comments in section 11.3.3)

12 *I can't see you while four o'clock this afternoon.*
This dialectal use of *while* to mean *until* is discussed in chapter 3.

13 *He omitted to lock his car door and found his radio and briefcase were missing when he got back.*
Some people find *omitted to lock* unacceptable. The use of *omit* with an **infinitive complement** *(to lock)* is common in England, though not acceptable in the USA, where you can 'omit something', but not 'omit to do something'.

14 *The two sisters are dead alike! You can't tell one from the other.*
You will probably find objectors to *dead alike*. Grammatically, *dead* is here used as an **intensifier**, an adverb with the meaning *very/completely/exactly*, but some would regard it as informal, even slangy. On the other hand, there are other phrases in which *dead* has this kind of meaning, and which are listed in dictionaries as Standard English:

dead stop/level/loss/calm/faint/silence/against/reckoning/shot/ahead

If these are acceptable, why not *dead alike*?

15 *Hopefully it's going to be a fine day, so let's take a picnic and go to the park.*
The use of **hopefully** as a **sentence adverb** or **disjunct** has been discussed in section 1.2.

Answers to Activity 1.7

Here are the answers to the examples of 'Bad Grammar' from the Victorian grammar book *A Manual of Our Mother Tongue*, taken from the original under the heading 'Corrections of Bad Grammar'.

1.   Leave Nell and me to toil and work.
2.   How sweetly the moonlight sleeps upon this bank.
3.   He would have spoken.
4.   He parts his hair in the middle. (centre means point)
5.   Homer is remarkably concise, a characteristic which renders him lively and agreeable.
6.   Whom are you speaking of? or, Of whom are you speaking?
7.   This is quite different from that.
8.   What sort of writer is he? – (not 'a writer')
9.   I have business in London, and shall not be back for a fortnight.
10. 'The boy stood on the burning deck,
     Whence all but him had fled.'

Activity 1.9

(i)   Find different informants – that is, people who will give you their own responses to the sentences in the Acceptability Test. Your informants should be as different from each other as possible, in age, education, social background, occupation, both male and female, etc.

(ii)   Read the sentences to them. Ask them if there is anything that sounds wrong, and to explain as exactly as they can what is wrong. Tell them that this is not a test of their own use of English, and that if they find the sentences perfectly acceptable, they should say so.

(iii)   Get your informants talking about 'good English', and what they think about the language. Ask them if they themselves speak 'correct English'. If you can record your conversations (with the permission of your informants), you will find it far more revealing and helpful to study the recording, rather than relying on your memory of the interviews.

(iv)   See how differences in attitude relate to different kinds of informant.

Activity 1.10

List other usages of English which are controversial. Try to describe their linguistic features in relation to Standard English.

   (It is useful to keep newspaper cuttings on this subject, and to write down in a notebook examples you hear.)

Activity 1.11

(i)　Read the following extracts from a book published in 1864. They give us further evidence of confident prescriptive attitudes to the English language in the mid-nineteenth century. The author was the Dean of Canterbury, Henry Alford DD.

(ii)　Identify the features of speech or writing that he is talking about, the beliefs about language that underlie them, and say whether you agree or disagree with him.

(iii)　Look up the derivations of *vulgarism, deterioration, vitiated* and *legitimate,* and comment on quotation (d).

THE QUEEN'S ENGLISH
Stray Notes on Speaking and Spelling

(a)　An American friend of ours, after spending two or three days with us, ventured to tell us candidly that we 'all spoke with a strong English accent'.

(b)　There is an offensive vulgarism, most common in the Midland counties, but found more or less everywhere: giving what should be the sound of the *u* in certain words, as if it were *oo*: calling 'Tuesday', *Toosday*; 'duty', *dooty*. And this is not from incapacity to utter the sound; but it arises from defective education, or from gross carelessness.

(c)　Write good manly English.

(d)　The language, as known and read by thousands of Englishmen and English-women, is undergoing a sad and rapid process of deterioration. Its fine manly Saxon is getting diluted into long Latin words not carrying half the meaning. This is mainly owing to the vitiated and pretentious style which passes current in our newspapers.

(e)　*Desirability* is a terrible word. I found it the other day, I think, in a leading article in *The Times. Reliable* is hardly legitimate.

Activity 1.12

Read the following extract from a report on *The Teaching of English in England,* published in 1919. Is the distinction between 'English' and 'a dialect of English' a correct one?

(a)　The great difficulty of teachers in Elementary Schools in many districts is that they have to fight against the powerful influence of evil habits of speech contracted in home and street. The teachers' struggle is thus not with ignorance but with a perverted power.

(b)　The position of the English language in the world affords another argument for all English children being taught English as distinct from a dialect of English.

1.4   This is the six o'clock news – belt up!

If you ask the question, 'Who speaks good English?', you will be almost certain to find that most people will say either 'the Queen', or 'BBC announcers'. It was the policy of the BBC from its earliest days in the 1920s to employ as announcers only those who spoke what was considered, by those with authority in the BBC, to be the best English – the accent that (it was said) everyone would understand – **RP, Received Pronunciation**.

In England RP is the **prestige accent** (though not in other English-speaking countries). If you speak it, you may be judged differently from another person who doesn't, either better or worse, depending upon who is listening. It is a fact that our judgement of what a speaker says is influenced by his or her accent.

An experiment was set up in which a lecturer who could speak both RP and a marked regional accent gave the same lecture, several times, to a series of different audiences who did not know the real purpose of the experiment. Lectures spoken in RP were judged by a majority of listeners to be superior *in content* to those spoken in the regional accent. How you speak, therefore, (your accent), affects people's judgements of what you say (your meaning).

How might this affect our response to listening to the news on television or radio? Does broadcast news in England have to be read in RP? If the news were to be read by an announcer with a broad Glaswegian accent, would it be taken seriously? Tom Leonard, a Glasgow poet, wrote a poem about reading the news. *(The poem is read by Tom Leonard on the accompanying cassette tape section 1.)*

Activity 1.13 —————————————

(Answer the questions before reading the commentary.)

(i)   Rewrite the poem in Standard English prose, and discuss what has happened to the poem in the process.

(ii) What is Tom Leonard really saying?

This is thi
six a clock
news thi
man said n
thi reason   5
a talk wia
BBC accent
iz coz yi
widny wahnt
me ti talk   10
aboot thi
trooth wia
voice lik
wanna yoo

scruff. if   15
a toktaboot
thi trooth
wia voice
lik wanna yoo
scruff yi   20
widny thingk
it wuz troo.
jist wanna yoo
scruff tokn.
thirza right   25
way ti spell
ana right way
ti tok it. this
is me tokn yir
right way a   30
spellin. this
is ma trooth.
yooz doan no
thi trooth
yirseltz cawz   35
yi canny talk
right. this is
the six a clock
nyooz. belt up.

Commentary

The poem is spoken in a marked Glasgow accent by a newsreader. But newsreaders, even on Scottish regional programmes, don't sound like this, nor is the text what they might say. The poem makes us realise the attitude of superiority that Tom Leonard believes to belong to RP speakers. RP is one accent of many, but it is popularly judged to be better than others, to the extent that many people believe that RP is English spoken without an accent.

By inverting the relationship between present-day RP (a Southern English educated accent in its origins) and working-class Glaswegian Scottish, Tom Leonard jolts us into examining snobbish attitudes towards a Scottish urban accent. The poem could only have been the voice of a BBC newsreader if the past history of Scotland and England had been different, and if Glasgow were the capital of Great Britain. The Glasgow dialect would then have been Standard English, and RP would have been educated Glasgow Scots, because the centre of political and economic influence would have been in Glasgow, not London.

Prestige dialects and accents do not arise because of their beauty or linguistic superiority, but because those who originally speak them are influential, and others copy them.

During the 1939–45 war, the Yorkshire broadcaster Wilfred Pickles was employed to read the news in his Halifax accent, but the attempt to use his popularity as an entertainer to make the news more homely completely failed. *(Listen to section 2 of the cassette tape.)* There were many complaints. People 'couldn't believe the news' if it was read in a regional dialectal accent. 'If a toktaboot thi trooth lik wanna yoo scruff yi widny thingk it wuz troo.'

If, in addition, 'yooz doan no thi trooth yirseltz cawz yi canny talk right', it makes the possession of a prestige accent essential for *understanding the truth*, as well as for getting on in the world. Is this an argument to be taken seriously? (The historical development of Standard English is discussed in chapter 2, and dialectal accent and attitudes to pronunciation in chapter 4.)

1.5   Is there a language trap?

The debate about the use of Standard English and the status of dialectal English continues to arouse controversy, but sometimes there is misunderstanding on both sides of the debate about what the other means. Linguists have said, and continue to maintain, that 'all dialects of a language are rule-governed systems'. This is intended to imply that a dialect of English is just as consistent in the way its sentences are formed as is Standard English. It is not a debased form of Standard English which has been imperfectly learned.

In real life, however, it does matter what your accent is, and whether or not you speak or write Standard English, depending on where you are and who you are speaking or writing to. It has been claimed that some teachers have taken the statement about the 'equal validity' of the dialects too literally, and have failed to teach or insist upon the use of Standard English. On the other hand, parents have been known to object to English lessons in which the dialects were discussed and analysed, on the grounds that this was teaching 'bad English'.

The arguments become difficult to refute, because strong emotions are bound up with attitudes to what people believe to be 'good, correct English'. One object of this chapter 1 is to try to point towards an objective assessment of language use in contemporary society.

Activity 1.14 ⸻

(i)   Read and discuss the following extracts. (i) is from *Accent, Dialect and the School* by Professor Peter Trudgill, published in 1975, and (ii) is from *The Language Trap: Race, Class and the 'Standard English' Issue in British Schools*, by Professor John Honey, published in 1983.

(ii)   Discuss the practical consequences of using dialectal and non-standard English in situations where Standard English is expected.

NB   *These short extracts cannot properly summarise all the arguments put forward by either author. You should try to read more from the original texts.*

(i) From *Accent, Dialect and the School* by Professor Peter Trudgill:

There are no linguistic reasons for saying that any language is superior to any other. All languages, that is, are equally 'good'. There is no way of evaluating any language more favourably than any other. Linguists have found that all languages are complex systems which are equally valid as means of communication. ... They are also no different in their expressive   5
capabilities. ...

The fact that no one language is 'better' than any other is important for the role of language in education. This is because the same thing is equally true of different varieties of the same language. Just as there is no reason for arguing that Gaelic is superior to Chinese, so no English dialect can be   10
claimed to be linguistically superior or inferior to any other. All English dialects are equally complex, structured and valid linguistic systems.

(ii) From *The Language Trap: Race, Class and the 'Standard English' Issue in British Schools*, by Professor John Honey:

It is a serious matter that our educational system (and others) continue to turn out, as they do, an annual crop of total illiterates, and no less serious that from otherwise able pupils we produce students who are in some sense semi-literate. Yet the inability of our schools to turn out pupils with satisfactory standards of English is not simply due to the legacy of an   5
inappropriate English curriculum or to a shortage of appropriately qualified teachers. Another powerful factor has been at work, especially over the past decade, and its effect has been to undermine attempts by teachers to meet the demands of parents and employers that pupils should be able to speak and write 'good English'. This is the notion, propounded originally by a   10
group of specialists in linguistics, and widely influential among educationists and especially among teachers of English and those who train them, that for schools to foster one variety of English is contrary to the findings of the science of linguistics. For has that newly established discipline not demonstrated that all languages, and all varieties of any one   15
language, are equally good? Therefore, to emphasise any one variety, i.e. standard English, in preference to the dialect spoken in the pupil's home, is not only unjustifiable in scientific terms, but it does irreparable harm to the self-esteem of the child whose dialect is discriminated against.

2. Dialects and Standard English – the past

2.1 How the English language was brought to Britain

The English language was brought to the island Britannia in the first half of the fifth century AD by settlers called Angles from across the North Sea. Britannia was the Latin name for the island, which had been a colony of the Roman Empire since the conquest, which began in 43 AD. The inhabitants are referred to as Britons or Celts. When the Roman legions were withdrawn from Britannia early in the fifth century to help in the defence of the Empire, the Britons were left to defend themselves against attacks from the west and north (present-day Ireland and Scotland). The Angles were at first invited from across the North Sea to assist the Britons in defending the country, and were granted lands in the eastern part of the island,

> nevertheless, their real intention was to attack it. At first they engaged the enemy advancing from the north, and having defeated them, sent back news of their success to their homeland, adding that the country was fertile and the Britons cowardly. Whereupon a larger fleet quickly came over with a great body of warriors, which, when joined to the original forces, constituted an invincible army. These new-comers were from the three most formidable races of Germany, the Saxons, Angles, and Jutes.
>
> (from Bede's *History of the English Church and People*, translated by Leo Shirley-Price)

The invaders spoke dialects of a language family which scholars now call **West Germanic**; the Britons spoke dialects of **Celtic**. In time, the country became known as *Englalond* – Angle-land – and the language as *Englisc*. We now call the language of this early period, up to about 1100 or 1150, **Old English**. The Britons were called *Wealas* in Old English, which is the same as the modern English word *Welsh*. Many of them were driven westwards, to settle in Wales and Cornwall. Later on, there were migrations of Britons into France, to the northern parts known as Bretagne (or Brittany) and Normandy. Today Celtic languages are still spoken (for example Welsh, Scots Gaelic, Irish Gaelic and Breton), though there are hardly any words of Celtic in the English language.

Although we speak of Old English as a **language**, there was no single standard version of it. There were four distinct dialects:

- Northumbrian – spoken north of the river Humber,
- Mercian – in the Midlands from East Anglia across westwards to the Welsh border,
- Kentish – in the south-east; and
- West Saxon – in the south and south-west.

They are called dialects because they were mutually intelligible varieties of the same language. That is, you could talk with a speaker of another dialect and be understood, though mutual understanding could be difficult. There is evidence of this difficulty as late as the fourteenth century, when John of Trevisa wrote, in the southwestern dialect of **Middle English**:

Al the longage of the Norþumbres, and specialych at York, ys so scharp,
slyttyng and frotyng, and unschape, þat we Souþeron men may þat longage
unneþe undurstonde.
All the language of the Northumbrians, and especially at York, is so sharp,
piercing and grinding, and unformed, that we Southern men can that language
hardly understand.

The evidence for the different dialects comes from the surviving manuscripts of the period. When the same words are regularly spelt differently, we can assume that they were pronounced differently, because Old English was spelt more or less as it sounded.

The establishment of a **standard language** depends upon the kind of social and political organisation in a country which did not develop in England until the sixteenth century.

2.2 Britain before the English came

We rely for much of our knowledge of the early history of England on *The History of the English Church and People*, written in Latin by Bede and completed in 731 in the monastery of Jarrow, in Northumberland. To introduce you to some of the important historical events that were to affect the development of the Old English language, here are two extracts from Bede's *History*. The book has been translated from Latin into English at different later periods, so we can also illustrate, at the same time, changes in the language itself, by using four translations: (a) twentieth, (b) sixteenth, (c) fourteenth and (d) ninth century. The ninth-century Old English texts have word-for-word translations.

A description of 'Britannia', the Roman colony

(a) In old times, the country had twenty-eight noble cities and innumerable castles, all of which were guarded by walls, towers, and, barred gates.

(b) This Iland had in it sumtimes xxviii cities, beside an innumerable sort of castles whiche also wer well and strongly fensyd wyth walles, turrettes, gates, and bullwarkes.

(c)   The kyngdom of Bretayne was somtymes i-hight wiþ eiʒte and twenty noble citees, wiþ oute welle many castelles þat were wiþ walles, wiþ toures, wiþ ʒates, wiþ barres, stalworþliche i-buld.

(d)   Wæs þis ealond geo gewurþad mid þam æþelestum ceastrum, twega wana þrittigum, þa þe wæron mid weallum and torrum and geatum and þam trumestum locum getimbrade, butan oþrum læssan unrim ceastra.

Was this island once made splendid with the noblest cities, two less-than
thirty, which were with walls and towers and gates and the
firmest bars built, besides other lesser innumerable towns.

(*þa þe* was the relative pronoun *which, that*.)

The first inhabitants of Britain

(a)   The original inhabitants of the island were the Britons, from whom it takes its name, and who, according to tradition, crossed into Britain from Armorica, and occupied the southern parts.

(b)   At the first this land was inhabited of none other nation but only of the Brittanes, of whom it receiveth his name: which Britannes comyng out of Armorica (called now little Britany) as it is thought, chose unto them selves the sowth parte of this land.

(c)   Bretouns wonede first in þis ilond. þei come hider and took hir cours from Armorik, þat now is þe oþer Bretayne; þey helde long tyme þe souþ contrayes of þe ilond.

(d)   On fruman ærest wæron þysses ealondes bigengan Bryttes ane, fram þam hit naman onfeng. Is þæt sæd þæt hi comon fram Armoricano þære mægeþe on Breotone, and þa suþdælas þysses ealondes him gesæton and geahnodon.

In beginning first were of-this island's inhabitants Britons only, from them it
name received. Is it said that they came from Armorican the people into Britain,
and the southern-parts of-this island (for)-them(selves) settled and appropriated.

Commentary

The Old English extracts are in the West Saxon dialect. You will notice several words which are still in modern English, though their spelling, and often their pronunciation also, has changed:

ealond	(*island*)	timbr-	(*timber* = *build*)
þrittig	(*thirty*)	oþer	(*other*)
wær-	(*were*)	læs	(*less*)
weall	(*wall*)	ceaster	(*-caster, -chester*)
torr	(*tower*)	nama	(*name*)
geat	(*gate*)	suþ	(*south*)
loc	(*lock, bar*)	sett-	(*set down*)
sæd	(*said*)	fram	(*from*)

Activity 2.1

Compare the list with the way the words are spelt in the texts, and write them out with their endings, or **suffixes**, which have been omitted in the list.
You should find the following: *-um, -on, -an, -de, -on, -es, -as, -a, -e.*

These suffixes are essential in the grammar of Old English, and one of the most important changes in the language has been the gradual loss of almost all of them. Suffixes are also called **inflections**. Old English was a highly inflected language. Notice also the words translated by *the*: *þam, þære*; there are eight other forms for *the.*

Old English was written down using the Roman alphabet, but other useful letters were adopted to represent English sounds that did not occur in the pronunciation of Latin. Two of these letters, reproduced above, are <þ> ('thorn'), for which we now use <th>, and <æ> ('ash'), for which we now have to use <a>, and so can no longer distinguish in spelling between the vowels of *ash* and *father*, /æ/ and /ɑ/. Other Old English letters, not usually reproduced in modern printed versions, were <ʒ> ('yogh') for <g>, and <ð> ('eth'), an alternative letter for <þ>. Middle English writing introduced <g> and kept <ʒ>, to distinguish between two different sounds.

Other Old English words in the two extracts above have been lost. The reason for this will be clearer when you examine two later historical events which had profound effects on the language.

2.3   The Vikings

The Angles, Saxons and Jutes, over a period of two hundred years, had gradually occupied almost the whole of England, but after about three hundred years of settlement, with the country divided into seven kingdoms, Vikings from Scandinavia began a series of raids on the north and east of England, at first for plunder, and then for occupation and settlement. The events were recorded in the contemporary *Anglo-Saxon Chronicle*.

In the following extracts, the inflections are printed in bold type. Those that are suffixes are separated from the stem by a hyphen:

> dcclxxxvii Her com-**on** ærest III scip-**u** Norþmann-**a** of Hereþeland-**e**,
> and þa se geref-**a** þær to rad, and h-**i** wold-**e** drif-**an** to þes cyning-**es** tun-**e**,
> þ-**y** h-**e** nyst-**e** hwæt h-**i** wær-**on**, and h-**ine** man ofsloh þa. þ-**a** wær-**on**
> þ-**a** erest-**an** scip-**u** Denisc-**ra** mann-**a** þe Angelcynn-**es** land **ge**-soht-**on**.

> *AD 787 Here came first 3 ships of-Northmen from Herethaland*
> *and then the reeve there to rode, and them wished to-drive to the king's town,*
> *because he knew-not what they were, and him one slew then. Those were*
> *the first ships of-Danish men that English-people's land sought*

After a hundred years of intermittent warfare, the king of Wessex, Alfred, finally defeated the Vikings, but had to allow them to occupy the northern and eastern parts of England, which were known as the Danelaw.

dccclxxviii Her Ælfred cyning gefeaht wiþ eal-**ne** her-**e**, and h-**ine** geflym-**de**, and h-**im** æfter rad oþ þæt geweorc, and þær sæt xiiii niht, and þa seal-**de** se her-**e** h-**im** gisl-**as** and myccl-**e** aþ-**as**, þæt h-**i** of h-**is** ric-**e** wold-**on**, and h-**im** eac gehet-**on** þæt h-**eora** cyning fulwiht-**e** onf-**on** wol-**de**, and h-**i** þ-**æt** gelast-**on**.

AD 878 Here Alfred king fought against all (the) enemy & him put-to-flight, & him after rode to the fort, and there sat 14 nights, and then gave the enemy to-him hostages and great oaths, that they from his kingdom would (go) & him also promised that their king baptism receive would and they that performed.

Activity 2.2 ─────────────────────────────────

Compare the Old English texts with the word-for-word translations underneath. What differences in word-order are there between Old English and present-day English?

You can still hear something of the effects of the Viking settlement by listening to present-day northern dialects of English. The Vikings spoke dialects of a Scandinavian language, now called **Old Norse**, which was not so different from Old English that speakers of the two languages could not communicate with each other. Both languages were Germanic. Many of their words were similar. But the grammatical inflections were different, so that where Vikings and English lived near each other and had regular speech together, the suffixes tended to be left off.

This speeded up the loss of word-endings, which was taking place anyway in Old English because the inflections were unstressed syllables. But the Vikings also had words in Old Norse that did not have their Old English cognate equivalents, and many of these remained in Northern dialects. Some have in fact replaced Old English words, and have spread throughout Standard English and the other Southern dialects, for example:

they	sister	skin
them	call	sky
their	egg	skirt (*cf.* shirt)
kneel	leg	take

These words were all Old Norse. So the source of English dialects today, including Standard English, lies partly in the four dialects of Old English, and also in the blend of Old Norse dialects spoken by the Viking settlers in the Danelaw, which eventually merged with English.

2.4   The Norman Conquest

The second historical event of the greatest importance is probably known to everyone through the date – 1066. This was the conquest of England by William, Duke of Normandy. The Normans (= *Northmen*) came of Viking stock also, but after settling in northern France, they had adopted the French language. The dialect they spoke is known as Old Northern French.

mlxvi And þa hwile com Willelm eorl upp æt Hestingan, on Sancte Michæles
mæssedæg, and Harold com norþan, and him wiþ gefeaht ær þan þe his here
come eall, and þær he feoll, and Willelm þis land geeode and com to Westmynstre,
and Ealdred arcebiscop hine to cynge gehalgode.

*AD 1066 And meanwhile came William earl up at Hastings on Saint Michael's
mass-day, and Harold came from-the-north, & him with fought before his army
came all and there he fell, and William this land occupied & came to Westminster,
and Ealdred archbishop him as king consecrated.*

The effect on the English language was not to be fully felt for two hundred years or
more, but by the end of the fourteenth century, in the time of the poet Chaucer,
hundreds of words of French origin had been taken into the English of educated
people. Here is a short extract from Chaucer's *Canterbury Tales*, written in the
1390s. The words of French origin have been printed in italics.

> In *Flaundres* whilom was a *compaignye*
> Of yonge folk that *haunteden folye*,
> As *riot, hasard, stywes*, and *tavernes*,
> Where as with harpes, *lutes*, and *gyternes*,
> They *daunce* and *pleyen* at dees bothe day and nyght,
> And eten also and drynken over hir myght,
> Thurgh which they doon the devel *sacrifise*
> Withinne that develes temple, in cursed wise,
> By *superfluytee abhomynable*.

After 1066, authority in government, land-ownership and the Church was almost
completely given to French-speaking Normans. The writing of Old English was
much reduced, and when we look at the written evidence for the language from about
1150 to 1450 (**Middle English**), we find marked differences from Old English in
spelling, as well as changes in vocabulary, word-forms and grammar.

Once a spelling system is adopted and becomes standardised, writers ignore those
changes in pronunciation that always develop, firstly between different dialect
speakers, and secondly between one generation of speakers and another. This had
begun to happen before the Norman conquest. In the tenth and eleventh centuries,
West Saxon was becoming the standard written language. West Saxon spelling was
used in writing in the other dialect areas of England, and changes in the
pronunciation of West Saxon itself were not systematically recorded in the spelling.
This process was interrupted as a result of the Norman conquest. The Old English
tradition was lost, and French-speaking scribes, when writing English, tended to
write what they heard. As a result, we have plenty of evidence of the differences
between Middle English dialects.

Today we have a spelling system which has remained almost unchanged since the
middle of the eighteenth century, and which even then represented the pronunciation
of English at the end of the fourteenth century. This helps to explain why English
spelling seems so remote from its pronunciation. Pronunciation has changed a lot in
six hundred years, but the spelling has not kept up with it.

2.5   The establishment of Standard English

As the short extracts from Bede's *History* showed, the changes that have taken place in the English language can be demonstrated by examining the same texts in versions written down at different times. Here for example is the same text in two versions one hundred years apart in time. It is from John of Trevisa's account of the English language, firstly in his own English of about 1385, and then in a modernised version printed by William Caxton in 1482. The fourteenth century text has present-day punctuation; Caxton's has the original punctuation.

Activity 2.3

(i)   Examine the two texts in detail, and list the changes from fourteenth to fifteenth century English that you can see in (a) spelling, (b) word inflection and (c) grammar.
(ii) Write out the Caxton text in modern English, and describe the differences between the two versions.

(1) 14th century text (John of Trevisa)

(Note the use of both <3> and <g>. Which sound or sounds do they represent in this text?)

Also Englischmen, þey3 hy hadde fram þe bygynnyng þre maner speche, Souþeron, Norþeron, and Myddel speche (in þe myddel of þe lond), as hy come of þre maner people of germania, noþeles, by commyxstion and mellyng furst wiþ Danes and afterward wiþ Normans, in menye þe contray longage ys apeyred, and som useþ strange wlaffyng, chyteryng, harryng and garryng, grisbittyng.

[apeyred = impaired, spoiled; wlaffyng = stammering; chyteryng = chattering; harryng = snarling; garryng = grating; grisbittyng = grinding of teeth]

(2) 15th century text (William Caxton)

also englysshmen though they had fro the begynnyng thre maner speches Southern northern and myddel speche in the middel of the londe as they come of thre maner of people of Germania. Netheles by commyxtion and medlyng first with danes and afterward with normans In many thynges the countreye langage is appayred/ffor somme use straunge wlaffyng/chyteryng harryng garryng and grisbytyng /

Activity 2.4

(i)   Study the following list of the derivations of the words in the Caxton text.
(ii) Make a separate list of your own of the words that came from Old English, Old Norse, or French.
(iii) What is the proportion from each source? Do any particular kinds of word belong to one source?

(NB A short text like this will not necessarily provide an accurate guide to the proportions of OE, ON and OF words in the language as a whole.)

afterward	OE æaftanwearde	*langage*	OF langage
also	OE ealswa	*londe*	OE land
and	OE and	*maner*	OF maniere
appayred	OF empeirer	*many*	OE manig
as	OE alswa	*medlyng*	OF medler
begynnyng	OE beginnan	*middel*	OE middel
by	OE bi/be	*netheles*	OE næfre + þe + læs
chyteryng	ME ('*imitative*')	*normans*	OF Normans
come	OE cuman	*northern*	OE norþerne
commyxtion	Latin commixtio	*of*	OE of
countreye	OF cuntree	*people*	OF peuple
danes	ON danir	*somme*	OE sum
englysshmen	OE englisc + menn	*Southern*	OE suþerne
ffor	OE for	*speche*	OE spræc
first	OE fyrst	*straunge*	OF estrange
fro	OE fram	*the*	late OE þe
garryng	OE georran	*they*	ON ðeir
Germania	Latin	*though*	OE þoh
grisbytyng	OE gristbitung	*thre*	OE þry
had	OE hæfde	*thynges*	OE þingas
harryng	OE ('*echoic origin*')	*use (vb)*	OF user
in	OE in	*with*	OE wiþ
is	OE is	*wlaffyng*	OE wlaffian

Caxton's English, like Chaucer's a century before, was an educated London dialect, which became established during the sixteenth and seventeenth centuries as the written standard throughout the country, so that from this time we gradually cease to be aware of the spoken dialects of English.

Standard English today comes from this dialect, that of educated speakers from the area bounded by London, Oxford and Cambridge, which were the centres of political and economic power and of learning, and so the most influential. There have been some changes since, of course, but comparatively few. The following quotation from George Puttenham's *The Arte of English Poesie*, (1589), advising writers which forms of English to use, demonstrates how the prestige of London English led to its adoption as the standard:

> Ye shall therefore take the usuall speach of the Court, and that of London and the shires lying about London within lx. myles, and not much above.

The spelling system was not fully standardised until after the publication of Dr Samuel Johnson's *Dictionary* in the mid eighteenth century.

2.6 How to analyse an historical text

2.6.1 *Old English*

The Bible is an obvious source of study of English at different periods, because we have translations going back to the Old English of King Alfred's time in the late ninth century.

The short Old English texts in the preceding sections show that it would be very difficult to read ninth-century English without learning the language. The vocabulary, spelling and word forms are unfamiliar.

To show you a little more about the way inflections and other kinds of changes in word form conveyed meaning, here is the beginning of the parable of the Good Samaritan in West Saxon Old English of the eleventh century, with a short explanation:

> Sum man ferde fram Hierusalem to Hiericho, and becom on þa sceaþan, þa hine bereafodon, and tintregodon hine, and forleton him samcucene.

sum man	*some man* in the sense of *a certain man*.
ferde	the third-person singular, past tense, of the verb *feran, to go, journey*. The *-de* suffix became modern English *-ed*, the **regular past tense** ending = *(he) journeyed*.
becom	the third-person singular, past tense, of the verb *becuman, to meet with*, which is marked by the change of vowel from <u> to <o> = *(he) met with*. It is the same verb as *become/became* today, but has changed in pronunciation (and therefore in spelling), and in meaning.
þa sceaþan	*þa* is literally *those*, and the following *þa* means *who*. *sceaþan, thieves*, is the **plural** of the noun *sceaþa, a thief*.
hine	means *him*, the **object** of the verb.
bereafodon	the third-person plural, marked by *-on*, and the past tense, marked by *-od*, of the verb *bereafian*, (modern *bereave/bereft*), meaning *to deprive*; *(they) deprived (him of* ...). Notice the restricted meaning of the verb today.
tintregodon	the third-person plural and past tense of the verb *tintregian, to torture*.
forleton	the third-person plural and past tense of the verb *forlaetan, to abandon*. Notice the change of vowel to mark past tense in this verb, not the suffix *-od*.
samcucene	means *half-alive*. The **prefix** *sam-* is the Latin *semi-*. The suffix *-ne* shows that the word is in agreement with *hine = him*. *cucu* is another form of the word *cwic*, meaning *alive*. Again notice the change of meaning in modern English *quick* (same pronunciation, but different spelling). The word still meant *living* in the phrase *the quick and the dead* in the King James Bible of 1611.

2.6.2 *Middle English*

If we move on another three hundred years, to the late fourteenth century, we find that we can read the South Midland dialect of John Wyclif's Middle English translation as easily as we can read Chaucer's London dialect of the same period:

> A man cam doun fro Jerusalem in to Jerico, and fel among theues, and thei robbiden hym, and woundiden hym, and wente awai, and leften the man half alyue.

The only significant differences from modern English are the *-en* and *-iden* suffixes on the verbs, which are the same as the Old English *-on* and *-odon* inflections, but pronounced differently. The *en* suffix eventually disappeared completely, leaving just the *-ed* past tense suffix.

2.6.3 *Early Modern English and Modern English*

A detailed comparison of the complete parable in the 1611 translation (the *Authorised Version* of King James I) and in a modern version published in 1952, will show how a linguistic analysis can be used to discover facts about change at each language level: spelling, choice of vocabulary, word-forms and grammar.

Both versions are translated from the original Greek of the New Testament. English in the sixteenth and seventeenth centuries is called **Early Modern English**. There are still important differences between the language then and now, as you will know if you have studied any Shakespeare plays in detail.

Activity 2.5 ——————————————

Examine the spelling, the differences of vocabulary, and the structure of words and sentences in the two versions of the parable, and describe the differences between them.

(1) From the 1611 King James Bible

A certaine man went downe from Hierusalem to Jericho, and fel among theeues, which stripped him of his raiment, and wounded him, and departed, leauing him halfe dead. And by chaunce there came downe a certaine Priest that way, and when he saw him, he passed by on the other side. And likewise a Leuite, when hee   5 was at the place, came and looked on him, and passed by on the other side. But a certaine Samaritane as he iourneyed, came where he was; and when hee saw him, hee had compassion on him, and went to him, and bound vp his wounds, powring in oile and wine, and set him on his owne beast, and brought him to an   10 Inne, and took care of him. And on the morrow when he departed, hee tooke out two pence, and gaue them to the hoste, and saide vnto him, Take care of him, and whatsoeuer thou spendest more, when I come againe I will repay thee. Which now of these three, thinkest thou, was neighbour vnto him that fell   15 among theeues? And he said, He that shewed mercie on him. Then said Jesus vnto him, Goe, and doe thou likewise.

(2) From *The Four Gospels*, translated by E. V. Rieu

'A man going down from Jerusalem to Jericho fell into the hands of brigands, who not only robbed but stripped and wounded him, and then made off, leaving him half dead. A priest, who happened to be going down by the same road, saw him and passed by on the other side. In the same way too a Levite, when   5 he reached the spot and saw him, passed by on the other side. But a Samaritan also came upon him as he went along the road and was filled with compassion directly he saw him. He went up

to him, bandaged his wounds, applying oil and wine, put him on
his own mount, and took him to an inn, where he attended to his   10
comfort. And in the morning he produced two shillings, gave
them to the innkeeper and said: "Take care of him; and on my
way back I will repay you any further charges." 'Which of these
three, do you think, proved himself a neighbour to the man who
fell into the brigands' hands?' 'The one,' he replied, 'who treated   15
him with compassion.' And Jesus said to him: 'Go and do as he
did.'

Commentary

1   The Early Modern English text

(a) *Spelling*: The words fall into groups, according to the spelling conventions they
observe:

(i)			
certaine	Samaritaine	tooke	mercie
downe	oile	hoste	goe
halfe	owne	saide doe	
hee	Inne	againe	

Formerly, in the Middle English period, a final <e> on a word would have been
pronounced. It was all that was left of most of the Old English inflectional endings.
By the time of the 1611 Bible translation, final <e>s were no longer pronounced, but
they survived in spelling in a fairly random way, because spelling was not yet
standardised. Sometimes printers would add an <e> to a word to fill up a line of type.

(ii)	Hierusalem	iourneyed	mercie

The rules for the use of <i>, <y> and <j> were not yet fixed as in modern spelling.
<i> and <y> had been interchangeable for a long time to represent the vowel /i/.
Letter <j> was at first an alternative form of <i>, used, for example, as the final letter
when writing numbers; ij (2), iiij (4).

(iii)	theeues	Leuite	whatsoeuer	vnto
	leauing	gaue	vp	

The distinction between the vowel /u/ and the consonant /v/ was not represented in
the spelling. The letters <u> and <v>, like <i> and <j>, were alternative forms of the
same letter, (compare <A>, <a> and <ɑ>), and were used for both sounds. The form
of the letter was determined by its place in the written word. If either sound began a
word (**word-initial**), then letter <v> was used,

vp	vnto	verily	victuals

If either sound was in the middle (**word-medial**) or at the end (**word-final**) of a
word, then letter <u> was used,

ouer	fiue	thou	multitude

The **digraph** (two letters representing one sound) <ou> was often written <ow>, as
in *powring*.

(b) *Word forms*:   The only important differences which this text illustrates are in the forms of *thinkest* and *spendest*.

The suffix *-est* in the present tense of a verb marks the older regular use of the pronoun *thou/thee* (second-person singular). The verb ending shows **agreement** (or **concord**) with the pronoun. Today we use *you* whether we are addressing one or more than one person, and *thou* has been dropped out of use in most church services, where it was common until the 1970s. (The other verb inflection which is now lost was *-eth*, used with the third-person singular *he/ she/ it – he beareth, she giueth, it hath*.)

(c) *Vocabulary*:   Some of the words are now out of date in everyday usage; they are now **archaisms**:

raiment   likewise   hoste

There are also set phrases, **collocations**, which are no longer in current use:

went down from   fel among   had compassion
on the morrow   powring in oile *etc.*

There is no clear boundary between features of interest in the vocabulary, and those in the grammar.

(d) *Grammar*:   The differences between Early Modern English and present-day English grammar, apart from those in (b) above, are relatively small, but **word order** shows some contrasts:

there came down a certaine Priest
doe thou likewise
thinkest thou?

To ask a question in English today when using the simple present tense (e.g. *you think*) or simple past tense (e.g. *you thought)*, we have to introduce the **auxiliary verb** *do*:

do you think?   did you think?

This form of the verb phrase is called **interrogative mood**.

To give a command or make a direct request, we would now say, for *do thou likewise*, in which *do* is being used as a **main verb**:

go and do it   you go and do it

This form of the verb is called **imperative mood**. Notice also the very frequent use of the **conjunction** *and* to link clauses and also to begin sentences. We do this in ordinary spoken English, especially when telling a story. The 1611 version of the parable has twice as many instances of *and* as the modern version to join clauses or begin sentences, which makes it sound much closer to oral narrative.

2   The 1952 translation
(a) *Spelling*:   Our spelling system has been standardised for over two hundred years, and we only misspell deliberately for special reasons (for example cf. Dialect in

Literature in chapter 9). So there is nothing to be said about the spelling of this translation. It is standard spelling.

(b) *Word forms*:   The inflections of verbs and nouns conform to the rules of Standard English.

(c) *Vocabulary*:   Any translator of the Bible into modern English must be influenced by the style of the 1611 version. So we find words that are perhaps not frequently used in modern English, or which sound literary or formal, especially in some phrases:

> fell into the hands of *brigands*
> *applying* oil and wine
> put him on his own *mount*
> he *attended to* his comfort
> I will repay you any *further charges*

Notice also how the translator uses the words of the King James Bible in 'leaving him half dead' and 'passed by on the other side'.

(d) *Grammar*:   There is more variation in sentence structure and in the use of linking words between clauses than in the 1611 translation. The word *and* occurs less frequently, and the use of the **relative clause** construction, and the **non-finite verb** contributes to the variety.

Compare:

A man *going down from* ...	A certaine man went down from ...
[non-finite verb]	[main clause]
A priest, *who happened* ...	And by chaunce there came down ...
[relative clause]	[main clause]

This chapter has outlined very briefly the historical background to English. The language was brought here from the Continent 1500 years ago. Its main word-stock is Germanic, from Old English and Old Norse; many hundreds of French words were adopted in the Middle English period. The other principal source of our vocabulary, not so far mentioned, is Latin. Many Latin words were used to coin English words by writers, especially in the sixteenth and seventeenth centuries. But if you are interested in words and where they came from, or their **etymology**, a good dictionary or history of English will show you how English speakers have adopted words from many other languages.

We have looked at some examples of older English, and shown how the differences can be described in terms of spelling, vocabulary, word-form and grammar. Old English and Middle English, like modern English, consisted of distinctive dialects, but Standard English as we know it today did not begin to emerge as the accepted *written* form of the language until the later fifteenth century. Since then, Standard English has become the ordinary spoken form of English for many people – the form discussed in chapter 1, widely thought of as 'correct English', or even as 'the English language'.

The important thing to remember is that all the dialects of present-day English spoken in England, including Standard English, and the dialectal accents associated with them, including RP, are traced back directly to the dialects of Middle and Old English.

Activity 2.6

Here is a short extract from St Luke's Gospel in Middle English and Early Modern English.

(i) Compare the spelling, vocabulary, word structure and grammar with present-day Standard English (the verses are numbered).

(ii) Use the list which follows, containing the origins of the words in the Early Modern English text, to find out the proportion of Old English, Old Norse, French or Latin words in the extract.

(1) Middle English (*c.* 1380)

21   And thei axiden hym, and seiden, Maister, we witen, that riȝtli thou seist and techist; and thou takist not the persoone of man, but thou teichist in treuthe the weie of God.

22   Is it leueful to vs to ȝyue tribute to the emperoure, or nay?

23   And he biheld the disseit of hem, and seide to hem, What tempten ȝe me?

24   Shewe ȝe to me a peny; whos ymage and superscripcioun hath it? Thei answerden, and seiden to hym, The emperouris.

25   And he seide to hem, ȝelde ȝe therfor to the emperoure tho thingis that ben the emperours, and tho thingis that ben of God, to God.

Early Modern English (1611)

21   And they asked him, saying, Master, we know that thou sayest and teachest rightly, neither acceptest thou the person of any, but teachest the way of God truely.

22   Is it lawfull for vs to giue tribute vnto Cesar, or no?

23   But he perceiued their craftines, and said vnto them, Why tempt ye me?

24   Shew me a peny: whose image and superscription hath it? They answered, and said, Cesars.

25   And he said vnto them, Render therefore vnto Cesar the things which be Cesars, and vnto God the things which be Gods.

Function words

det = determiner; ccj = coordinating conjunction; scj = subordinating conjunction; prep = preposition; pn = pronoun.
OE = Old English; OF = Old French; ON = Old Norse

a	*det*	OE an	of	*prep*	OE of	vnto	*prep*	ME unto
and	*ccj*	OE and	that	*scj*	OE þæt	vs	*pn*	OE us
but	*ccj*	OE butan	the	*det*	late OE þe	we	*pn*	OE we
for	*prep*	OE for	their	*pn*	ON ðeira	which	*pn*	OE hwilc
he	*pn*	OE he	them	*pn*	ON ðeim	whose	*pn*	OE hwæs
him	*pn*	OE him	they	*pn*	ON ðeir	ye	*pn*	OE ge
it	*pn*	OE hit	thou	*pn*	OE þu			
me	*pn*	OE me	to	*particle*	OE to			

Nouns

any	OE ænig	*peny*	OE penig
Cesar/Cesars	Latin	*person*	OF persone
craftines	OE cræftig + -ness	*superscription*	Latin superscriptionem
God/Gods	OE god/godes	*things*	OE þingas
image	OF image	*tribute*	Latin tributum
Master	OE mægester	*way*	OE weg

Verbs

acceptest	OF accepter	*perceiued*	OF perceivre
answered	OE andswarode	*render*	OF rendre
asked	OE acsode/ascode	*said/sayest/*	OE sægde/sægst/
be	OE beon	*saying*	secgende
giue	OE giefan	*shew*	OE sceawiaþ
hath	OE hæfþ	*teachest*	OE tæcest
is	OE is	*tempt*	OF tempter
know	OE cnawaþ		

Adjectives

lawfull	ON lagu + OE full

Adverbs

neither	OE nahwæþer	*therefore*	OE þærfor
no	OE nan	*truely*	OE treowlice
rightly	OE riht + -ly	*why*	OE hwi/hwy

Activity 2.7

Spelling and printing conventions in the past were different in some details from today's. Here are two **facsimiles**:

(i)   part of William Tyndale's translation of The Pentateuch (the first five books of the Old Testament), first printed in 1530; and

(ii)   the title page and a single page of Jonathan Swift's Proposal for 'Correcting, Improving and Ascertaining' the English language, published in 1712. *(Ascertaining* means *making certain, fixing permanently.)*

Compare the facsimiles with modern printed English in terms of letter-forms and spelling. Then look at differences in vocabulary and grammar.

The fyrst boke of Moses,   VIIL. I–II

The .VIII. Chapter. [Fo. X.]

1   AND god remēbred Noe & all ẏ beaſtes & all ẏ catell ẏ were with hī in ẏ arke And god made a wynde to blow vppó

2   ẏ erth, & ẏ waters ceaſed: ād ẏ fountaynes of the depe ād the wyndowes of heavē were ſtopte and the rayne of heaven was

3   forbiddē, and the waters returned from of ẏ erth ād abated after the ende of an hundred and .L dayes.

4   And the arke reſted vppó the mountayns of Ararat,

5   the .xvii. daye of the .vii. moneth.   And the waters went away ād decreaſed vntyll the .x. moneth.   And the fyrſt daye of the tenth moneth, the toppes oſ the mounteyns appered.

6   And after the ende of .XL. dayes. Noe opened the

7   wyndow oſ the arke which he had made, ād ſent forth a raven, which went out, ever goinge and cominge agayne, vntyll the waters were dreyed vpp vppon the erth

M.C.S. After the sendyng forth of theraue & the doue Noe went forth of the arcke. He offreth sacrifice. The malyce of mannes heart.

A

PROPOSAL

FOR

Correcting, Improving and *Ascertaining*

THE

English Tongue;

IN A

LETTER

To the Most Honourable

ROBERT

Earl of Oxford *and* Mortimer,

Lord High Treasurer

OF

GREAT BRITAIN.

LONDON:
Printed for BENJ. TOOKE, at the
Middle-Temple-Gate, Fleetstreet. 1712.

Sea ; and though not of such immediate Benefit as either of these, or any other of Your glorious Actions, yet perhaps, in future Ages, not less to Your Honour.

My LORD; I do here, in the Name of all the Learned and Polite Persons of the Nation, complain to Your LORDSHIP, as *First Minister*, that our Language is extremely imperfect; that its daily Improvements are by no means in proportion to its daily Corruptions; that the Pretenders to polish and refine it, have chiefly multiplied Abuses and Absurdities ; and, that in many Instances, it offends against every Part of Grammar. But left Your LORDSHIP should think my Censure too severe, I shall take leave to be more particular.

3. Dialects and Standard English – the present

3.1 Standard English – a dialect

When Chaucer wrote *The Canterbury Tales* at the end of the fourteenth century, there was no Standard English – that is, no single form of the language whose vocabulary and grammar were written throughout the country. He wrote in the educated variety of the London area, where he lived and worked. William Langland wrote *Piers Plowman* in the South Midland dialect. The York Mystery Plays were written in the Northern dialect. The poem *Sir Gawain and the Green Knight* is in the West Midland dialect of Lancashire or Cheshire. The writer John of Trevisa used a South-Western dialect.

The contrast with the situation today is not as great as it may seem if we think of Standard English today as one dialect among many. The English language, then and now, from a linguistic point of view, consists of the sum of all its dialects, which today include Standard English. This view is, however, not the popular one we looked at in chapter 1, which sees Standard English as 'the English language', and the dialects as a number of substandard varieties.

But even if Standard English is defined as one dialect among many, it is no longer a **regional dialect**. It has spread throughout the country as the educated variety of English, and is taught to foreign learners of English, so it is natural that people should come to look on the other dialects as imperfect versions of English. To the linguist, however, all dialects of English are equally regular in their own forms and rules.

Dialect words can, of course, fail to convey their meaning if they are unfamiliar to a listener. The number of words still regularly used in dialects, and which are not part of the vocabulary of Standard English, is much smaller now than a generation or two ago. Easier travel, people moving from one area to another, the influence of film, radio and television, and the effects of over a century of compulsory education, will all have influenced the vocabulary of dialects. Almost everyone can now hear Standard English, in a wide variety of its styles, every day, and a large amount of American English also. But in spite of the loss of words from the vocabulary of the regional dialects, there is still plenty of evidence of dialectal grammar.

3.2 Present-day dialectal forms

The most noticeable differences between present-day dialects and Standard English in England lie in quite a small set of grammatical features, illustrated in the sentences below. Some of them were included in the Acceptability Test in chapter 1.

Activity 3.1

Before reading the commentary which follows the dialectal sentences, identify and describe the words or constructions which are non-standard. Are any of the sentences difficult to understand? If so, can you say why?

1. I didn't have no dinner yesterday.
2. My Dad seen an accident before he come home the other day.
3. My sister have a boy friend and she see him every day.
4. That was the man what done it.
5. John fell over and hurt hisself.
6. Mary's more nicer than her brother.
7. She spoke very clever.
8. Leave your things here while you come back.
9. Our teacher can't learn us anything.
10. (a) I want this coat cleaning. OR This coat needs cleaning.   (b) I want this coat cleaned OR This coat needs cleaned.
11. She gave it her friend.
12. (a) I were going down the road.   (b) We was going down the road.
13. If you're tired, why don't you lay down?
14. The water was dripping out the tap.
15. Will you go and buy me two pound of apples?
16. You can gan out to play now.
17. We never had TV them days when I were a lad.
18. She wanted for to go till the theatre.

Commentary

In these sentences the dialectal forms are not identified as belonging to any particular region of England. They are all authentic, but many of them are widespread. They illustrate variations in the grammar of English, which we can place together as **non-standard**. You would expect them to be spoken with a dialectal accent also, but this is being treated as a separate topic for study.

One of the purposes of this book is to encourage you to listen to varieties of English speech objectively. You should learn to identify the differences accurately, comparing them with Standard English vocabulary and grammar. Whether you like a particular·dialect or accent is not relevant.

1 *I didn't have no dinner yesterday* (cf. Acceptability Test no. 8)
If spoken in a normal way, it means the same as Standard English *I didn't have any dinner yesterday*, or more formally, *I had no dinner yesterday*. That is:

/I didn't have no **dìnner yésterday**/

It is not true that two negatives necessarily make a positive in language, even if they do in mathematics. Many languages make more than one item negative in a sentence; Old English and Middle English did, which is where the present-day dialects that use the **double** or **multiple** negative get it from. It is Standard English that has changed. Here are some examples:

Old English (the negative word was *ne*, before the verb)

> *ne* þurfan ge *noht* besorgian
> = *ne* need you *not* fear
> = you need *not* fear (*Standard English*)

(the word *noht* reinforces the negative *ne*, and is the origin of modern English *not*)

Middle English (from the *Peterborough Chronicle* for 1137)

> for *ne* wæren *nævre nan* martyrs swa pined alse hi wæron
> = for *never* weren*'t no* martyrs so tortured as they were
> = for never were martyrs tortured as they were (*Standard English*)

The Middle English example is a **multiple negative** because three items in the sentence carry the negative – *ne, nævre* and *nan*.

The double or multiple negative in present-day dialects is therefore a survival of older forms of the language, not badly learned Standard English.

There is another linguistic construction, however, in which two negatives do make a positive. The *Oxford English Dictionary* records its first example from 1657:

> The study of antiquity was *not un*usefull...

The use of *not* with an adjective or adverb which has a negative prefix like *un-* or *in-/im-* is still quite common, though usually in a formal style, nor does the quotation mean exactly the same as,

> The study of antiquity was usefull...

But this is not the same construction as the preceding examples from Old and Middle English and dialects.

It is possible to speak sentence 1 in such a way as to imply the positive, by using **contrastive stress**:

/I didn't have **nŏ** dinner **yésterday**/

But this is quite clearly different from the unmarked normal intonation pattern which implies the negative, and is in everyday use in many English dialects.

2 *My Dad seen an accident before he come home the other day*
Standard English would have *saw* and *came*, the **simple past tense** of *see* and *come*. The regular past tense in English consists of the **base form** of a verb, e.g. *walk*, to which the suffix *-ed* is added in writing. (The pronunciation varies, but will not be discussed here.)

She *walked* to the station to meet me.

The form of the verb called the **past participle** is exactly the same as the past tense in regular verbs. Together with *have* it forms the **present perfect tense**:

She *has walked* to the station every day.

or the **past perfect tense**:

She *had walked* to the station every day.

There is, however, a large set of **irregular verbs,** most of them very common, whose past tenses and past participles are not formed by adding *-ed*. These irregular verbs are in fact the oldest in form, going back beyond Old English in time to Germanic, and finally to the language from which most European languages have developed, called **Indo-European.** As a result, they tend to resist change. Grammarians have called them **strong verbs,** and the regular verbs **weak.**

So our modern irregular verbs are the remnant of the Old English strong verbs, and show a variety of different kinds of change in their forms. Here are a few examples:

(a) *One form only:*

base form	past tense	past participle
let	let	let

In this group of verbs, the base form, and therefore the present tense also, is the same as the past tense and past participle:

I *let* him go there whenever he wants to.	(*present tense*)
I *let* him go there yesterday.	(*past tense*)
I have *let* him go, although I didn't want to.	(*past participle*)

Type (a) is a group of verbs that have lost the distinction between base form, past and past participle forms. There is only one form. Compare *cost, hit, hurt, put, set, shut, spread* and so on.

(b) *Two forms:*

	base form	past tense	past participle
(i)	swing	swung	swung
(ii)	come	came	come

Type (b) verbs have two forms. In b(i) the past tense and past participle have 'fallen together', taking the form of the OE past participle. Type b(ii) has the same form for the base/present tense and past participle.

(c) *Three forms:*

base form	past tense	past participle
see	saw	seen
do	did	done

Type (c) verbs have three forms. The past tense and past participle are different from each other and from the base/present tense form.

The changes that took place in verb forms between the Old English and Middle English periods, and then further changes up to today, are very complicated.

Different changes took place in each of the different dialects, and so survive into modern dialects. The examples given above all show Standard English forms, but many dialect verbs are non-standard in form.

In the dialects represented in sentence 2, the past tense and past participle of *see* have fallen together, both taking the form of the past participle as in standard type b(i) above:

	infinitive	*present tense*	*past tense*	*past participle*
dialect	see	I see	I seen	(I have) seen
Old English	seon	ic seo	ic seah	sewen

In the verb *come*, a similar thing has happened, but since the past participle had the same root vowel as the infinitive in Old English (*cumen/ cuman*), these dialects have the same vowel for all three forms, like type (a) in Standard English:

	infinitive	*present tense*	*past tense*	*past participle*
dialect	come	I come	I come	come
Old English	cuman	ic cume	ic com	cumen

The important point that this rather detailed description shows is, that though at first the dialectal forms sound wrong if you are used to Standard English, they can be explained in linguistic terms in exactly the same way as Standard English forms. It is simply that different choices were made among the varied **speech communities** forming the speakers of English in the past. These choices are not conscious or deliberate, but pronunciation is always changing, and leads in time to changes in word form.

3 *My sister have a boy friend and she see him every day.*
Standard English is *has* and *sees*. The present tense of verbs uses the base form, except that the third-person singular adds an -*s*:

I see	I have
you see	you have
he sees	**she has**
they see	they have

Dialects using the base form for the third-person singular, and not adding the -*s*, have taken to its conclusion the process of simplifying or **regularising** the forms of the present tense. Standard English speakers and other dialect speakers have not taken this step.

4 *That was the man what done it.*
Two non-standard features, *done* for *did* (past tense) and *what* for *who* or *that*:

That was the man who did it.

The use of *done* for the past tense is another example of the alternative forms described for sentence 2.

What has a number of functions in Standard English, and it is not surprising that its use in some dialects overlaps with that of other **pronouns** like *that, which* and *who*. In this sentence it is functioning as the **relative pronoun**.

	Standard	Dialectal
	The woman who came...	The woman what came...
	The man who I saw...	The man what I saw
or	The man whom I saw...	
	The girl that called...	The girl what called...
	The pen which he gave me...	The pen what he gave me...
or	The pen that he gave me...	

In some dialects, *as* is used as the relative pronoun:

The chap as called last night was an old friend.

5 *John fell over and hurt hisself.*
The standard form is *himself.* Why? Look at the following lists of **personal pronouns**:

object	*possessive*	*object* + *-self*	*possessive* + *-self*
me	my	meself	**myself**
him	his	**himself**	hisself
her	her	**herself**	herself
it	its	**itself**	itself
us	our	usselves	**ourselves**
you	your	youselves	**yourselves**
them	their	**themselves**	theirselves

Standard English uses *my/our/your* + *self/selves*, but not *his/their* + *self/selves*, and there seems to be no logical reason why.

me/him etc. are **object pronouns**:
He saw *me.*   I saw *him.*
my/his etc. are **possessive pronouns**:
This is *my* bike.   That's *his* bike.

Dialects using *hisself* and *theirselves* are consistently using the *possessive pronoun* + *self/selves* to form the **reflexive pronoun**, and Standard English is here inconsistent. It is another example of regularisation in the dialects.

6 *Mary's more nicer than her brother.*
We form the **comparative** of an adjective in Standard English either by adding the suffix *-er*, or by using *more* + the adjective,

She is *nicer* than he is.
She is *more intelligent* than he is.

The 'double comparative' is a feature of some dialects, similar in some ways to the double negative because the comparison is reinforced by being doubled.

7 *She spoke very clear*
In Standard English the **adverb** form is *clearly.* Most adverbs in English today end in *-ly*, because they are **derived** from adjectives, e.g. *slow/slowly, bad/badly, deep/*

deeply. But a few common ones derive from Old English adverbs, some of which ended in the suffix *-e*, which was then pronounced as a syllable. This suffix has now disappeared, leaving some adverbs without one, for example:

OE *fæst-e*	He ran *fast* to avoid trouble.
OE *wid-e*	They searched *far* and *wide*.
OE *dun-e*	Please sit *down*.
OE *ut*	Have you put the cat *out*?
OE *lat-e*	She went out *late* in the evening.
(*which contrasts with*	Have you seen her *lately*?)

8 *Leave your things here while you come back*
If you do not live in the north of England, you may never have heard this use of *while*. The standard form is:

Leave your things here until you come back.

It is said that the notices placed at unmanned level crossings, when they were first introduced, stated,

> **STOP WHILE LIGHTS SHOW**

Since this means, for some dialect speakers,

> **STOP UNTIL LIGHTS SHOW**

instead of

> **STOP WHEN LIGHTS SHOW**

you can see how dangerous the notice was. If you were to ask someone in a shop what their opening hours are, they might reply:

We're open from nine in the morning while five in the afternoon.

or you could be asked,

Can you wait while Friday?

9 *Our teacher can't learn us anything.*
In Standard English, to *learn* means to *acquire* knowledge. In some dialects, it also means to *impart* knowledge. How can one word have two opposite meanings? This is not so unusual as you might at first think. For example,

I rent a flat *from* a landlord.
The landlord rents a flat *to* me.

are both acceptable Standard English. But the corresponding second sentence of,

I learned it *from* the landlord.
The landlord learned it *to* me.

is no longer acceptable Standard English.

To learn comes from an Old English verb *leornian*, and its meaning in the true sense of to *impart* and to *acquire* knowledge is recorded in writing, and therefore in educated usage, up to the nineteenth century. It is therefore only comparatively recently that the meaning equivalent to *to teach* has become non-standard, but it survives in spoken English in many dialects.

Here are some examples of its use, meaning *to teach*, taken from the *Oxford English Dictionary*:

1382   Who *lerneth* a scornere, doth wrong he to himself. (Wyclif's *Bible*)
1535   Lede me in thy trueth and *lerne* me. (Coverdale's *Bible*)
1666   That my Father might *learn* me to speak without this wicked way of swearing. (Bunyan)
1801   They *learn* us to associate a keen and deep feeling with all the good old phrases. (Coleridge)
1876   Thou hast *learned* me all my skill. (William Morris)

10   *I want this coat cleaning. This coat needs cleaning. I want this coat cleaned. This coat needs cleaned*

These forms are all in common use, but in different parts of Britain. The standard forms are probably *This coat needs cleaning*, and *I want this coat cleaned*, but perhaps it is a matter of stylistic variation.

11   *She gave it her friend.*
Standard usage would require either,

> She gave it to her friend.
> *or*   She gave her friend it.

We are here talking about the **direct object** and **indirect object** of the verb. To *give* implies something which she gave (the direct object, DO), and a person to whom she gave it (the indirect object, IO).

She gave	her friend	a birthday present.
	IO	*DO*
She gave	a birthday present	to her friend.
	DO	*prepositional object*

The term *indirect object* is best reserved for the form without the preposition *to*, and in Standard English and most other dialects it precedes the direct object. If a **prepositional phrase** (PrepP) with *to* (or *for*) is used, then it follows the direct object. But if pronouns are used instead of nouns, the meaning can be slightly confusing:

She gave him it.	She gave it him.
She gave her friend it.	She gave it her friend.

Both pairs seem acceptable, because common sense tells us that it is unlikely that she would give a person (*him/her friend*) to a thing (*it*), and the meaning *She gave him to it* is less probable. In any case, the sentence would be spoken in a context in which the referents of *him* and *it* were known.

12   *I were going down the road. We was going down the road*
Standard English conjugates the verb *be* in the past tense as follows,

> I/he/she/it *was*   we/you/they *were*

This is more or less as it was in Old English,

ic/he/heo/hit *waes*   we/ge/hi *waeron* & þu *waere*

but many dialects have brought the past tense of *be* in line with all other verbs, which have only one form for the past tense (one more example of regularisation in the dialects). Some dialects have *was*, in the past tense (as in *we was*), others have *were* (as in *she were*). They are not muddling their usage, but simplifying it. The two sentences in 12 are not from the same dialect.

13 *If you're tired, why don't you lay down?*
A favourite mistake for teachers to mark wrong, but still a common usage. Standard English distinguishes two verbs,

base form	present tense	past tense
lie	I lie	I lay
lay	I lay	I laid

The past tense of *lie* has the same form as the base and present tense form of *lay*, so the confusion is easy to understand. But the use of *lay* meaning *lie* was common in written English, and not formerly regarded as a **solecism** (bad grammar).

c. 1300   Sathanas, y bynde the, her shalt thou *lay*.
          (a mystery play, *The Harrowing of Hell*)
1625   Nature will *lay* buried a great time, and yet revive.
          (Francis Bacon's essay *On Nature*)
1818   Thou dashest him again to earth, there let him *lay*.
          (Byron)

In grammatical terms, Standard English *lie* is **intransitive** and is not followed by a direct object – you can't *lie something* – while *lay* is transitive and is followed by an object – you can *lay the table*, and hens *lay eggs*. Some dialects use *lay* as an intransitive verb.

14 *The water was dripping out the tap*
Standard English *out of*. Variation in the use of **prepositions** is widespread between the dialects of English, including the standard. Prepositions can be simple (one word) or complex (two or more words), and the possible combinations allow many variations. For example:

along	along with	away	away from
off	off of	together	together with
by means of	on top of	in front of	in relation to

15 *Will you buy me two pound of apples?*
This is very common. You might expect the plural form *pounds*, as the word *two* implies more than one. There are, however, many **noun phrases of measurement** in which the noun remains singular. For example:

I walked three mile into town.

This is probably directly descended from the Old English, when *three miles wide* would have been *þreora mila brad* which is literally *of-three of-miles broad*. *Two pounds* was *twegen punda*, literally *two of-pounds*.

In Old English, as we have already seen, words were inflected to show their grammatical relationships in a phrase or sentence. Modern English tends to use prepositions, or word order, for the same purpose.

The words for *of-miles* and *of-pounds* in expressions of measurement in Old English were *mila* and *punda*. (The *-a* inflection marks the **possessive plural** form.) These words eventually became *mile* and *pound* because the ending was dropped, and many dialects still use this grammatical form without the *-s* plural.

In fact it is quite usual in Standard English to talk of a *three-foot ruler* or a *ten-mile walk* or a *thousand-metre race*, so it could be argued that this is not dialectal at all, but common to all varieties of English.

16 *You can gan out to play now.*
The Old English verb for *go* was *gan*. The vowel /ɑ/ was a long vowel, and *gan* changed to *gon* in early Middle English, in the south of England, and later lost the final /n/ to become *go*. This change did not occur in the north, and *gan* is still common usage in the north-east of England.

17 *We never had TV them days when I were a lad*
Non-standard features are the use of *never* for the negative *We didn't have TV...*, the use of *them* for the **demonstrative pronoun** where Standard English has *those*, and the omission of a preposition before *them days* – *in those days*. The use of *never* may not be accepted as dialectal, but as an informal feature of Standard English grammar also. Dialects and styles do not have fixed definable boundaries. *I were* has already been discussed.

18 *She wanted for to go till the theatre.*
For occurs with *to* in Standard English in constructions like,

> *For* me *to* understand this is easy.
> What he wants is *for* her *to* visit her mother.
> The idea is *for* him *to* go next week.

Some dialects retain both *for* and *to* in constructions where Standard English omits *for*:

> I want *for to* go to Widecombe Fair.

The use of the preposition *till* to indicate direction of movement, where most dialects and standard English use *to*, is a survival from Northern dialects of Old English. The Old Norse word for *to,* spoken by the Danish and Norwegian settlers in the Danelaw in the East Midlands and north of England, was *til*. When Chaucer in the late fourteenth century wanted to portray the speech of two young men from the North of England, *til* was one of the words he used, so that the phrase *to and fro* is spoken as *til and fra*.

These examples of non-standard dialect illustrate some of the principal differences between Standard English and the dialects today, most of them from England. It is not a complete list, nor does it attempt to specify the characteristics of any regional dialects but it illustrates some of the most common differences. Because we are sensitive to even small changes in word-form or grammar, our judgements of a dialect speaker may rest upon very few items of difference. The detailed linguistic commentary on the dialectal sentences has been done for two reasons:

(i) to show you how to make an objective analysis of a piece of language before you go on to evaluate it, and

(ii) to illustrate the fact that Standard English is just as arbitrary in its choices of words and structures as other dialects and languages – you can't argue for Standard English on any grounds of its superior logic or structure. There are other and different kinds of reason for accepting and using it.

Activity 3.2

The following sentences are from Sir Thomas Malory's *Le Morte Darthur*, and they illustrate the form of literary English of five hundred years ago which was to become Standard English. The book was printed by Caxton in 1485.

Identify those features that are nowadays regarded as non-standard or dialectal, and relate them to the dialectal sentences of Activity 3.1.

1. And in the meanewhyle I and my sistir woll ryde untyll your castell.
2. His castell is here nerehonde but two myle.
3. But in no wyse I wolde nat that he wyste what I were.
4. Than was syr Gareth more gladder than he was tofore.
5. Hit was never done by me, nother by myne assente this unhappy dede was never done.
6. Ryght so come this damesell Lyonett before hem all.
7. For such yonge knyghtes as he is, whan they be in their adventures, bene never abydyng in no place.
8. We shall be full sore macched with the moste nobleste knyghtes of the worlde.
9. And than sir Trystrams and his bretherne rode togydyrs for to helpe sir Gareth.
10. If I may nat have hym, I promyse you I woll never have none.

Activity 3.3

Compare the following descriptive definitions of Standard English:

(i) Standard English is ... 'normal English'; that kind of English which draws least attention to itself over the widest area and through the widest range of usage. It is particularly associated with English in a written form, and we find that there are sharper restrictions in every way upon the English that is written (and especially printed) than upon English that is spoken. (Randolph Quirk, *The Use of English*, 1962)

(ii) The standard is that speech variety of a language community which is legitimised as the obligatory norm for social intercourse on the strength of the interests of dominant forces in that society.   (Norbert Dittmar, *Sociolinguistics*, 1976)

Activity 3.4

The following sentences are authentic examples of contemporary dialectal speech.
(i)   Listen to the speakers on the cassette tape, section 3.
(ii)   Identify and describe the dialectal features of vocabulary and grammar in relation to the forms of Standard English. (Aspects of dialectal *pronunciation* are discussed in chapter 4.)
You should find one or more examples of the following dialectal forms, some of which have not so far been discussed in this chapter:

Verbs
Regularisation of present tense with loss of third-person singular -s inflection.
Regularisation of present tense with addition of -s inflection.
Regular -ed inflection applied to past tense and/or past participle of irregular (strong) verbs.
Different vowel in past tense or past participle of irregular verbs.
Different distribution of the forms of the verb *be*.

Nouns
Irregular forms of the plural.
Singular noun in expressions of measurement with plural number.

Pronouns
Interchanging of subject and object personal pronouns.
Retention of second-person singular pronoun *thou/thee/thine*.
Use of personal pronoun *them* for the demonstrative pronoun *those*.
Use of *what* as a relative pronoun.

Adjectives
Double comparative of adjectives.

Prepositions and particles
Use of *till* as preposition of direction.
Use of *for to* with verb infinitive.

Negatives
Double and multiple negatives.

Vocabulary
Learn used with the meaning *to impart knowledge*.
Non-standard vocabulary.)

Recorded regional dialect speakers *(cassette tape section 3)*

1. If she know she got it coming cushy she ain't got to bother, have she?
   (*Berkshire*)
2. I seed the advertisement in the newspaper and our Dad said to I, 'If thee carsn't do that as good as some of the men, that's a poor job.'
   (*Gloucestershire*)
3. All them men had all to get motor transport for to get till it, and come in their own cars and one thing and another, so there must be something in a drum for all them people for to go for to hear them drums.
   (*Belfast*)

4. And there were never a betterer mental arithmetic reckoner than my father, but not with a pen. Well, he could set 'em down, but not write letters, nor my mother couldn't – not till I got big enough – even write her name, and we learned her to just write it, and that were all they could do them days.
   (*West Yorkshire*)

5. We used to have cookers out there and everything, and we used to cook our trotters there – all come up in trays, all jelly – they used to nosh 'em there like. It was really beautiful.
   (*London*)

6. One of the teachers, the teacher what I had last – I were only about five and I were staying to school dinners – and she made me eat a big load of mashed potatoes.
   (*Lancashire boy*)

7. I was sitting here writing a letter to dear Willie's mother. Her's up to Brent, her was working but now her of course has gone. And I was blowed right up there.
   (*Devon*)

8. I'm not sprucing you. They knew every kid in the village, and if they come through the village and they see you, they always used to call you 'master', and you always used to touch your cap and call them 'sir'.
   (*Sussex*)

9. A good boss was a good boss. He were paying for the stuff that I were supposed to make perfect or as near perfect as possible. It's his money. It's his building. It's all that. He's kept your childer for so many year while you work for him, style of thing – hasn't he?
   (*Lancashire*)

10. I usually just sub, but then again, I'm a defender. I likes playing defender more than anything else.
    (*Plymouth boy*)

11. I used to work in Marks and Spencer's. We've always kept friends with the people in there, you know. And then I worked on the station for nineteen year.
    (*Carlisle*)

12. When I heard the knocking I never thought nothing like that could ever happen.
    (*Norwich*)

3.3 Creole English

During the last forty years, new dialects have appeared in England that were formerly to be heard only in the dominions and colonies of the former British Empire. Families who emigrated from the West Indies to Britain in the 1950s and 1960s found that although they spoke English, it was different in many ways from the English they heard in Britain. Their language had developed from the early days of slavery in the West Indies, as far back as the seventeenth century, when a simplified form of English – a **pidgin** – was used for giving orders and communicating. A pidgin language is a **contact language** which develops and is used by two sets of people when neither knows the other's language. A pidgin may in time develop into a first language, or **mother tongue**. Linguists then call it a **creole**. A creole, like any other first language, grows to serve all the purposes of language in a society.

Some of the differences between a West Indian creole and other forms of English can be heard in the following story told by a small boy who had recently come to live in England in the 1960s. It is most unlikely that this particular form of creole will now be heard in England in the 1990s, because West Indian creoles have continued to develop and therefore change in the process. They remain a clear marker of speech communities.

This transcription is not edited or tidied up, and includes the hesitations and self-corrections which the boy makes, because some of them are significant clues to his knowledge of English. Ordinary spelling is used but without forms of written punctuation, and pronunciation and intonation are not indicated. Momentary breaks are marked with the sign (.).

Activity 3.5

Listen to the cassette tape recording and follow the transcription. Then make a list of all the non-standard features in vocabulary, word-form and gammar, together with the Standard English equivalents.

3.3.1 *The Mango Tree* (cassette tape section 4)

every night we don't go to bed soon and in the morning (when) we wake up soon and we race one another to go to the mango tree (.) and every morning my big brother always racing me and get more mango than me

when we have a mango we don't carry it down (.) because you know (.) when   5
we go to school them other will eat it off and when we come from school in the evening we go for them and eat them

and always my granma (.) my granma (.) when we hided (.) the mango in the ground he (.) he (.) she always find it (.) and eat them off and when we go and   10
look for them there was none mango but the seed and the skin

and when we come down and ask where (.) where (.) where the mango we cannot have ..?.. (.) and my granny say he (.) she eat them off (.) and she say you (.) we musn't hide no more in the ground (.) and (.) in the grass we hide   15
them and he still find them

one morning I find one dozen mango and I hide them in the bush and my brother come (.) run home soon and come and eat them off and I didn't get none (.) and I tell my granny and sh.(.) and I tell my granny and he beat him   20
[*teacher*: she beat your brother?] yes (.) he say she mustn't eat off the mangoes and me don't get any (.) and she tell him to stop it

every time when my granny beat him always my dog (.) my dog come in and bark at him (.) and he lick after the dog and the dog run away   25

Commentary

This is a simple narrative typical, in its structure, of any young child's story-telling with its succession of clauses linked by *and* and *when*. The non-standard features must be grouped into sets in order to explain them:

(i) *Tense*
Is the boy telling his story in the present tense, which is common enough in oral narrative, or in the past tense? In Standard English, we use the base form of a verb for the **infinitive**, e.g. *to come*, and for the **present tense**, e.g. *I come*, except for the third-person singular, with *he/she/it*, which has an *-s* added:

I, we, you, they *come* / he, she, it *comes*

For the **past tense** we either change the vowel of the verb,

I, he, she, it, we, you, they *came*

or we add *-ed*

I, he, she, it, we, you, they *raced*

All the verbs used by the boy are in the base form, except for the single use of *hided*. In creole English, verbs are not inflected to show present or past tense, just like a small set of verbs in Standard English already discussed (see section 3.2, page 40), neither does the third-person singular verb take an -s.

This does not mean that you cannot tell past from present in creole, but that you don't do so by inflecting the verb. If necessary, you use a separate word, like *did* or *been*. Different dialects of a language, like different languages, convey similar meanings but in different ways. Some dialects are more developed and complex than others, as is Standard English compared with creoles of English. It can be assumed therefore that the boy's narrative is in the past tense.

(ii) *Nouns*
A second set of differences is in the form of the **nouns**, e.g. *mango* for *mangoes* (except once). Creoles do not mark nouns for plural. Standard English nouns usually inflect with an *-s,* but there are a few with **zero plural** – for example *sheep* / *salmon* / *deer* / *grouse* – so creole usage is not altogether different.

(iii) *Gender*
Thirdly, there is, to us, confusion in the boy's use of *he/she/him/her*. He hesitates when he wants to refer to his granny, and gets the pronouns wrong: *and I tell my granny and he beat him.*

Standard English distinguishes **masculine, feminine** and **neuter** gender in the singular third-person pronouns,

he, him, his/she, her, her/it, it, its

Creoles do not mark third-person singular pronouns for gender, just as Standard English does not mark any other pronouns for gender. This probably explains the boy's confusion. He has not been in England very long, but he is already using *he* and *she*, *him* and *her*, and sometimes getting them wrong from our point of view.

These are the three main differences between the grammar of the boy's English and that of Standard English. Notice the double negatives. The small differences of vocabulary do not cause any problems of understanding – *soon* for *early*, *eat off* for *eat up*, and *lick after* for *run after*.

Remember that creoles and other dialects are all rule-governed varieties of a language, internally consistent. A creole speaker learning to use another dialect is bound to mix up the two sets of rules. According to the social situation, an English dialect speaker will often use both dialectal and standard forms during the same conversation. So we heard the boy using *mangoes* once, and *hided*, and he got *she* right most of the time.

The next story is told by a small girl who had come to England from the West Indies. It gives a fascinating insight into a way of life in which a belief in ghosts and the supernatural is commonplace. She is using a mixture of creole and standard forms.

Activity 3.6

Listen to the tape recording, and write down the words you hear to fill in the blank spaces in the following transcription. One of your problems will be to decide whether or not you can hear the *-ed* past tense inflection on some verbs, and the *-s* inflection for plural or possessive on nouns.

Activity 3.7

Having identified what you think the girl said, list her non-standard forms and their standard equivalents. Then describe her use of both creole and standard forms under these headings:
1 Use of the base form of the verb and inflected past tense forms.
2 Use of the verb *be* as a linking verb.
3 Use of double negatives.
4 Use of plural inflections on nouns.
5 Use of possessive inflections on nouns.
6 Use of pronouns marked for gender.
7 Unfamiliar vocabulary.

3.3.2 *The Red Bird* (cassette tape section 5)

once upon a time there was a man ...1... Mr Lenny Campbell
his wife ...2...
and one day my brother ...3... (.) and he ...4... a big bird up on the tree
it was a red bird
and then he ...5... his catapult and ...6... to ...7... it   5
Alec ...8... to ...9... it
and when he ...10... to ...11... it [*sentence not completed*]
when he ...12... the bird off the tree (.) his hand ...13... right behind his back
and he couldn't ...14... back from his back

he ...15... to pull it from his back but he couldn't   10
and so he ...16... to Mr Lenny Campbell (.) and Mr Lenny Campbell ...17...
'what can I do about it?'
and he ...18... 'I cannot do ...19... about it so you'd better ...20... to your
granny at once and ...21... her before your hands all ...22... together'
and so my brother ...23... (.) and when he ...24... to my granny (.) my granny   15
...25... 'what have you been ...26... with your ...27...?'
and he said 'I ...28... just shooting a bright bird off the tree (.) a red one (.) and
then my ...29... ...30... behind me'
and so my granny ...31... 'all right (.) come on'
and she ...32... me to the shop (.) to go and get two ...33... of corn meal   20
and I ...34... to get it (.) and some bana-bush
and she ...35... it and she ...36... all around the ...37... (.) and ...38... it all over
his ...39...
and then the next morning it ...40... too bad (.) but he could hardly move his
...41...   25
and then my granny ...42... him to go outside and stand up by the same tree
again and try and get a catapult and throw [*sentence not completed*]
and there would be another bird and he must ...43... after it
but there wasn't a bird (.) it was the ghost (.) it was Mr Lenny ...44... ...45...
ghost   30
she ...46... (.) and she didn't have a peaceful place to rest (.) so she was all
around the place (.) and she ...47... everything to try and kill ...48... husband

3.3.3 *Coming to England*

The next text is a transcription of the story of a ten-year-old girl's journey from
Jamaica to England, to join her parents living in the West Midlands. By the time of
the recording, she had already acquired much of the dialectal accent of the region,
but her vocabulary and grammar showed features of a mixture of Jamaican creole
English, the West Midlands regional dialect, and also the Standard English she was
being taught in school.

The story was recorded in a classroom at her primary school. The transcripion has
been edited to omit most of the non-fluency features like hesitations and repetitions.

Activity 3.8 ⎯⎯⎯⎯⎯⎯⎯⎯⎯⎯⎯⎯

Read the transcription and describe the dialectal features of the girl's language.
Say which features you think belong to Jamaican creole English, West Midlands
English or Standard English.

When I was coming from Jamaica in the plane (.) I was with one of the nurse
and we wasn't glad to come over here (.)
and then my Mum was coming up the airport to meet me (.) and when they
came I didn't know it was them (.) I was frightened and then (.) my dad look
strange and my Mum (.)   5
and then they went to the coffee and bought some orange and some tea and
some sandwich but I didn't have it (.) I only taste a bit and I feel sick (.)
and then we come over (.) we was coming back (.) we came about five
o'clock in the morning (.) cos we was late coming home (.) we've lost our
way (.)   10
and then we was coming home (.) it was about ten o'clock in the night (.)
and then we saw a car (.) it was upside down (.) it just crash across the other
field (.)
my Dad went out and he have a look (.)
and he saw that the glass came out of the car and it wasn't broken (.)   15
it came out like the door there and it wasn't broken (.)
and then he went up to the phone
and then when the ambulance come the lady was injured and the other one
was killed (.) the man what was driving was killed (.)
and when we come home (.) we went in the house and I was ever so   20
frightened
and we went in the room (.) and I said 'Is this your room?' I call (.) I said 'Is
this your room?'
She says 'Yes' (.)
then I say 'I don't want to stay in here cos I don't like the room' (.)   25
she said 'Why I'm your mother you know (.) didn't you know?' (.)
and then I says I didn't know (.) 'I don't like you' (.)
and then my Dad said 'You'd better like her cos she's your Mum and I'm
your Dad' (.) and then I call the other little boy in the room (.) cos he called
my Mum 'Mummy' (.)   30
you know (.) cos he used to her (.)
he couldn't call her name properly (.) he call her Mummy (.) and his name is
Steve (.)
I says 'Steve come here' (.) I said 'Is this my Mum?' (.) he says 'I don't
know' (.)   35
and then after where that I'm believing that it was my Mum she show me a
picture (.) a married picture what she send to me in Jamaica (.) and I
remember her

3.4 Pidgin English

Most pidgin languages are spoken only, and not written, but sometimes a pidgin is
used as an official language, and a writing system is invented for its spelling, for
example in Papua New Guinea.

In Vanuatu (the former New Hebrides islands in the Pacific), which was
administered as a 'condominium' by Great Britain and France until 1980, when
independence was achieved, the pidgin language Bislama is used as a common
language, or **lingua franca**. Among about 100,000 people, there are 115 languages
still in use, so Bislama is useful for Vanuatuans to communicate with each other.

A written system using the Roman alphabet was devised for a translation of the New Testament published in the 1970s, based on **phonemic** principles – that is, one letter representing one sound– so you must not expect to be able to recognise words by just looking at them. You must try to hear them, as if you were reading a phonetic script, and then you will probably understand them.

Most of the vocabulary of Bislama is derived from English. Here is a short news report from the former *New Hebrides News*, first in Bislama, second in a literal word for word translation, using the original English words and finally in a modern English version. The grammar of Bislama is not that of English. This applies especially to the common word *i* and a suffix *-em/-im*. Try to work out what the word and suffix are for, and also to describe some of the other grammatical features of Bislama that differ from English.

HEMI FAERAP MO I SEKEM AELAN!!

1 I kat wanfala samting we i foldaon long Sarere moning Jun 17 bitwin Merelava mo Gaua.

2 Olgeta pipol long Merelava oli talem se olgeta i lukim samting i foldaon from skae mo i kat faea bihaen long tel blong hem.

3 Taem i kasem solwora hemi faerap.

4 Olgeta i ting se hemi bom sipos nomo volkeno blong Gaua.

HIM I-FIRE-UP MORE I-SHAKE-HIM ISLAND!!

1 i-got one-fellow some-thing that i-fall down along Saturday morning June 17 between Merelava and Gaua.

2 Altogether people along Merelava all-i-tell-him say altogether i-look-him something i-fall down from sky more i-got fire behind along tail belong him.

3 Time i-catch-him saltwater him i-fire up.

4 Altogether i-think say him i-bomb suppose no more volcano belong Gaua.

EXPLOSION SHAKES ISLAND!!

1 There was something that fell between Merelava and Gaua on Saturday morning June 17th.

2 All the people on Merelava reported (that) they saw something fall from the sky and there was fire behind in its tail (= *and it had a tail of fire*).

3 When it hit the sea it exploded.

4 They thought it was a bomb or else a volcano on Gaua.

And to conclude, here is the Lord's Prayer from the New Testament (St Matthew's Gospel, chapter 6, verses 9 to 13) in Bislama:

> Papa bilong mifala, yu yu stap antap long heven,
> Mifala i wantem we nem bilong yu i tabu.
> Mifala i wantem we kingdom bilong yu i kam,
> Mo we olgeta man long wol oli wokem olgeta samting we yu yu
> wantem, olsem olgeta long heven oli stap wokem.   5
> Mifala i askem yu bilong tedei yu givem kakai long mifala, i stret
> bilong tedei nomo.
> Mifala i askem yu bilong yu fogivem mifala from ol samting
> nogud bilong mifala,
> Olsem we mifala i stap fogivem ol man we oli stap mekem i   10
> nogud long mifala.
> Mifala i askem yu bilong yu no tekem mifala i go long sam
> samting we bambae oli traem mifala tumas,
> Mo bilong yu blokem Setan i no kam kasem mifala.

Glossary of words that may be difficult to understand:

blong and *long*	*(belong/along): are the only two prepositions in Bislama, so use the most appropriate English preposition to translate them.*
mifala	*(me-fellow):* we / us
stap	*(stop):* live, *or indicates* **progressive aspect** *on the verb*
we	that
nem	name
kam	come
mo	*(more):* and
olgeta	*(altogether):* all
wol	world
wokem	work
olsem	*(all same):* just as
kakai	food
stret	*(straight): means something like* as it should be
nomo	*(no more):* only
bambae	*(by and by): indicates the future,* will
traem	*(try); in the sense of* test
tumas	too much
blokem	*(block):* prevent
kasem	catch

NB   *i* is a grammatical **predicate marker**, that is, it precedes the predicate of each clause. There is no equivalent in English, and it cannot be translated. *-em/-im* are verb suffixes which mark **transitive verbs**.

4. Regional accents and Received Pronunciation

4.1 The difference between dialect and accent

When people talk about regional English, they often use the words *accent* and *dialect* rather loosely and interchangeably. For example, they could say of someone, 'She has a broad northern accent' or, 'She speaks a strong northern dialect', and both statements might be understood as meaning more or less the same thing. The linguistic distinction between accent and dialect has already been referred to in previous chapters: the term *accent* (sometimes *dialectal accent*) refers only to the system of pronunciation a speaker uses; *dialect* refers to a speaker's grammar and vocabulary.

In this chapter a method for analysing and comparing accents will be demonstrated, which you can use for describing other samples of regional English not represented here.

Activity 4.1

On section 6 of the cassette tape, Mrs Amy Cook from the village of Wotton-under-Edge in Gloucestershire is interviewed about her work. A transcription of the interview is printed below.

Listen to the recording twice, noting down the features of Mrs Cook's speech that give away her regional origins. Unless you came from Gloucestershire, you probably would not be able to place the speaker in a particular village or even in the county. But you would be able to identify her as coming from somewhere in the south-west of England.

Answer the question, 'What is it about Mrs Cook's speech that marks her out as a West Country person?'

(The interviewer's questions are not transcribed)
well for a start call me Ame (.) everybody else do ... I'm the only one
(.) in the whole of Gloucestershire (.) after twenty six year (.) nineteen
thirty nine when war broke out (.) I seed the advertisement in the
newspaper (.) and our dad said to I well he said if thee carsn't do that
as good as some of the men he said that's a poor job (.) well I thought   5
myself well I wouldn't let the old man down so I had a go (.) that's
nineteen thirty nine and I'm still going strong ...

well it was on account of the money (.) they was paying (.) they was
paying more for an hour than what I was getting where I was before ...

all sorts sk. (.) it's got grass-cutting to do (.) in the winter put down   10
the grit (.) it's got siding (.) channeling (.) I've even put up signposts
... even put up signposts ...

no (.) I er I'm classed as a roadworker (.) I do all the jobs all (.) all but
the manual labour which is carried out by the men ...

all round Hutton (.) Coombe (.) Sinnel (.) Blackwaters and er all   15
round Worlds End Lane and up Sinnel Lane again and that's my
worst piece on my area is Sinnel Lane (.) all the fish and chip paper is
chucked up the bank and the kids is on the top of the lane scorting the
bloody stones down (.) and it ain't a bit of good to sweep it up
because it's just as bad in ten minutes after ...   20

they do (.) and it ain't no good to have litter baskets ...

not a bit of good (.) and it ain't no good to tell them (.) cos they'll
they'll say all right to thee face and behind thee back there's (.) b. and
we's just as bad as ever ...

well (.) take them on the average and they been't too bad (.) but still   25
there's (.) there's ways and way (.) means for improvement ...

oh toffee papers sweet papers lollipops (.) there's sticks (.) all the
ruddy lot ...

all on it (.) you can get barrowfuls ...

no er (.) no not in the least (.) you er you can meet all sorts in the   30
course of a day (.) some'll say good morning Ame some'll say good
night some'll say good old Ame and some do say different ...

oh some do say good old Ame (.) some do say bugger her ...

no not at all (.) no the cos there's cars is going by all day (.) kick up a
heck of a dust (.) well it's a mystery to I in all these years I haven't   35
had my beauty spoiled ...

it is ...

well if you (.) you see the dust I do get ...

Commentary

Pronunciation belongs to a different level of language from vocabulary and grammar. You will have discovered features from all three levels in the tape and transcription.

Some will be **phonological**, that is, to do with the way the speaker pronounces vowels and consonants, and with the rhythm and pitch of her speech. It is these features which, together, make up her Gloucestershire **accent**.

Other features you will have noted are to do with the particular words she uses (vocabulary or **lexis**), the endings she gives to words like nouns and verbs and the way she combines words together to form sentences (**grammar**). These lexical and grammatical features form the basis of Mrs Cook's West Country **dialect**.

Activity 4.2

List any dialect words in the transcription, and say what you think they mean.

Activity 4.3

List the features of dialectal grammar in the transcription, giving the Standard English equivalent and identifying the differences in the way shown in chapter 3.

4.2 Accent

Activity 4.4

(i)   Attempt a description of Mrs Cook's accent, using the twenty-six symbols of the Roman alphabet to write down her pronunciation of vowels and consonants.

(ii) Comment on her use of intonation, or speech melody.

Commentary

It is necessary to differentiate between the two aspects of pronunciation mentioned in Activity 4.4. Some of the features that mark Mrs Cook as coming from Gloucestershire are **segmental**, that is, they are to do with the way she produces the individual sound-segments from which speech is made up, already referred to as **vowels** and **consonants**.

Other features are the speed (or **tempo**) and **rhythm** of her delivery, the placement of **stress**, and the fluctuations in the **pitch** and **loudness** of her voice. These are said to be 'overlaid upon' her speech, and so are called **supra-segmental**. Another term for them is **prosodic** features.

(i) *Supra-segmental features*

The supra-segmental aspects of her Gloucestershire accent are compared, as is customary in English language study, with the regionally neutral accent called **Received Pronunciation** (RP), which has been referred to in chapters 1 and 3.

Activity 4.5

Listen to the passage beginning *nineteen thirty-nine* and ending *I'm still going strong* (lines 2 – 7), and describe the differences between the Gloucestershire accent and of RP in terms of: (a) rhythm and tempo, (b) pitch range and movement, (c) use of pauses, and (d) patterns of stress.

Commentary

Firstly, the tempo is extremely fast and the rhythm is staccato – almost like a machine-gun.

Secondly, the pitch of the voice is constrained within a narrow band of the speaker's range. Rather than her voice rising and falling like an RP speaker's might, she keeps it relatively high and level throughout the passage.

Thirdly, the passage has few 'natural breaks' within it. As explained in section 4.4 below, all speech is divided into blocks known as **tone-units**. Compared with the RP passages on the tape, Mrs Cook's speech is characterised by long, unbroken tone-units. The overall effect of the rhythmic and pitch features makes for a delivery reminiscent of an auctioneer calling for and repeating bids.

Finally, there is variation from RP in her placement of primary stress in words of more than one syllable. For example, her pronunciation of the word *adver`tisement* differs from the RP pronunciation *ad`vertisement* - the third syllable, not the second, is stressed, with a consequent change in the pronunciation of the vowel.

(ii) *Segmental features*

Many of her vowels and consonants are different from an RP speaker's. One very obvious difference is in the stressed vowel in the words *paper* and *again*. As in RP, the sound is not a **simple vowel** but a **diphthong** – the speaker glides from one vowel sound to another. The beginning part of the diphthong is similar to the one an RP speaker would use in the word *feet*, and the second part is similar to that in RP *cat*.

Mrs Cook's pronunciation of *paper* and *again* might therefore be represented as *peeaper* and *ageean*. This pronunciation is restricted to a small area to the south-west of the Cotswold Hills. Some of the consonant features you will have noticed are characteristic of West Country speech more generally.

One such feature is the /r/ sound in words like *cars*, *roadworker* and *thirty*. Even though we have the letter <r> in the spelling of these words, RP, together with most regional accents, does not have the /r/ in pronunciation. This is a comparatively recent development. Until the seventeenth century, all accents of English did pronounce the sound. Today only a few accents retain /r/ sounds before other consonants and at word endings. These accents, which include some of East Lancashire, much of Scots and the West Country, are called **rhotic** (*rho* is the Greek name for the letter <r>).

Finally, there are two further related consonant features which distinguish West Country speech from that of other regions. These are the sounds we represent in writing by the letters <s> and <f>. You will have noticed that in words such as *sweep*, *seed* and *before*, the speaker replaces the sounds [s] and [f] with [z] and [v], *zweep*, *zeed*, *bevore*.

4.3 Boundaries of regional variation

Although we have been speaking of 'West Country English' as if it were a single, homogeneous variety, this is an idealisation of the facts. It has already been pointed out that Mrs Cook's pronunciation of *paper* is not common to the whole of the South West.

Activity 4.5 ────────────────────────────

Listen to the second sample of West Country speech on tape. Mr Fred Archer also lives near the Cotswolds, in Ashton-under-Hill, which is to the north-east of Wotton-under-Edge. Identify those features of Mr Archer's pronunciation which are similar to, and those which are different from, Mrs Cook's.

he wore a (.) a thing like a pinafore smock made out of sacking (.) with erm (.) some binder-twine round the middle (.) and he got his battered old trilby (.) and he used to keep his clay pipe stuck in his frock when he wasn't smoking it (.) and he smelt a mixture of Jeyes Fluid (.) Stockholm tar (.) twist tobacco (.) cider (.) and erm   5 (.) well and sheep I should say (.) not that he wasn't clean mind you I mean he was a clean man but it was just er (.) the (.) you know the (.) the smell of him (.) and er (.) everything seemed to be erm (.) for a purpose now he (.) had his thumb nails (.) a bit on the long side for getting the maggots out of the sheep you see (.)   10 he er grew them specially for that he never cut his thumb nails very much (.) for maggoting the sheep you see ...
that's right yes (.) and erm (.) then erm (.) he got (.) about three teeth at the front (.) which er (.) he used to use for castrating the   15 lambs and they came in very handy (.) he drew the (.) he did the castration with his teeth you see and er (.) and then another spare time job of his was doctoring cats (.) he used to put a pair of steel spectacles on the (.) end of his nose and he looked real professional when he was doing that ...   20

Commentary

One consonant feature common to both speakers is the distribution of /r/ sounds. Like Mrs Cook, Mr Archer produces /r/s at the ends of words like *pinafore*, *tar* and *cider*, and before other consonants in words like *purpose*. However, if we turn our attention to [s] and [f] , the two speakers are obviously different.

In *pinafore* and *cider* we find Mr Archer using [f] and [s] rather than [v] and [z]. On the basis of recordings such as this, linguists have found that the feature of **rhoticity** (sounding /r/ wherever it occurs in spelling) extends much further north and east than does the tendency to replace [f] and [s] with [v] and [z].

In describing the extent of any single accent feature, linguists use the concept of **isophones**. An isophone is a line on a map that indicates where one accent feature stops and another begins. Thus, on the map below, the solid line is an isophone showing the extent of two different pronunciations of the vowel in words like *cup* and *love*.

The isophone runs from the Bristol Channel on the west coast to the Wash on the east coast. People living north of the line tend to pronounce *cup, love, cut, mud,* etc. with a vowel very similar to, or the same as RP *put, cushion, butcher*. People south

North of the solid line, the vowel spelt <u> is pronounced by dialect speakers as [ʊ], and south of the line as [ʌ], e.g. [kʊp] versus [kʌp], [lʊv] versus [lʌv]. North of the broken line, the vowel spelt <a> is pronounced by dialect speakers as [æ], and south of the line as [ɑ], e.g. [gɹæs] versus [gɹɑs], [pæθ] versus [pɑθ].

of the line would use a different vowel in these words. They would therefore distinguish between pairs of words like *put* and *putt*. For some northern speakers, these words may be **homophones** – words with different meanings but the same pronunciation.

The second, broken line on the map is the isophone relating to the pronunciation of *grass, glass, path,* etc. To the south of the line, the vowel in these words is similar in quality to that used in *cart* and *jar*, whereas to the north of the line tends to be the same as that used in *cat, pat* and *mass*.

You will notice that although the two isophones do not follow exactly the same line, they do approximately coincide. This, in fact, reflects a general tendency for isophones to come in bundles or clusters – where we find one isophone, very often there is another nearby.

In the West Country area between the lines marked —·—·—·—·—, dialect speakers tend to pronounce the <th> of words like *thumb* as [ð].

To return to the different pronunciations of [s]–[z] and [f]–[v] in the south-west, you will see from the map on page 65 that the two isophones reflecting the north-eastern limits of the [z] and [v] also take broadly similar routes. There is a third isophone which follows the other two, though Mrs Cook's speech does not illustrate this. This is the pronunciation of <th> in words like *three* and *thumb*. People to the south-west of the line of the isophone tend to make no distinction between the <th> of *three* and *thumb* and that of *those* and *they*, both being pronouned with the <th> in RP *those* and *they*. People to the north-west of the line, however, do make the distinction found in RP.

Accent boundaries are not arbitrarily placed. Very often they correspond to other types of boundary such as natural geographical barriers, the past limits of trading circuits and socio-political boundaries.

Before the development of motorised transport and other modern technology, natural boundaries like rivers and mountain ranges formed barriers to communication. As a result, the linguistic communities on each side of the boundary tended to develop in isolation from one another, each evolving its own distinctive pronunciation patterns, which have persisted into present-day English.

Market and trading patterns have also had a significant effect on the limits of accent variation. Until quite recently, rural villages conducted their agricultural trade almost exclusively through nearby centres of marketing and commerce. Even though two villages might be near to one another with no natural barrier between them, people from each village might seldom meet one another because they belonged to different trading circuits, and used different market towns. The isophones separating the speech represented by Mrs Cook from that represented by Mr Archer could partly be explained in these terms. Wotton-under-Edge fell within the sphere of influence of Bristol and the south-western market centres, whereas Ashton-under-Hill was within the trading circuit of the West Midlands towns.

Socio-political boundaries are also very important in determining the limits of accent features. For example, at the England–Scotland border in the north-west of England, there is no natural barrier that can explain the abrupt transition from English English to Scots English in the space of the few miles between Carlisle and Gretna Green. People living on opposite sides of socio-political boundaries may use different systems of speech to assert their different cultural identities. Accent is a means of aligning yourself with certain groups of people and of distinguishing yourself from other groups.

The study of dialectal features works in exactly the same way as the study of accent just outlined. The boundaries of non-standard lexical and grammatical features called **isoglosses** can be plotted on a map to show the extent of their usage. Just as bundles of isophones make up accent boundaries, so bundles of isoglosses are said to make up **dialect boundaries**. The positions of isoglosses and dialect boundaries can often be explained by reference to natural barriers and socio-political boundaries also.

4.4 A framework for accent study

So far, in comparing features of regional accents with RP we have been using the ready-made resources of the Roman alphabet and English spelling system. Although some description of features of regional pronunciation is possible using these resources, they are, nevertheless, very limited. Some obvious limitations can be illustrated from the features of West Country speech already identified. For example, it was noted that in the words *paper* and *again*, the vowel used in Mrs Cook's area began with a sound like the vowel of RP *feet* and ended with a sound like the vowel of RP *cat*. The diphthong was represented by the sequence *eea*. In many respects, this was an arbitrary choice of letters. The vowel of RP *feet* is sometimes represented by <ea>, as in *bean*, or <e>, as in *be*, or <i> + consonant + <e>, as in *police*. Her pronunciation could just as easily have been represented as *peaaper*, or *peaper* instead of *peeaper*. Why any one rather than the other?

Another kind of difficulty concerns the West Country pronunciation of /r/ before other consonants and at word endings. How might we spell this pronunciation of *car*, for instance? We cannot put an <r> on the end of the word because one is there already.

The pronunciation of *thumb* with the <th> sound of RP *that* also causes problems. There is no difficulty in hearing two different <th> sounds in English, but there is no convention in ordinary spelling for distinguishing between them. Both are written <th>.

Because of difficulties like these, linguists have developed a special system of symbols for representing pronunciation. This is known as the International Phonetic Alphabet (IPA). The complete system has symbols for transcribing all speech sounds, not only those of English, together with a set of marks, or **diacritics**, which allow the transcriber to make subtle distinctions between sounds. For beginning purposes, however, many of the symbols and most of the diacritics can be ignored. You will be able to make significant progress using only a sub-set of forty-five symbols.

Received Pronunciation is used as the reference accent, the one with which samples of regional speech are compared, so the selected symbols reflect the sound distinctions an RP speaker would make.

4.4.1 How to make a phonetic transcription

List of symbols to transcribe the segmental sounds of RP English

IPA symbol		RP pronunciation
Simple vowels		
i	bead	[bid]
ɪ	bid	[bɪd]
ɛ* (see note on p. 69)	bed	[bɛd]
æ	bad	[bæd]
ɑ	bard	[bɑd]
ɒ	cod	[kɒd]
ɔ	board	[bɔd]
ʊ	put	[pʊt]
u	shoe	[ʃu]
ʌ	cup	[kʌp]
ɜ	bird	[bɜd]
ə	about, porter	[əbaʊt], [pɔtə]

IPA symbol		RP pronunciation
Diphthongs		
ɛɪ	pay	[pɛɪ]
aɪ	pie	[paɪ]
ɔɪ	boy	[bɔɪ]
əʊ	go	[gəʊ]
aʊ	hound	[haʊnd]
ɪə	beer	[bɪə]
ɛə	bear	[bɛə]
ʊə	cure	[kjʊə]

Consonants		
p	pit	[pɪt]
b	bit	[bɪt]
t	tip	[tɪp]
d	did	[dɪd]
k	kick	[kɪk]
g	give	[gɪv]
f	five	[faɪv]
v	vine	[vaɪn]
θ	thumb	[θʌm]
ð	this	[ðɪs]
s	some	[sʌm]
z	zoo	[zu]
ʃ	shoe	[ʃu]
ʒ	measure	[mɛʒə]
h	hot	[hɒt]
ʧ	charge	[ʧɑʤ]
ʤ	gin	[ʤɪn]
m	mouse	[maʊs]
n	nice	[naɪs]
ŋ	sing	[sɪŋ]
l	leaf	[lif]
r e.g. RP = [ɹ] *(continuant)*	run	[ɹʌn] RP
e.g. Scots = [ɾ] *(tap)*		[ɾʌn] Scots
j	yacht	[jɒt]
w	wet	[wɛt]

ʔ   The **glottal stop**, which occurs in some people's pronunciation of the medial consonant of words like *butter,* pronounced as *bu'er,* [bʌʔə]or [bʊʔə]. See section 4.6.

There are two principles underlying this system of sound symbols:

(i) each symbol has a fixed and stable value, that is, it is used consistently to represent the same sound. For example, although in ordinary spelling the letter <e> sometimes represents the sound in *bet* and sometimes the sound in *be*, in phonetic transcription the sound [ɛ] always represents the vowel in *bet*.

(ii) one symbol represents one segment in the 'speech chain', with only a very few exceptions. This is simpler than ordinary spelling, where a sequence of two or more letters may be used to represent one sound. For example, the vowel in *through* is represented by four letters, <ough>, in spelling, but with one, [u], in phonetic transcription.

The use of IPA symbols provides a solution to the sorts of transcription problems already identified. In describing the pronunciation of *car*, for example, we write simply that an RP speaker says [kɑ], and a West Country speaker says [kɑɹ]. Similarly, because the system has a symbol for both of the <th> consonants, we write that RP speakers say [θɹi] and [ðæt], and some West Country speakers say [ðɹi] and [ðæt].

Activity 4.7

Listen to section 8 on the tape, where the sounds relating to the phonetic symbols are illustrated, with particular attention to the vowel sounds. Notice that there are twenty vowels in RP, and learn to distinguish them clearly.

4.5   Practical exercises in broad phonetic transcription

Activity 4.8

Section 9 of the tape contains a passage spoken in RP. Listen to it and make a segmental transcription using phonetic symbols.

Commentary

In using phonetic symbols, you have transcribed the successive speech **segments** of the words. As mentioned in section 4.2, however, the **supra-segmental** features of pitch, loudness, rhythm and tempo are also important elements of natural speech.

In the transcription printed below, the passage has been divided into sections known as **tone-units**. The boundaries of tone-units may be marked by a variety of features, including abrupt changes in pitch and/or loudness, short pauses, and lengthening of the last speech sound in the unit.

Within each tone-unit one syllable, called the **tonic syllable**, is more prominent than the others. This extra prominence is caused mainly by a definite movement of pitch over the syllable, which may continue over any following syllables within the tone-unit. Pitch movement can be rising (e.g. Ként), falling (e.g. wèather), rising-falling (e.g. Nôrth), or falling-rising (e.g. Sŭmmer). Different meanings and attitudes are conveyed by such pitch movements, called **tones**. In the transcription, tonic syllables are underlined. Other syllables in tone-units carry stress also, but the tonic syllable, which usually specifies new information, stands out more.

Segmental and supra-segmental features may be transcribed separately or together. The following transcription of the passage in Activity 4.8 uses ordinary spelling, and indicates the supra-segmental features of tone units, tonic stress and pitch movement only.

> on the first day of British Sŭmmer Time I the winter
> wèather I has still got much of the cóuntry I in its
> grĭp I with ĭcy roads I as far south as Ként I and
> Hàmpshire I but it's still the Nôrth I that's móst
> affected I with the wòrst conditions I now moving
> north-wèstwards I into Scòtland I

Activity 4.9

(i)   Using phonetic symbols, make a segmental transcription of the second RP passage on the tape, section 10.

(ii) Divide the transcript into tone-units, underline the tonic syllables and mark in the tones above the tonic syllables, using the notation given above.

You may find it difficult to agree on a common solution to supra-segmental analysis in these exercises, especially in the placing and type of the tonic syllable. More practice will be needed before you become confident in an analysis of these features, if this is the first time you have attempted one.

4.6   A practical exercise in describing a regional accent

Section 11 of the tape contains three samples of speech by two speakers from the town of Ashington in Northumberland. A transcription of each sample in ordinary spelling appears opposite.

Activity 4.10

Listen to the Ashington speakers, following the speech from the transcriptions.

1. even so (.) on Saturday nights (.) you'll probably remember the street fights (.) I've often heard my wife er (.) tell me (.) that (.) she's seen them out (.) standing in the street in their er linings (.) sparring up and fighting (.) that was quite common on a Saturday night

2. times as far as I can remember when I was a young lad times was very very hard in Ashington (.) make no mistake about it (.) we were getting nothing (.) nothing (.) I'm only sixty seven year of age (.) and from about five year old till I was married until I started work we lived in dire poverty

3. we worked for nowt man (.) nothing (.) seven and fourpence a shift (.) I remember the first pay I got when I was married (.) I produced eighty ton of coal and I had thirty-nine bob (.) to take home to my wife (.) I'd ten bob rent to pay out of that

Activity 4.11

Now compare the Northumberland accent with RP. Follow these instructions step by step to make a systematic description, beginning with the vowels:

(i)   Identify the words that contain vowels pronounced [aʊ] in RP, as in *about, out,* and write down the phonetic symbol for their Northumberland pronunciation.

(ii) Repeat the exercise for the RP vowels [ɜ], *(shirt);* [ɒ], *(job);* [ɔ], *(law);* [ɛɪ], *(say).* You may find that an RP vowel has more than one pronunciation in Northumberland speech.

Activity 4.12

Next, examine the consonants:

(i)   Try to work out the pronunciations of <r>, which is particularly different from RP in the first extract.

(ii) Identify the final consonant in words ending in <-ing> in their spelling.

(iii) Note the pronunciation of <t> in the middle of a word.

Commentary

(i) *The vowels*

1 The vowel [aʊ] in RP, as in *about*, *out*, tends to be pronounced [u]. The relationship between RP and Northumberland pronunciation can be set down as follows:

RP	Northumberland	Evidence
[aʊ] ↔	[u]	*out* (extract 2), *about* (extract 3)

where the arrow ↔ indicates a consistent relationship between the two vowels.

2 The relationship between the other vowels is:

RP	Northumberland	Evidence
[ɜ] ↔	[ɔ]	*worked, thirty, first*
[ɒ] ↔	[ə]	*bob*
[ɔ] ↔	[aʊ]	*fourpence*

3 The vowel /ɛɪ/ has more than one **realisation**. In the word *pay* (extract 2), it is like a long RP [ɪ] sound. This is the most usual realisation for this accent, and can be represented by placing a colon after the [ɪ] symbol to denote lengthening,[ɪː].

A second realisation is found in the word *eighty* in the same sample. Here the vowel is very similar to the RP *buy*, [aɪ]. This replacement with [aɪ] occurs only in the word *eight* and its compounds *eighteen* and *eighty*.

The third realisation is found a few words later in *take*, RP [tɛɪk], where the vowel is pronounced [ɛ]. This pronunciation is also highly restricted and occurs in two words only, the other being *make*.

RP	Northumberland	Evidence
[ɛɪ] ↔	*[ɪː]	*pay*
	*[aɪ]	*eighty*
	*[ɛ]	*take*

* = the standard form for the Northumberland accent.

(ii) *The consonants*

The first prominent consonant feature is the pronunciation of <r>. The difference between the pronunciation of <r> in Northumberland and in RP is most noticeable in extract 1, *remember* and *probably*. The realisation of <r> in RP (called a **continuant**) is represented by the IPA symbol [ɹ]. The Northumberland <r> is similar to the 'rolled' [r] of French and German, but instead of being produced with the tongue behind the tooth ridge at the front of the mouth, it is made with the back of the tongue against the **uvula** (the small 'finger' of fleshy tissue that hangs down from the very back of the palate). The symbol for this **uvular roll** or **trill** (not included in the list of sounds) is [ʀ].

Another common consonant feature in Northumberland, but not restricted to it, is the replacement of [ŋ] with [n] at word endings. This is most noticeable in extract 1, in *linings* (a dialect word for men's combination underwear) and *sparring*.

A third consonant difference is in the realisation of /t/. The word *Saturday* in extract 1 does not have the [t] that occurs in RP *top*. Some people might say that there is no consonant at the end of the first syllable, and a novelist might substitute an apostrophe for the letter <t> and write the word as *Sa'urday* (cf. chapter 9 on dialect in literature). In phonetic terms, however, there *is* a consonant there, produced within the **larynx** (behind the 'Adam's apple'). It has the technical name **glottal stop**, and is symbolised as [ʔ]. It occurs in many accents, and is often referred to as 'sloppy pronunciation' when used in words like *better* and *butter*.

RP		*Northumberland*	*Evidence*
[ɪ]	↔	[ʀ]	probably, remember, street
[t]	↔	[ʔ] *(word-medial and final)*	Saturday
[ŋ]	↔	[n] *(word-final)*	linings, sparring

Activity 4.13

Listen to the two samples of the London accent on the tape (sections 12 and 13).

(i) Transcribe the speech.
(ii) Identify the differences in vowel and consonant pronunciation between the London accent and RP, and describe them in the way which has been demonstrated.

4.7 Social evaluation of accents

On the whole, regional accents tend to be stigmatised together with the words and grammar of their dialect. The description of accents is often pejorative, that is, they are disparaged and not valued highly. The claims made against the use of regional accents fall into three main types:

● they are simply incorrect ways of speaking;
● they are ugly, and lack aesthetic appeal;
● they are lazy and imprecise.

Activity 4.14

(i) Question informants about their opinions on regional accents.
(This topic could be added to the questions in the Acceptability Test in chapter 1, or form the subject of a separate investigation.)
(ii) Discuss the opinions that you discover, and say whether there is any relationship between the social class of the person interviewed and their attitudes towards regional accents.
(iii) Discuss the validity of these views on regional accents.

Commentary

(i) *The 'incorrectness' view*
This raises the main topic of chapter 1 again. Just as there is a strong tendency for people to look upon the regionally neutral system of Standard English as the correct

one, and then to use it as a 'measuring rod' for evaluating regional dialects, so the regionally neutral accent, RP, is used to measure regional accents.

To what extent is RP the correct way of speaking? If a large number of people agree that one form of behaviour is the correct form, then that behaviour becomes the standard by which they judge others. However, it is important to remember that such standards are matters of fashion and convention.

For example, at one time all accents of English were rhotic. The sound of <r> was pronounced before consonants and at the end of words by everyone. However, in the seventeenth century it became fashionable in Court circles to drop the pronunciation of <r> except where it occurred before vowels. The accent associated with the court had social prestige, and developed later into present-day RP. The dropping of <r> spread to other regional accents. Today the pronunciation of *car* and *part* as [kɑ] and [pɑt] is generally more socially acceptable than the West Country older pronunciation [kɑɹ] and [pɑɹt] .

In parts of the United States, however, the situation is reversed. The pronunciation with [ɹ] present has more prestige, and the non-rhotic accents have low status and are called 'incorrect'.

RP, therefore, cannot be the correct pronunciation in any absolute sense. What counts as correct is a a matter of social convention, relative to time and place.

(ii) *The 'ugliness' view*

You may hear people talking about Northern accents as 'flat', or Glasgow vowels as 'harsh', or saying that the Birmingham accent is 'not melodious'. When speakers of British English are presented with samples of accents and asked to rate them on a scale according to how pleasant they sound, they broadly agree that RP should come near the top, together with certain south-eastern accents. Highland Scots and West Country are usually rated highly too.

Accents from Newcastle, Liverpool, Glasgow and Birmingham, however, are rated negatively. These ratings are often justified on the grounds of ugliness, harshness and so on, but it can be no coincidence that the accents which receive the poorest ratings are all from industrial cities. It seems that people are reacting to the **social connotations** of the areas from which the accents come.

This is confirmed by the reactions of speakers who are unfamiliar with the social connotations of the accents about which they are asked to make aesthetic judgements. They often rate the accents of the big industrial cities more highly than those of RP and the rural south and south-west.

(iii) *The 'impreciseness' view*

The words *lazy* and *sloppy* are often used to express this negative view of regional accents. The glottal stop replacement of <t> is frequently cited as an example. But if you examine accents which have a glottal stop where RP has [t] it becomes clear that the use of [ʔ] is by no means sloppy or haphazard. Not every /t/ can be realised by [ʔ]. The possibility of realisation is governed by the position of /t/ within a word.

No accent of British English allows /t/ at the beginning of a word (*word-initial*) to be pronounced as [ʔ]. The word *top* is never pronounced [ʔɒp]. The possibility of replacement can only apply to a /t/ in the middle of a word (*word-medial*), or at the end (*word-final*). Thus we find pronunciations such as [bɛʔə] for *better* and [bɛʔ] for *bet* in a number of accents. Far from being sloppy, the use of the glottal stop is an orderly business, governed by linguistic rules concerning the position of the /t/ sound.

Another aspect of the 'impreciseness' argument suggests that children with regional accents may have difficulties in learning to read and write. One well-aired example concerns the 'dropping of aitches', which is characteristic of London, Yorkshire and Lancashire accents, and others. Children who drop an initial /h/, the argument goes, will have difficulty in distinguishing between pairs of words such as *hill* and *ill* in writing.

However, *all* accents, including RP, contain many pairs of words that are **homophones**, that is, words that are pronounced the same but spelt differently. Is there not equal difficulty in distinguishing *hour* from *our*? Consider also the tendency in RP to pronounce *tower* and *tar* as homophones, [tɑ].

A measured, linguistic consideration of people's negative reactions to regional speech leads again and again to the view that, no matter what other reasons are put forward in explanation, the issue is really one of social prejudice. An objective study of accent can help to modify the instant reaction that we all tend to have towards an accent which is marked as socially inferior.

4.8   Accents and social variables

Accents vary not only geographically, but according to certain **social variables**, that is, accents are associated with different social groups.

The first, and most obvious, social grouping related to accent is **social class**. Although we often label regional accents as coming from particular geographical areas – a city or a county, for example – it is clear that not everyone in that area will speak in the same way. Social class seems to stand in *inverse* relationship to regional accent. That is, the higher up the social and occupational ladder we look, the fewer regional features we find. Thus, although people in professional jobs from different areas of the country may have some pronunciation features that are regional, the differences between them are less marked than for unskilled manual workers.

The second and less obvious feature is **gender**, or the differences between women's and men's speech. Recent research has shown that within any social class, men show a greater tendency than women to use the 'broadest', most regionally marked, pronunciation. The reasons for this are not yet clear, but one possibility is that teachers and parents may tend to correct girls' speech more than boys'.

When you have studied this chapter, you should be much more aware of the differences in pronunciation that you hear, and able to say more precisely which features are the most marked, in terms of vowels and consonants, pitch and intonation. Your opinions on the controversial aspects of attitudes towards dialect and accent may have changed, but these remain your own, and you must question everything that has been said here, except the objective linguistic facts.

Activity 4.15

Read again the extracts from Peter Trudgill's and John Honey's books at the end of chapter 1, and apply the arguments specifically to regional and social accents.

Discuss the debate between the view that would stress the linguistic validity of all accents, and the view that the social consequences of speaking a marked regional accent must be a first consideration.

5. Spoken English and written English

5.1 Speech and writing as media for language

We all learn to talk before we learn to read and write. Chapter 6 describes in more detail how children learn to talk. This chapter discusses the principal differences between **speech** and **writing** as media for language. That is, we assume that the same **language**, English, underlies talking and writing, listening and reading. Language in this sense is abstract, something we know. When we use it, it must be made concrete, and transmitted and received by one or more of the human senses.

Consider the alternative realisation of language that is available to the deaf, **signing**. Like writing, sign language is read with the eye, but uses the human body itself to signify the words. And what is available to those who are both deaf and blind? Communication through the sense of touch alone is possible, as the life of Helen Keller made clear.

Speech consists of sounds, and writing of marks on a surface, and this fundamental difference produces equally marked contrasts in our use of the two media. Some of the differences are the result of the fact that we listen to speech, which is impermanent (unless tape-recorded), and usually we can see who is talking to us. Hence there is always the possibility of **feedback** between speaker and listener. The telephone is a special case, and produces its own characteristic features of discourse. We must read writing. It is permanent and can be re-read. We do not usually see the writer, so communication is one way only. There is no feedback during the interchange.

These differences of **substance** (sound or marks on a surface), and of **function** (what we can do with spoken or written language), result in differences of **form** and **style**. Rather than list these differences, we shall look closely at some authentic speech and writing, and help you to discover for yourself what these examples show.

Transcribing speech into writing freezes it in a form that we can study. If speech can be turned into writing, and writing can be read aloud, you may wonder whether there can be any essential differences. There are, as you will find out.

5.2   Making a transcription

In transcribing speech into writing you have the choices of method discussed in chapter 4: ordinary or phonetic spelling, with or without an indication of certain supra-segmental features. Your choice will depend upon the purpose for which you are making the transcription.

For the dialogue in section 5.3, ordinary spelling, or **orthography** is used, as the chapter focuses on aspects of speech in which segmental features of pronunciation are not important. Features of the spoken language are shown as follows:

   (i)   **Pauses** – a momentary break or *micropause* of less than half a second is shown as (.), and a longer pause is shown as a figure in seconds, e.g. (0.5), (2.0). A pause which includes an audible intake of breath is marked <h>.

   (ii) **Capital letters** are used only to mark people's names, abbreviations like *TV*, the first letter of the first word in a person's speaking turn, or loudly spoken words.

   (iii) **Quietness** is marked by putting a raised <°> before and after the quietly spoken words.

   (iv) **Unfinished words** are marked with a dash < – >. Where there is an overlap between the speakers, the places where the overlap begins and ends is marked by brackets < [ ] >.

   (v)   **Stress** is marked by <u>underlining</u> the stressed syllable of the word.

   (vi) **High and low pitch** – for raised pitch put <↑> before and after the relevant words; for lowered pitch put <↓>.

   (vii) **Pitch movement** – put < ´ > above the vowel of the syllable for noticeably **rising** pitch, <`> for **falling** , <ˆ> for **rising–falling** and < ˇ> for **falling–rising** pitch.

   (viii) **Pronunciation** which is distinctive or unusual is transcribed using IPA symbols (listed in chapter 4).

   (ix) **Indecipherable** text is marked (*********), each asterisk representing a syllable.

Features that break the flow of speech are quite usual and necessary. Remember that when you speak spontaneously you are doing at least three things at once: planning what to say next, saying what you have planned, and monitoring what you are saying in order to check that it is what you meant to say. It is, therefore, not surprising that ordinary spontaneous speech in conversation is broken up by hesitations, false starts, self-corrections, repetitions, fillers and so on. They have been referred to as **normal non-fluency features** of speech. They are not part of the vocabulary or grammar of language, and by definition cannot be a feature of a written document (except in rough drafts with alterations, which we don't usually let others read).

In the following transcription, the non-fluency features are printed in italics.

(NB The commentary in section 5.3 is deliberately restricted to a discussion of ways in which speech contrasts with writing in its **structure**. Other important aspects of spoken language related to the functions of intonation, pitch and stress are not discussed here, but in chapter 8.)

5.3   Dialogue 1: making a model village

A nine-year-old girl called Romy had a conversation with her father, which was tape-recorded. She had been amusing herself in the holidays by making a model village market, after watching a Blue Peter programme on television. Her father got her to talk about it and then asked her to write down what she had been telling him about the market she had made.

Notice that he asks questions, partly to start the dialogue and to keep it going, and partly because he wants to question things she hasn't made clear. Some parts of their talk will show features that belong to **discourse**, or **verbal interaction**. One will complete another's utterance, for example. Certain words, like *Well...*, when starting a sentence, have a discourse function.

Activity 5.1 _____

Transcribe the first minute of the conversation before looking at the transcription printed below, making sure that you include everything you hear.

Activity 5.2 _____

Then listen to the whole conversation, following it with the transcription.

Activity 5.3 _____

Make a list of the ways in which Romy's use of English in speech differs from her use of the language in writing.

One important clue to the difference can be presented in the first place as a question: can you divide Romy's speech into **sentences**?

5.3.1   *Transcription of the spoken dialogue* (cassette tape, section 14)

F	So what have you been <u>mák</u>ing Ro?	
R	*h* (3.0)	
	° *Well I was ma- I've been making a mar-* °	
	I've been making a ↑ <u>màr</u>ket ↑ *h*	
	(3.0)	5
	and I made it out of ↑ <u>màtch</u> ↑ sticks and (1.0) *h em*	
	<u>match</u>boxes *h*	
	and (.) at the bottom of the <u>match::</u>boxes *I I put h*	
	I put <u>matches</u> (.) *for* for four ↑ <u>legs</u> ↑	
	(1.0) and then *h* I put four matches at the <u>top</u> *h*	10
	and I put a <u>roof</u> at the top (1.0) *em* out of <u>pa:</u>per *h*	
	and then I made little things to put <u>on</u> it *h er*	
F	↑ You've been making <u>what</u>? a <u>màr</u>ket? ↑	

R	° Yeah °	
F	*So* and you've been using *match*::(.) match<u>bò</u>xes?	15
R	° And <u>match</u>sticks °	
F	What did you use the ↑ <u>bòx</u> ↑ part for?	
	(1.0)	
R	That was for the <u>tà</u>ble	
F	Oh <u>I</u> see (.) the <u>stàll</u> was it?	20
R	<u>Yeah</u> *h and* (.) and then I made lots of <u>thóse</u> *h*	
	(3.0)	
	and later on I'm going to (.) finish it off by making a	
	village <u>squà</u>re	
	h and I make the village square by	25
	(3.0)	
	h well I'm going to pu	
	I'm going to put *er h* benches for (.) <u>bén</u>ches	
	and I'm going to put <u>bí</u>::ns around the place and <u>bus</u>-stops	
	h and I'm going to put my ↑ <u>màr</u>ket ↑ on *h*	30
	(3.0)	
	em	
F	Have you made any things to go ↑ <u>òn</u> ↑ the stalls?	
	(1.0)	
R	Yes *I made f-*	35
	h I've made <u>frŭi</u>::t and (1.0) *h* <u>brĕa</u>::d and (.) <u>flŏ</u>:wers *and*	
	(.)	
F	° What did you <u>use</u> to make all those things? °	
R	*h* Well (.) for my ↑ <u>frùit</u> ↑ and the <u>bread</u> em I used	
	<u>plas</u>ticine	40
	h and (.) for my flowers I used crepe <u>pà</u>per	
	(2.0)	
F	° So how how did you make (1.0) the fruit (.) with the	
	<u>plas</u>ticine? °	
R	I just came to put them in the shape of the ↑ <u>frùit</u> ↑	45
	(3.0)	
F	What <u>rôlled</u> them *or s.*?	
R	Well it depends what kind of a <u>shape</u> really	
	if they're bananas I made them in a long line and ↑ <u>cùrved</u> ↑	
	them	50
	h and if they were apples ° I made them into a <u>bàll</u> °	
	h and I had (.) pears what *I* (.) I had quite a <u>trouble</u> with	
	making those *h*	
F	° Why's <u>that</u>? °	
R	Because I couldn't quite get it the quite <u>shape</u> *it*	55
	it was <u>pointed</u> at the top when it went <u>round</u>	
	h and it went into a great big ↑ <u>bà</u>::ll ↑	
	h it looked a bit funny so I had to try and get it so it was	
	kind of <u>slò</u>:ped ° into a ball °	
F	° Oh I <u>see</u> ° (.) did you have *er* (.) *have* to ↑ <u>pàint</u> ↑ them?	60

R   *h* Yeah I painted them <u>blà:ck</u>
      (1.0) ↑ <u>òh</u> ↑ (1.0) I painted the ↑ <u>stàlls</u> ↑ black
      (1.0)

F   ° Oh I <u>see</u> (.) but I meant the <u>fruit</u> (.) did you ⎡ (1.0) ⎤
                                                    ⎣ R no ⎦   65
      have to <u>paint</u> them? °

R   No because *they had the c-* the plasticine was ↑ <u>còloured</u> ↑

F   ° Ah I <u>see</u> (.) so what colours did you use for <u>what</u>? °

R   *h* Well for the apples I used <u>grĕe:n</u> *h*
      (2.0)   70
      and fo:r (.) bananas I used <u>yĕllow</u>
      h for the (3.0)
      ↑<u>nò</u> ↑for the apples I used <u>rèd</u>
      (2.0)
      and for the *h* pears I used <u>grĕe:n</u>   75
      (3.0) *er* (1.0) *and I* (1.0)
      that's all I could really ↑ <u>màke</u> ↑ those kind of fruits
      but I made (1.0) about <u>twò</u> of each kind *h* (2.0) *and* (.)
      and I used <u>bròwn</u> for my bread rolls
      and just h put them into a kind of   80
      (3.0)
      em a <u>rèc</u>tangle

F   Rect<u>àn</u>gular shape?

R   Yeah *h* and put a <u>line</u> at the top to make it more like <u>bread</u>
      because *h* sometimes they put lines in the <u>mĭddle</u>   85

F   When they're <u>bàking</u> them?

R   Yeah ⎡ *h*   ⎤
            ⎣ F mm ⎦
      R (2.0) *em*

F   You said you made ↑ <u>flòwers</u> ↑ didn't you?   90

R   Yes I just <u>screw:ed</u> up some (1.0) crepe <u>pàper</u> *it* (.) and *it* (.)
      it ↑ <u>dĭd</u> ↑ look a bit like *em* ° <u>flówers</u> °

F   Were they in <u>bùnches</u>?
      (2.0)

R   No I just put (1.0) *I just put* lines of (.) screwed up <u>pàper</u>   95

F   But they look ⎡ (1.0)   ⎤ ° quite like <u>flowers</u> °
                   ⎣R ↑ yèah ↑ they look⎦

R   ° <u>Yèah</u> °

F   And <u>thèy</u> were all ° different colours as well °

R   ° Yeah °   100

F   So you've got <u>bréad</u> (1.0) <u>flówers</u> (1.0) <u>frúit</u> (1.0) ° what
      <u>èlse</u>? °
      (1.0)

R   <u>Wéll</u>
      (3.0) *well h*   105
      I had a <u>matè:ri</u>al stall *h*
      and for that I got<u> matchsticks</u> again *h and got*
      and got little bits of (.) mat<u>èri</u>al

and got little bits of (.) ma<u>tè</u>rial
and rolled them <u>ròund</u>   110
and then put them on the ↑ <u>stàll</u> ↑

F   ° Oh that was a good i<u>dèa</u> ° (.) was ↑ that ↑ <u>yòur</u> idea?
(3.0)

R   We:ll (.) I got it while *h* I was watching Blue <u>Pèter</u>
that's how I got the i<u>dèa</u>   115

F   For <u>èv</u>erything?
(2.0)

R   *h* <u>Nò</u> (.) well *h they made* they made the ↑ <u>stàlls</u> ↑ a bit
different to me *h* and *they just* they didn't make a <u>vïll</u>age

     [(.)   ] they just (.) made these <u>stàlls</u>   120
     [F mm]

F   But what about [ði:] (2.0) the ma<u>tè</u>rial rolls did

R   Oh yes <u>that</u> [bit   ]
                   [F that] was <u>their</u> ° idea? °

R   ° Yeah °   125

F   ° Yeah °

R   They didn't use <u>plàs</u>ticine for the *h* bread rolls *they* (.)
they made it out of special <u>bàk</u>ing stuff (.) *stuff* what
won't go <u>mòu:ld</u>y though (1.0)
° they made <u>real</u> *br-* (1.0) *real* (.) things h °   130
I've forgotten what they used for the ↑ <u>frùit</u> ↑ though
(3.0)

F   <u>ók</u> well that sounds (.) ° as if you've been having a good
<u>tïme</u> ° (.)
can I go and have a <u>lòok</u> at it now?   135

R   <u>Yès</u>

5.3.2   *Romy's writing*

The market I made

These are the things I used. I used dead matches and match box's and
plasticene. First I stuck the matches at the bottom of the match box's
for legs. Then I stuck four at the top of the match box and then made a
roof out of paper. Later on I painted it black. When it had dried I made
the things to go on them. I made fruit, bread, flowers, then I made a
material shop by rolling material round matches. I made the bread and
fruit with plasticene. The flowers were made out of screwed up crate
paper. Then I'm going to make a villige to put the stalls on.

Commentary

Her written version is much shorter than the conversation. She omits quite a lot of the
information she talked about, and she also puts some of it in a different order. This is
to be expected from a nine-year-old. Writing takes more thought and effort than

talking. But she has written enough for us to notice some important differences. Look first at the **structure**, or how the bits of information are linked and related.

In her writing, Romy correctly places a capital letter at the beginning, and a full-stop at the end of her sentences (except, perhaps, sentence 7?). Setting out a text in columns is often helpful in sorting out its sentence structure. If a sentence consists of more than one **clause**, each clause is put on a separate line. Words which have a linking function are separated from the main part of the clause, as follows:

	Linking words	*Clauses*
1		These are the things I used.
2		I used dead matches and match box's and plasticene.
3	First	I stuck the matches at the bottom of the match box's for legs.
4a	Then	I stuck four at the top of the match box
4b	and then	Ø made a roof out of paper.
5	Later on	I painted it black.
6a	When	it had dried
6b		I made the things to go on them.
7a		I made fruit, bread, flowers,
7b	then	I made a material shop,
7c	by	rolling material around matches.
8		I made the bread and the fruit with plasticene.
9		The flowers were made out of screwed up crate paper.
10a	Then	I'm going to make a villige
10b		to put the stalls on.

If her spoken response to her father's first question is printed as if it were written language, it looks like this:

> I've been making a market **and** I made it out of matchsticks and matchboxes **and** at the bottom of the matchboxes I put matches for four legs **and** then I put four matches at the top **and** I put a roof out of paper **and** then I made little things to put on it.

It is fully **grammatical**, but not **acceptable** as good written English because it consists of a series of clauses all joined, or **coordinated**, by *and*. Compare the linking words in her writing. What is normal and goes unnoticed in speech would look wrong in writing. It is a matter of convention, so she changed her spoken English to conform to an acceptable style in her writing, though without really knowing how.

The question in Activity 5.3 asked what a **sentence** is in speech. There are no capital letters or full stops to tell us. In Romy's first utterance there are six **main clauses**. Is it one sentence just because she happened to pause at that point? Suppose she had gone on uninterrupted with *and... and then... and then...*?

Can we define a sentence? Here, for example, is a confident definition from a Victorian grammar book called *The Analysis of Sentences* (1859):

> Language is the utterance of our thoughts in words. The complete utterance of a single thought is called A Sentence.

Activity 5.4

Discuss this definition of a sentence, apply it to Romy's talk, and to her writing. Is it a satisfactory definition?

Commentary

(i) *The functions of the word* and

In her opening utterance, Romy uses *and* five times to join her clauses. In her writing, she uses *and* only once for this purpose. Her other uses of *and* are for joining **phrases** and **words**. She avoids the normal spoken use of *and* as a kind of all-purpose linker, or **continuer**. Listen to the tape-recording again, and notice how she uses intonation, stress and pauses like spoken punctuation, to divide up her speech into manageable units of information. The function of written punctuation marks is partly equivalent to some of the functions of intonation, stress and pauses. That is why we can read aloud from a written text. But it will always sound like reading aloud, and not like spontaneous speech.

In a similar way in reverse, we have seen that speech doesn't look like authentic writing when transcribed. So the **coordinating conjunction** *and* has two uses in speech. Firstly as a grammatical word, joining sentences, clauses, phrases and words, just as in writing. Secondly, and only in spoken English, as a linking word or continuer between groups of clauses (or **clause-complexes**) where its function is not just grammatical, but also part of conversational exchange, telling a listener, 'Don't interrupt, I haven't finished.'

(ii) *Deletion*

If *and* joins two clauses, and the second clause has the same grammatical subject as the first, the second subject may be **deleted**. For example, Romy's written sentence (4) omits *I* in the second clause (4b) – 'and then Ø made a roof out of paper' (the sign Ø is used to mark a deleted item). When you find examples of deletion, or **ellipsis**, you have direct evidence of *and* as a grammatical conjunction.

Activity 5.5

The writing has 15 clauses, but *and* is used only once to coordinate clauses. Her talk has 66 clauses (not counting *yes* and *no* and other very short responses), and 25 uses of *and* between clauses. The difference is very marked.
Examine the uses of *and* in Romy's talk, and divide them into the two categories.

Activity 5.6

Write out Romy's spoken narrative in clauses, separating out the linking words. Here is part of it as an example:

Father	**Romy**
how did you make the fruit with the plasticene?	I just came to put them in the shape of the fruit
what rolled them?	well it depends what kind of a shape really
	if they were bananas
	I made them in a long line
	and Ø curved them
	and if they were apples
	I made them into a ball
	and I had pears
	what I had quite a trouble making those

To sum up so far, spoken English tends to be marked by features of non-fluency which are often only apparent when speech is transcribed and read, because they are a normal part of our way of talking.

Particularly when telling a story, we link our spoken clauses together with *and* so that the boundaries of sentences may be impossible to determine. This is not so in writing, because we learn not to use *and* like this, and punctuation clearly marks the beginning and end of sentences. In this way, the style of spoken English is usually in marked contrast to that of written English.

The grammatical structure of speech is often less complex than that of writing. This is not very noticeable in Romy's speech and writing, because at nine years old she has not yet acquired the skills of complex writing, but you can see it more clearly in the following transcription and text, spoken and written by her older sister.

These stylistic features of spoken and written English are, of course, always associated with the context in which we use either medium. As a result, we say that spoken English tends to be more **informal** than written English, because we usually use writing for purposes that are **formal** (although there are occasions when we speak formally and write informally, of course.)

Using a tape-recording of a conversation, we are in fact eavesdropping on people we don't know. We cannot see them, and so have to guess at their gestures and facial expressions (called **paralinguistic** features), and the kind of place in which they were talking (the **context of situation**). It is possible that some references made by the speakers cannot be properly understood, and so remain inexplicit, because language is only a part of how we communicate meaning.

Activity 5.7

Examine the transcription and listen again to the tape to find:

(i) some examples of inexplicitness of language, and
(ii) supply some of the probable paralinguistic gestures and visible signs used by the speakers.

5.4   Dialogue 2: at the riding school

Romy's elder sister Rebecca, who was twelve years old, was recorded in a similar conversation and then wrote about her experiences at riding school. Here first is the unedited text of her writing, followed by an unedited and unmarked transcription of the opening part of her talk.

5.4.1   *Rebecca's writing*

When you go to a riding school everything apart from riding the horse will be done for you. However if you have a horse of your own you have to do everything yourself.

Before you mount (get on) a horse it has to have a saddle and bridle put on it, this is called 'tacking up'.   5

When saddling a horse you need a saddle and a girth. A girth is a long strap which, when the saddle has been put on the horse's back, is buckled to one side and is then brought under his stomach and buckled tightly to the other side of the saddle. This stops the saddle from falling off.   10

Lift the saddle high above the horse's back and then bring down gently so that the front (pommel) of the saddle is over the horse's withers. Slide the saddle down onto the horse's back until it fits snugly. The sliding down of the saddle is done so that the hairs on the horse's back all lie down the right way. Looking from   15
the back of the horse you should be able to see a channel of light between the lining of the saddle. You should also be able to slide your hand under the pommel of the saddle, this is so that air can get to the horse's back.

The first thing you will learn, when having your first riding   20
lesson, is to mount correctly.

Face the horse's tail, hold the reins in your left hand and rest this hand on the pommel of the saddle. Turn the stirrup iron towards you.

Slip your left foot into the stirrup iron. Turn round so you are   25
facing the horse's side then spring up. Swing your right leg over the saddle then lower yourself gently into the saddle.

There is a special position when riding. This position in no way should appear stiff. Your back should be straight, yet relaxed, your arms should hang from the shoulders, with your elbows bent   30
and slightly touching your sides of your body. Your hands should be 6" apart and must keep a 'feel' of the horse's mouth. The ball of the foot should be on the stirrup iron, the heel pushed down and the toes in a natural position.

The paces   .   35

A walk is slow pace and easy to master, but the trot is more difficult. The trot is a bumpy pace and to make it comfortable to ride, the rider rises for one bump and sits down in the saddle for another.

To make a horse canter you make him go into a trot by   40
increasing your leg pressure on his side. But instead of rising for
one bump and sitting down in the saddle for another you sit down
in the saddle all the time. If you wish to make the horse canter in
a circle his inside leg must go farther than the outside one. To
make the inside leg go farther you put your inside leg on the girth   45
and your outside leg behind the girth. Then increase your leg
pressure against his sides and he should go into a canter, if he
does not use your stick against his side.

To make your horse jump you must ride him on towards the
jump, if he runs out to the left pull his right rein and kick him   50
with your left leg and vice versa. When taking off and going over
the jump your horse will stretch out his neck, lean forward and
give him lots of rein so you do not restrict his head.

5.4.2   *Transcription of part of the spoken dialogue* (cassette tape section 15)

F   ok. Reb (.) are you going to tell me something about riding?
 (2.0)
R   yeah what do you want to know?
 (2.0)
F   h well (.) when you go riding (.) to the riding school (.)   5
 what's involved?
R   well first we just mount (2.0)
 and w.(.) we mount by going to the left side or the near side
 of the pony (.)
 and we put our left foot in the stirrup (1.0)   10
 and then we sort of jump round until we're facing the
 pony's side (1.0)
 and then (.) and then we jump up (.)
 and then we swing our right (.) leg over
 and then go gently down to the saddle   15
 so we don't give the horse a fright if we went h bump down
F   oh so the horses are all (1.0) s.
 they've got the saddles on before you start then
 (2.0)
R   yeah ⌈yeah   ⌉ (.) you don't have to do anything about them   20
        ⌊F the bridles⌋
R   no (1.0) h but h
 but when we went on the Boxing Day ride we had to do that
F   put the saddles on?
R   yeah h and (1.0) what you do is you get the saddle and a girth   25
 which you tie round the pony's tummy well h
 it's sort of like a strap (.) with buckles on the end h
 and you get this saddle h you put (.) lift it quite high above
 the pony's head
 but not really really high (1.0)

well not the head but back h
and then you lower it down on to his withers
which is just above his back and slide it down h
and if you didn't slide it th. the hairs would all b. (.) be all
the wrong way h   35
and it'd hurt the pony because it'd rub against the saddle
(1.0) h
and then you've got to get the stirrups and (1.0)
I mean the h the girth (1.0)
and buckle it to one side and bring it under the (.) pony's   40
tummy (2.0) h
and then buckle it to the other side and h
often when you do that they blow their tummy out
so that when they're on a ride they h they can (1.0) bring the
 tummy back in (1.0)   45
and it'll be quite comfortable h
but but most people (.) kick them in the tummy and then
they go (1.0) thin
[*the conversation continues*]

Activity 5.8

(i)   Edit and mark the transcription.
(ii) Transcribe the remainder of the dialogue.

Activity 5.9

Collect examples of normal non-fluency features from the transcription, and classify them as hesitations, false starts, self-corrections or fillers.
   You will find that these categories overlap, so don't expect each example to fall neatly into one set or the other.

Activity 5.10

Take a 'paragraph' of Rebecca's talk and turn it into good written style. Then describe what you have done to the original to achieve this.

Activity 5.11

Is Rebecca's talk similar to Romy's in the frequency of the conjunction *and*?
Are the sentence boundaries or Rebecca's talk as clear as those of her writing?

Activity 5.12

Is the sentence structure of her writing simpler or more complex than that of her speech? Quote examples when commenting.

Activity 5.13

Examine the interaction between Rebecca and her father for features which show that they are in a face-to-face situation, using gesture as well as speech, aware of each other and reacting to each other. Give examples from the language used which give you the information.

Activity 5.14

Make a comparison between the following extract from her talk and the corresponding section of her writing. Look especially for features of vocabulary and grammar that you would describe as **formal** or **informal**. Which of these categories best fits the speech and the writing?

Saddling up

spoken:

	what you do is	
	you get the saddle and a girth	
	which you tie around the pony's tummy	
well	it's sort of like a strap with buckles on the end	
and	you get this saddle	5
	you lift it quite high above the pony's head	
but	not really really high	
well	not the head but back	
and	then you lower it down on to his withers	
	which is just above his back	10
and	Ø slide it down	
and if	you didn't slide it	
	the hairs would be all the wrong way	
and	it'd hurt the pony	
because	it'd rub against the saddle	15
and	then you've got to get the girth	
and	Ø Ø Ø buckle it to one side	
and	Ø Ø Ø bring it under the pony's tummy	
and	then Ø Ø Ø buckle it to the other side	

written:

When	saddling a horse	
	you need a saddle and a girth.	
	A girth is a long strap	
	which ..... is buckled to one side	
when	the saddle has been put on the horse's back	5
and	Ø is then brought under his stomach,	
and	Ø Ø buckled tightly to the other side of the saddle.	
	This stops the saddle from falling off.	
	Lift the saddle high above the horse's back	
and	then bring down gently	10
so that	the front (pommel) of the saddle is over the horse's withers.	
	Slide the saddle down onto the horse's back	
until	it fits snugly.	
	The sliding down of the saddle is done	
so that	the hairs on the horse's back all lie down the right way.	15

Activity 5.15

Select another pair of parallel extracts from Rebecca's speech and writing, and discuss their differences and similarities.

Activity 5.16

Use part of the conversation to identify some of the prosodic (supra-segmental) features of Rebecca's speech:

(i)   **intonation:** mark stressed syllables with the tone, or direction of pitch movement on them.

(ii) **stress:** find words which Rebecca speaks with contrastive stress, or extra emphasis.

(iii) **tempo, loudness** and **rhythm:** find examples of her delivery that are faster or slower, louder or softer than the norm, or show marked changes of rhythm.

In all these examples that you discover, relate the prosodic features to her meaning, or to the effect that she wishes to produce.

5.5   The relationship between spoken and written English

We have already seen that there are distinctive differences between the ways we use language to talk and to write. But how far does the system of writing match or copy the sounds of speech?

5.5.1 *Features of speech omitted in writing*

In speech there is no gap or pause between words. What we say is divided up into units of information called **tone units** (see section 4.5). There is no spoken equivalent of a capital letter to mark the beginning of a sentence. In writing, punctuation defines units of the grammar, with spaces between words, commas between some phrases, and full stops to mark the end of sentences. Paragraphs are indented to mark changes or developments in the topic.

In writing English, we only make an approximate representation of speech. We do not normally show **intonation** and **pitch,** or **stress, tempo** and **loudness,** those supra-segmental or prosodic features which are so important in communication of our meanings in talk (see sections 4.2, 4.5, 5.2 and 5.3). For example, we do not show the difference of stress pattern between *to insult, to record, to export* and *an insult, a record, an export.*

Activity 5.17

Use the text of a novel, short story or play to find out ways in which writers indicate features of intonation, pitch, stress, tempo or loudness in the speech of their characters.

5.5.2 *Using an alphabet of letters to represent sounds*

English has an alphabetical system of writing, that is, an **alphabet** of signs we call **letters** represents the **sounds** of the language, so that the words of English are written down using a system of **orthography** or **spelling** which is intended to match the pronunciation.

To convey meaning in writing, it is not necessary to use an alphabet related to the sounds of the spoken language. Signs can represent complete words, like Chinese **ideograms**, or syllables, as in Hebrew and Arabic scripts. In writing or printing English some signs to represent whole words may be used:

Activity 5.18

Write out the meanings of these signs, using words spelt with the Roman alphabet:
(i)   1; 2; 3; 4; 5; 12,567; 25,496,987
(ii)   ii, ix, xiv, mlccvii
(ii)   24 @ £1.95
(iii)   17.5%
(iv)   16 + 27 = 43; 347 ÷ 17 = 20.41
(v)   ♣ ♦ ♥ ♠
(vi)   ©

but the number of signs of this kind that we use in English is very small compared with the 'productivity' of an alphabet, which can reproduce hundreds of thousands of words using only a few letters.

In a perfect alphabetical system, one sound would be represented by one letter and vice versa, without irregularities or exceptions. Everyone knows, however, that our present-day spelling system is irregular and inconsistent, and it is both useful and interesting for students of language to examine some of the features of this irregularity and its causes.

We use a **Roman alphabet** of twenty-six letters, each of which has a lower and upper-case (or capital letter) form:

abcdefghijklmnopqrstuvwxyz
ABCDEFGHIJKLMNOPQRSTUVWXYZ

In order to emphasise certain words, or to show that we are referring to a word as a word, we use *italics* in printing and typing, though not in handwriting, when we have to make do with underlining or using CAPITALS to show emphasis – usually in informal writing like personal letters.

But you have already seen in section 4.4.1 that we need forty-four or forty-five symbols to make a phonetic transcription of the English RP accent, so it is obvious that our present system of spelling cannot be perfect in the sense just indicated – one letter one sound and vice versa.

All other European languages that use the Roman alphabet make use of extra signs called **diacritics**, which provide additional letters to mark differences of pronunciation, e.g. <â, ç, é, è, ê, î> in French, <ö, ü> in German, <ñ> in Spanish, and <å> in Norwegian. English, however, uses no diacritics.

When English was first written down by monks over a thousand years ago in the Anglo-Saxon period, the Roman alphabet was adapted for the purpose. Latin was the language of the Church and the monks were experienced in using that alphabet for writing and copying manuscripts. The 'fit' between the pronunciation and writing of Old English was good at first, especially as three other letters were added to the alphabet to represent sounds that were not in the Latin language – <æ> and <ð> or <þ> (see section 2.2). But the changes in pronunciation over the following centuries were not always matched by parallel changes in spelling (re-read the last paragraph of section 2.4).

5.5.3 *Imperfections and anomalies in our present spelling system*

In a broadcast about regional accents and people's attitudes to them, a Lancashire woman said:

b - a - r - t - h - it's not English, you know, [bɑːθ]. It should be [bæθ].
And [grɑːs], g - r - a - r - double s. It's not right.

She is arguing that the Lancashire pronunciation of *bath* and *grass* is 'correct', and the southern pronunciation 'wrong', because the spelling of the words does not contain <ar>, which is pronounced as [ɑː]. The vowel spelt with <a>, she claims, should be pronounced [æ]. She assumes that pronunciation depends upon spelling, but this is not so. In an alphabetic system of writing, spelling should follow pronunciation. In any case, the assumption that there is one 'correct' pronunciation of *bath* and *grass* is debatable.

One spelling, several sounds

(a) *Vowels*

Activity 5.19

(i) Discuss the validity of the Lancashire woman's assertions about the spelling and pronunciation of *bath* and *grass*.

(ii) The letters and digraphs (two letters representing a single sound) used to represent vowels are listed below with examples of words using the spellings. Transcribe the words using the phonetic alphabet in section 4.4.1. Include any different pronunciations of the same word if you know them. Are any single letters or digraphs used to represent one sound only? *(This list is not intended to be fully comprehensive.)*

Letter			Words			
a	sat	bass (singer)	water	ape	pass	many
	village	castle	all	was	vase	
e	set	be	complete	pretty	England	
i	sit	child	children	police	time	
o	dock	come	wolf	women	lose	do
	son	sole	so			
u	sun	busy	bury	sure	put	minute
	tune	putt				
ai	said	waist	again	plait		
ao	gaol					
au	aunt	flaunt	because	pause	gauge	laundry
ay	day	says	Sunday			
al	calm	palm	psalm			
aw	saw	gnaw	lawn			
ee	tree	seed	beet			
ea	leaf	dead	steak	idea		
ei	seize	either	Leicester			
eo	people	leopard	neon	leotard		
eu	feud	museum				
ey	key	they	eye			
ew	chew	new	sew			
ia	dial	hiatus	tiara			
ie	piece	die	ladies	society	friend	
io	biology	biological	nation			
iu	triumph	diurnal				
oo	blood	good	food	brooch		
oa	broad	oak				

Letter			Words			
oe	*toe*	*shoe*	*does*			
oi	*noise*	*abattoir*				
oy	*boy*	*foyer*				
ou	*count*	*group*	*trough*	*thorough*	*country*	*soul*
	though	*through*	*thought*	*cough*	*rough*	*bough*
ow	*know*	*knowledge*	*cow*			
ua	*truant*	*actual*				
ue	*blue*	*fluent*	*unique*			
ui	*juice*	*suit*	*suite*			

The following words are all spelt with an <r> after the vowel (called **post-vocalic <r>**). In some dialects of English speakers pronounce the <r>, e.g. in the south-west, parts of Lancashire and the Pennine area, the north-east, and throughout Scotland. Others, including RP speakers, do not pronounce it. Formerly it was pronounced in all dialects of English.

Activity 5.20

Transcribe the words into your own pronunciation. If you pronounce post-vocalic <r>, transcribe the RP version also.

ar	*part*					
er	*clerk*	*fern*	*heron*	*severe*		
ir	*bird*	*iron*				
or	*cord*	*word*	*store*			
ur	*turn*	*curious*				
ear	*heart*	*hear*	*heard*	*bear*		
our	*four*	*flour*	*flourish*	*tour*	*your*	*journey*
oor	*door*	*poor*	*moor*			
iar	*liar*					
ier	*fierce*	*drier*	*tastier*			
eir	*weird*	*their*				
are	*care*	*are*				
ere	*here*	*there*				
ire	*fire*					
ure	*sure*	*pure*				

(b) *Consonants*

The consonant letters are, on the whole, less varied in the different sounds they represent than the vowels. There are twenty-one consonant letters for about twenty-four consonant sounds, but the letters include <c>, <q> and <x> which could be replaced by other existing letters: <k> or <s>, <kw> and <ks>.

Activity 5.21

In the following list, the pronunciation of the words is transcribed into phonetic symbols.

(i) Write the conventional spelling of the words.
(ii) Comment on any spelling rules or conventions that are demonstrated.

The transcriptions assume an RP accent.

Consonants	*Transcribed words*				
[p]	stɒp	stɒpə			
[b]	rɒb	rɒbə	ɛb		
[t]	pæt	pætə	wɔːkt		
[d]	mæd	æd	mædə		
[k]	kaɪnd	kɒŋkə	keɪk	stʌmək	əkɔːdɪŋ
[g]	dɪg	dɪgə	gɑːd	gəʊst	
[ʧ]	ʧeɪn	raɪʧəs	wɒʧ	kwesʧən	neɪʧə
[ʤ]	ʤæm	ʤem	səʤest	əʤeɪsənt	mɪʤɪt	səʊlʤə
[f]	fɔːk	ɪnʌf	ɒf	fɪzɪks	sfɪə
[v]	vaɪn	veɪn	ɒv		
[θ]	θaɪ	θɪn	hiːθ		
[ð]	ðaɪ	ðɪs	siːð		
[s]	sɔː	pɑːs	saɪəns	æks	naɪs	dɪsiːs
[z]	rəʊzɪz	dɪzɪ	sɪzəz	siːzɪz	ɪgzækt	dɪziːz
[ʃ]	ʃuː	məʃiːn	əʃʊə	neɪʃən	mænʃən	mɪʃən
	kɒnʃəns	speʃəl	əʊʃən	lʌkʃərɪ	ʃiːt	ʃed
[ʒ]	vɪʒən	meʒə	beɪʒ		
[h]	hæŋ	huː	hiːt		
[m]	miːt	sʌmə	kʌm		
[n]	nuːn	fʌnɪ	sniːz		
[ŋ]	sɪŋ	sɪŋk	sɪŋə	æŋkə	lɪŋgə	streŋθ
[l]	lɔɪjəl	lʌl	pælɪd		
[r]	rʌb	fɜːrɪ	fjuːrɪ		
[j]	jes	spænjəl	mjuːzɪk	njuː	fjuːd	bjuːtɪ
	juːnɪən	juːrəp	jɒt		
[w]	west	wɪʧ	kwɪk	wʌn	kwaɪə	swiːt

One sound, several spellings

(a) *Vowels*

Just as we have seen that in our present spelling system, most letters in English are pronounced in more than one way, so the opposite is also the case – most English sounds have more than one spelling. If you were to try to make up a list of words containing all the different spellings for the twenty English RP vowels, you would find you needed about 220 different words.

The next activity will help you to discover the variations in spelling for some of the vowels of English

Activity 5.22 ———————————————————————————

The following alphabetical list consists of words containing the **simple RP vowels** [iː, ɪ, ɛ, æ, ʌ, ɑː, ɒ, ɔː, ʊ, uː and ɜː]. Sort them into sets according to the pronunciation of the vowel, and list the different spellings used for each vowel sound. (If a word contains two syllables, identify the stressed vowel.)

again	bury	daughter	heart	pass	says	was
all	busy	dead	her	people	seize	wolf
aunt	calm	do	journey	piece	set	women
be	chew	dock	juice	plait	shoe	word
because	clerk	does	key	police	sit	worsted
before	colonel	door	knowledge	pretty	son	yacht
bird	come	earth	leaf	purr	sun	
blood	complete	food	lose	put	sure	
blue	cord	four	many	rude	symbol	
bought	cough	friend	myrtle	said	tree	
broad	could	good	or	sat	turn	
build	country	group	part	saw	vase	

Activity 5.23 ———————————————————————————

The following alphabetical list consists of words containing the **RP diphthong vowels** [eɪ, aɪ, ɔɪ, əʊ, aʊ, ɪə, ɛə and ʊə]. Sort them into sets according to the pronunciation of the vowel, and list the different spellings used for each vowel sound. (If a word contains two syllables, identify the stressed vowel.)

air	buy	dough	gauge	mauve	sole	toe
aisle	care	ear	great	no	soul	tour
ape	child	eight	height	noise	sow (needle)	truant
bass (singer)	cow	either	here	oak	sow (pig)	waist
bear	cry	fierce	high	poor	their	weird
bough	day	fluent	house	pure	there	
boy	deer	folk	idea	sew	they	
brooch	die	gaol	isle	sewer	time	

(b) *Consonants*

The main variation in the spelling of consonants is the choice between a single or a double letter, which does not indicate the pronunciation of the consonant itself, but of its preceding vowel.

Activity 5.24

What 'rules' of spelling can you infer from the use of single or double consonants in the following spellings?

> *can, canning, caning, cane*
> *hop, hopper, hoping, hope*
> *pin, pinning, pining, pine*
> *tun, tunny, tuning, tune*

Other variant spellings for consonant sounds are generally the result of the **assimilation** or **elision** of sounds. This happens either in borrowed foreign words whose spelling has been kept, but whose pronunciation has been assimilated into English, or in sound changes to English words (see the following section 5.5.4 for an explanation of assimilation and elision). Such sound changes tend to result in what are usually called 'silent letters' in the spelling of words. For example:

> ***Borrowed foreign words***
> *pneumonia, debt, stomach, muscle, diaphragm, sign, science, rhythm*
>
> ***Changes in the pronunciation of English words***

Activity 5.25

The spelling of the following words in phonetic script contains what are usually called 'silent letters'. At one time they were pronounced. They are nearly all words from Old English, or taken into English from French at an early period, eleventh–fourteenth centuries.
Write out the words and identify the 'silent letters'. Check the derivations of the words in an etymological dictionary and discuss possible reasons why the letters are no longer pronounced.

kʌbəd	ni	naɪf	ʃɛpəd
sæmən	nəʊ *(verb)*	ɔːtəm	sɪzəz
læm	sɑːm	saɪn	raɪt *(with a pen)*
kəʊm	næt	tɔːk	rɒŋ
kɑːsəl	nɔː *(verb)*	ʃʊd	rɪst

Some 'problems' in English spelling

(a) *Homophones*

Words may be pronounced identically but have different meanings, e.g. *sight, site, cite* and *pear, pair, pare.* They are called **homophones.** Their distinction in writing is useful, but not essential, because there are also homophones which are not differentiated in writing, like *bear* (animal) and *bear* (carry).

Some words may be homophones in one dialectal accent of English, but not in others, e.g. *weigh* and *way* are differentiated in some Northern accents as [wɛɪ] and [weː], whereas *night* and *neat* may both be pronounced [niːt].

(b) *The question of spelling reform*
This is not the place to discuss spelling reform at any length. Proposals for reform have been made since the sixteenth century, but none has been taken up. Spelling reformers claim that our present system causes difficulties for some children learning to read. A system called the **Initial Teaching Alphabet (ITA)** was introduced in the 1960s and was popular in many infant schools for some time. It contained forty-five letters, so that children could match each of the contrastive sounds of English to a letter when learning to read and write. But it is no longer widely used.

One problem that would have to be solved in reforming the spelling to match pronunciation is that of variable dialectal accents. For example *walk to work* in RP would be [wɔːk tə wɜːk], whereas on Tyneside it would be something like [waːk tə wɔːk]. We accept present-day spelling as neutral to dialectal pronunciation – we know what a word means, and we say it in our own accent, whatever the alphabetical spelling might indicate.

Secondly, a reform to match pronunciation would obscure the relationship between many sets of words.

Activity 5.26

Identify the differences in the pronunciation of certain letters in the following sets of words. If you can, transcribe them using the phonetic alphabet.
Discuss the advantages and disadvantages of changing the spelling of the words.

> nation, national; nature, natural; sane, sanity
> wide, width; phone, phonic; tone, tonic
> courage, courageous; anxious, anxiety
> photograph, photography, photographic
> medicate, medicine; critical, criticize
> sage, sagacity; prodigal, prodigious
> grade, gradual; mode, modular
> resident, residential; expedite, expeditious
> fact, factual; quest, question
> revise, revision; divide, division
> sign, resign; gymnastics, gymnasium
> waited, walked
> cats, dogs, horses

Accurate spelling is generally regarded as an essential part of writing 'good English', but if the first thing you look for in a piece of writing is the accuracy of the spelling, then you will sometimes fail to notice the quality of the language in other respects. Here is an example of a six-year-old boy's writing following a lesson on 'riddles':

I am dlack I	and I go
goe evriy wer	outsid in tHe
los of pepl triy to	wind I Hav got a lat
cil me but tHay	of druvs and sists
mis all was I	wat is my nam
get in Hosis	

Activity 5.27

If you were the boy's teacher, what would you say to him, and what steps would you take to improve his spelling?

If you only look at the inaccurate spelling and lack of punctuation, you may be 'blinded' to the fact that it is a fully grammatical piece of writing, and a good attempt at producing a riddle:

> I am black. I go everywhere. Lots of people try to kill me but they miss always. I get in houses and I go outside in the wind. I have got a lot of brothers and sisters. What is my name?

(c) *Words spelt with* -ough

The details of the historical changes in pronunciation that have not been reflected by changes in our spelling system are too detailed and complex for this book, but -*ough* words are favourite puzzles for most people. A very brief explanation should be of interest.

Firstly, the eight variations in pronunciation can be remembered from this sentence:

> A **rough**-coated **dough**-faced **plough**boy strode **cough**ing and
> **hiccough**ing **thought**fully **through** the streets of Scar**borough**

There are two kinds of variation in pronunciation, firstly between the vowels, and secondly in the written consonant <gh>, which is either 'silent', or pronounced as [f].

rough	*dough*	*plough*	*cough*	**hiccough*	*thought*	*through*	*borough*
[rʌf]	[dəʊ]	[plaʊ]	[kɒf]	[hɪkʌp]	[θɔːt]	[θruː]	[bʌrə]

> **(Hiccough* is a later spelling of *hiccup*, 'under the erroneous impression that the second syllable was *cough*, which has not affected the received pronunciation, and ought to be abandoned as a mere error' (*OED*), so does not really belong to this group of words.)

All were Old English words except *cough*, which was borrowed from the Dutch word *kuchen* in Middle English:

> *ruh dah plog þoht þurh burh/burg*

The final consonant spelt <h> or <g> was strongly pronounced in Old English as a **fricative**, similar to modern German *ich* or *bach* (in phonetic script [ç] or [x]). The spelling changed to <gh> in the Middle English period. In the course of time the consonant was modified to [f] or entirely lost. The reason for the variations in vowel and consonant pronunciation today lies in the wide variety of dialectal pronunciations in earlier times. There is evidence of these alternative pronunciations, for example of *though* and *ought*, in Smollett's novel *Humphry Clinker* (1771), in which characters say,

> "but he would never be satisfied, even **tho'f** she should sweat blood and water in his service ..." "But then they **oft** to have some conscience."

Both characters are servants, and so speak the 'vulgar tongue' of the time. The choice of the established pronunciations of *-ough* words today is arbitrary, and the earlier 'vulgar' pronunciation is now standard in *cough, trough, rough* and also *chough, tough*.

(d) *Some historical changes*

A full acount of the changes in the spelling and pronunciation of English would occupy a long book, but here are just some of the interesting facts which help to explain anomalies in present-day spelling.

<o> pronounced as [ʊ]   The Old English spelling of *son, come, some, wolf, monk* was *sunu, cume, sum, wulf, munuc*. The vowel is pronounced [ʊ] just as it was in OE times (except for RP and southern dialect speakers' pronunciation as [ʌ]). The spelling with an <o> was adopted by scribes because the manuscript formation of letters like <u>, <i>, <w>, <n> and <m> was very similar (they are called 'minim' letters, and the <i> was not dotted), and could cause confusion in reading. So letter <o> was written for <u>, but the pronunciation was unchanged. This convention was borrowed from the writing of Latin.

initial <h>   There were many Old English words beginning with a strongly pronounced [h] that is now much weakened, so that some dialectal accents today have lost it altogether. But in the Middle English period, some new French words, spelt with an initial <h> which was not pronounced, were adopted. In some of them the influence of the spelling has reintroduced the pronunciation of the [h].

Activity 5.28

What is your pronunciation of the following words, which were adopted from French? Is there any rule that tells you when to pronounce the <h> and when not to?

honour	*horror*	*hostage*
honest	*hospital*	*hotel*
horrible	*host*	*hour*

Other French spellings   After the Norman Conquest of 1066, the introduction of French-speaking monks into the English churches and monasteries led to the adoption of a number of conventions of French spelling, for example:

(i)   letter <c> for [s] before <e> and <i>, as in *cease, cedar, cede, celery, cell, cement, centre, certify, city, citadel, cipher, circle, cistern, cite, citizen.*

(ii)   digraph <ch> for [tʃ], eg *chalk, cheese, choose, churl* for OE *cealc, cese, ceosan, ceorl*

(iii) digraph <sh> for [ʃ] eg *shade, shield, ship* for OE *scead, scield, scip*

(iv) digraph <qu> for [kw] eg *quell, queen, quick* for OE *cwellan, cwen, cwic*

(v) digraph <ou> or <ow> for [uː] (later [aʊ]), eg *cow, house, mouse* for OE *cu, hus, mus*

(vi) letter <v> was introduced for the sound [v] , eg *even, knave, drive, heavy, liver, vixen* for OE *æfen, cnafa, drifan, hefig, lifer, fyxen*, in which <f> was pronounced [v].

(vii) digraph <th> replaced letters <ð> and <ƿ>, and letter <æ> was dropped.

Activity 5.29

Have all these French re-spellings of Old English words been useful?

The spelling of <ar>, <er>, <ir>, <or>, <ur> and <yr>   The Lancashire woman quoted at the beginning of section 5.5.3 believed that the correct pronunciation of the spelling <ar> is [ɑː]. She ignored the fact that many English speakers pronounce the <r> after a vowel and at word endings still. Their dialects are **rhotic** (see Activity 5.20 and section 4.2). But before the eighteenth century, all speakers of English would have pronounced the <r> in words like *hard, herd, bird, lord, curd* and *myrtle*, and the vowels would have been short, and pronounced [a, ɛ, ɪ, ɒ, ʊ, ɪ].

The gradual loss of the [r] in some dialects led to a simultaneous change and lengthening of the vowels, so that in RP and some other dialects today they are pronounced as long vowels, and four have 'fallen together' to the same vowel [ɜː], [hɑːd, hɜːd, bɜːd, lɔːd, kɜːd, mɜːtəl]

5.5.4 *Pronunciation in normal speech*

If you compare the way a single word is pronounced slowly and then in a stream of speech, you will find it likely that one or more sounds that belong to the word are changed or lost. All consonants and vowels may be affected by their neighbouring sounds in a word or phrase – their **phonological environment** in linguistic terms – and also by whether they belong to a stressed or unstressed syllable – the **rhythmic structure** of the speech. This is caused by the continuous movements of the tongue and lips, sometimes anticipating a following sound, and sometimes simply 'skating over' a sound so that it is left out altogether. The 'merging' of one sound into another is called **assimilation**; the loss of a sound is called **elision.**

These processes are perfectly normal. Everybody's speech is full of assimilations and elisions, even those who accuse others of being 'slovenly' or 'lazy'. They have nothing to do with dialectal accents as such, because all accents are affected. Here are just a few examples to show what is meant. A detailed survey would require a good knowledge of phonetics.

Assimilation and elision of consonants

These three examples are taken from the RP spoken text in section 4.2. (cassette tape section 9).

(i) *first day* spoken slowly would be transcribed [fɜːst deɪ], but a final [t] before another alveolar stop consonant [d] requires you to make the same plosive sound twice in succession, once unvoiced and then voiced, which is difficult in a normal stream of speech. The tongue goes to make the first [t] sound, but it remains **unreleased**, and the [d] is sounded. The IPA sign for an unreleased sound is [˺], so we transcribe the actual pronunciation as [fɜːst˺ deɪ]. In very rapid speech, the [t] would disappear completely and be elided, [fɜːsdeɪ].

(ii) *has still* [hæz stɪl] is similar – same place of articulation (alveolar), but fricative instead of plosive, and voiced [z] followed by unvoiced [s] The first consonant [z] is assimilated with the second [s] , [hæstɪl].

(iii) In the pronunciation of the word *Scotland,* the plosive <t> sound is clearly heard, but because it is followed immediately by [l], a lateral consonant, the tongue is already moving towards [l], and so the <t> has a lateral release down the sides of the tongue, not at the tip. You probably will not have noticed this before, although it is the normal pronunciation before [l]. Try saying it yourself, and note the position of your tongue and the actual sound of the <t> as you speak. The IPA sign for [t] with lateral release is [tˡ]·

Examples of consonant assimilation   In the following examples in which one consonant follows another, the place of articulation of the first is assimilated to that of the second. (The IPA symbol [ɹ] represents the normal RP pronunciation of <r>.)

words	transcription		normal speech with assimilation
Great Britain	[ɡɹeɪt bɹɪtən]	⇒	[ɡɹeɪp˺bɹɪtən] (alveolar [t] ⇒ unreleased bilabial [p] before [b]
stand forward	[stænd fɔwəd]	⇒	[stæmb˺fɔwəd] (alveolar [n] + [d] ⇒ labiodental [m] + unreleased [b] before [f]
can get	[kæn ɡɛt]	⇒	[kæŋɡɛt] (alveolar [n] ⇒ velar [ŋ] before [g]
and produces	[ænd pɹədʒusɪz]	⇒	[æmpɹədʒusɪz] (alveolar [n] ⇒ bilabial [m] before [p]; [d] elided

These are a few examples only of the possible kinds of assimilation.

Examples of consonant elision   Certain consonants at the end of a syllable or word, or in a consonant cluster of three or more, tend to be elided in informal speech (often with assimilation also):

[t]	at least three	[ət liːst θɹiː]	⇒	[ətˡliːsθɹiː]
	extracts	[ɛkstɹækts]	⇒	[ɛkstɹæks]
[d]	changed to	[tʃeɪndʒd tu]	⇒	[tʃeɪndʒtə]
	received by	[ɹɪsiːvd baɪ]	⇒	[ɹɪsiːvbaɪ]
[v]	choices of method	[tʃɔɪsɪz ɒv mɛθəd]	⇒	[tʃɔɪsɪzəmɛθəd]

[ð]	*knock them down*	[nɒk ðəm daʊn]	⇒	[nɒkəmdaʊn]
[l]	*year-old plants*	[jɪəɹ əʊld plɑnts]	⇒	[jɜɹəʊdˑplɑnts]
[ɹ]	*referring to*	[ɹɪfɜɹɪŋ tu]	⇒	[ɹɪfɜːntə]
[n]	*in the holidays*	[ɪn ðə hɒlɪdeɪz]	⇒	[ɪðəhɒlɪdeɪz]
[k]	*asked her to write*	[ɑːskt hɜ tə raɪt]	⇒	[ɑːstətəraɪt]

Practice your awareness by listening carefully to the exact way in which people pronounce their words, and which sounds they leave out or modify. Listen to yourself also.

Reduction, modification and elision of vowels

In unstressed syllables, the vowel is always **reduced** in quality to [ə] or [ɪ], depending upon the phonological environment, as for example in *telegraph, telegraphy, telegraphic*, ['telɪˌgrɑf, tə'legrəfɪ, ˌtelɪ'græfɪk], (the sign <'> means *primary stress*, and <ˌ> means *secondary stress*). The vowel [ə], called *schwa*, is the commonest English vowel, but we have no letter of the alphabet for it, which helps to explain why children learning to spell often don't know whether to put *a, e, i, o* or *u* in spelling a word – *relevant/relavant, opportunity/oppertunity, separate/seperate* and so on.

Because [ə] is always unstressed, it is more likely to be elided in fast speech, together with other assimilations and elisions, for example:

interest	['ɪntəˌɹest]	⇒	['ɪntrest]	⇒	['ɪntrəs]
secretary	['sekrəˌterɪ]	⇒	['sekrəˌtrɪ]	⇒	['sekəˌtrɪ]
library	['laɪbrəˌrɪ]	⇒	['laɪbrɪ]		
extraordinary	['ekstrəˌɔdɪnərɪ]	⇒	[ɪk'strɔːdənrɪ]	⇒	['strɔːnrɪ]

Elision also occurs in sequences of words, as in,

after the election	['ɑftə ði ɪ'lekʃən]	⇒	['ɑfðɪ'lekʃən]
letter of apology	['letə ɒv ə'pɒləʤɪ]	⇒	['letrəv'pɒlʤɪ]

Sound changes

These examples of normal assimilation and elision can sometimes show evidence of a sound change. At any one time, variant pronunciations of the same sounds can be heard, between dialect speakers, between social classes, between young and old, and so on. Some of the variants eventually become more widespread, and lead to a recognisable change in pronunciation more generally, though this usually happens over several generations.

For example, there is evidence that the RP diphthongs [eə] and [ʊə] are becoming simplified to [ɛː] and [ɔː], *care, where, spare,* and *poor, moor, sure*. This is a possible change that you could yourself investigate by listening to other speakers, or by setting up your own experiment. For example, do speakers differentiate between and *poor/paw, moor/maw, sure/shore*?

This examination of assimilation and elision in ordinary speech is only a short survey, and does not try to illustrate all the kinds of simplification that you will find, but it should give you enough information to make you more aware of what goes on in normal talk.

Activity 5.30

There are plenty of examples of assimilation and elision in the father and daughter dialogue, section 5.3.1 (cassette tape section 14).
Choose a short section of the dialogue, listen to the pronunciation carefully while following the transcription in section 5.3.1, and make a broad phonetic transcription of what you hear. (You will need to transcribe the glottal stop [ʔ] as well as the recognised vowels and consonants of English.)

6. Learning to talk

6.1 Language learning – a complex skill

If you have had the experience of learning a foreign language, you will have some idea of the range of knowledge that is needed in properly speaking, reading and writing that language. You have to learn about pronunciation, spelling, words and their meanings, and how to construct sentences with the words in the right order. Then there are different ways of constructing messages so as to be interesting, logical, persuasive, tactful, polite and so on.

The way we learn a second language after we have already learned our first will differ from the way we learned the first one, because knowledge of our first language is bound to affect our learning of the new language, in helpful and unhelpful ways. Nevertheless, attempting to learn a new language can highlight the nature and complexity of the skills involved in knowing a language.

If we consider just what goes on when children learn their first language, we can begin to appreciate the true nature and complexity of the skills they have. All normal children learn to talk surprisingly quickly, and most of them, by the age of four, can talk on a wide variety of topics, using language that is clearly spoken, rich in vocabulary, varied in the patterns of sentence used, subtle in shades of meaning expressed, and appropriate to the situation and purpose.

We shall try to show more exactly what a four-year-old's skills in language use are by looking at successive stages in the development of speech. Argument still goes on about how a child can learn so effortlessly the complex skills that using language involves. After four years of learning a foreign language in school, when you were not a young child, could you speak it as fluently as your first language?

These attempts to explain how children acquire their first language have been set out as hypotheses, that is, principled guesses. They depend to some extent upon ideas about what language itself is, and research over the last twenty years or so has come up with three main hypotheses:

- Children learn language by **imitating** the people they hear talk to them – usually their parents and family.
- Children learn language because they are **programmed** to do so, just as a bird is programmed to build a nest or to migrate. This is not to say that a French child is

programmed to learn French and a Chinese child to learn Chinese, but that all children are programmed to learn any language they are exposed to in infancy, because all languages have certain **universal features**. Children, in this hypothesis, are supposed to have special mental capacities which are designed to make the task of language learning possible.

● Children learn language because they are very clever when compared with animals like chimpanzees, for example. Their intelligence is not so much different, as considerably greater, and so they are able to work out the intricate characteristics of language and its uses.

We shall not discuss these hypotheses and the evidence for and against each of them, but go on to describe what children's language is like at different stages in its development, by examining the spoken language of children under the age of four. We shall look at authentic samples of the language of children talking to their parents in the home, and for each example we shall ask the general question: What language skills enabled the child to say what he or she said, in the way he or she said it?

6.2 Pronunciation skills (cassette tape, section 16)

Firstly, some examples of a child's **pronunciation** in brief extracts from conversations between a mother and her young son, Danny. The conversations were video-recorded over a period of six months from the age of two to two and a half.

The extracts have been selected to illustrate three distinct stages of development in the six-month period.

Stage A

1	M	don't want the egg shell do you?
	D	[ʃaɪ ʃu] ugh.
2	M	what is it? cold?
	D	[kàʊ]
3	D	[sɪg]
	M	mḿ
	D	[ʃ̀ɪg]
	M	cheese?
4	M	what is it Dan?
	D	[kàːk]
	M	cart (.) yes the dustcart.

Stage B

1	M	mm yeah. it's a dustcart.
	D	[ə dùskat]
2	M	what's that?
	(2.0)	
	D	[wìl]
	M	yes it's a wheel (.) they've all got wheels haven't they?
3	D	[lɪki ka lɪki ka lɪki ka lɪki ka]
	M	yes that's a little car and that's a little car (.) so that's one little car (.) two little cars
4	M	alligator

	D	[æli æligeɪti gɒt æləgeɪti æləgeɪti ə ka]
	M	yes (.) alligator
5	D	[ðæts mɒk væn]
	M	a milk van yes

Stage C

	D	[aɪ gɒt kol **bred** naʊ]
1	M	cold bread
	D	mm
2	D	[aɪ dɒn wɒn ə go ə **wɒtʃət**]
	M	no (.) cos he's not there any more (.) they've moved

Naturally, we cannot, on the basis of these few examples, give anything like a complete description of the skills relevant to pronunciation that Danny has learned or developed. But we can begin to appreciate what is involved in pronouncing even these few utterances.

(i) *Sound segments*

In studying pronunciation, we try to identify the **segments** of sound the child makes. Different segments have different characteristics – they are particular kinds of **vowel** or **consonant**. They are organised in certain **sequences**, together with **stress** on some syllables and movements of **pitch**.

Activity 6.1 ————————————

(i)   List the different sound segments that the child produces.
(ii) Using the symbol C for a consonant, and V for a vowel, list the kinds of consonant–vowel sequences that make up the child's words.
(iii) List the words of more than one syllable, and underline the syllables that are stressed.
(iv) Comment on the child's and the mother's different uses of intonation. Are there any patterns of pitch movement?

Commentary

In answering these questions, it is helpful to consider what the answers would be if we were studying the mother's pronunciation. For example, in extract 1 illustrating stage A in Danny's language development, the mother uses five distinct vowel sounds: [o], [ɒ], [ə], [e], [u], whereas Danny uses only five vowels in all four stage A extracts: [aɪ], [u], [aʊ], [ɪ], [ɒ].

Furthermore, Danny's vowels can be unstable. In trying to pronounce *shell* he says [ʃaɪ] and [ʃu], and in only one case does his pronunciation of a vowel match his mother's, as you can see from the following list:

word	mother vowel	child vowel
shell	[ɛ]	[aɪ] and [u]
cold	[o]	[aʊ]
cheese	[i]	[ɪ]
(dust)cart	[ɑ]	[a]

So at this stage, the child can produce certain recognisable vowels, but they may vary when the child is repeating the same word, and they do not necessarily match the vowels of adult speakers.

If we then compare the **consonants** produced by Danny at stage A and compare them with his mother's, we again find obvious differences. The following consonants occur in Danny's speech: [ʃ], [k], [s], [g]. His use of them is unstable too. In pronouncing the first sound of the word *cheese* he uses both [ʃ] and [s], and neither of these is the same as the adult pronunciation [ʧ]. Here is a summary of the use of consonants in the stage A extracts:

word	mother consonant	child consonant
shell	[ʃ-l]	[ʃ⁻]
cold	[k-ld]	[k⁻]
cheese	[ʧ-z]	[s-g] and [ʃ-g]
(dust)cart	[k-t]	[k-k]

If you examine stages B and C, you will find that Danny has learned to produce other vowels and consonants, sounds that are stable in their characteristics and also more like the corresponding adult sounds in the same words. For example, at stage A he pronounces *shell*, which has the sound [l] at the end, without a consonant in that position. This is perhaps because he cannot or will not pronounce the sound in **word-final** position, whereas at stage B he is pronouncing *wheel* as [wiːl], that is, he is now using [l] in word-final position. You will also notice that *wheel* has the vowel [i] in his pronunciation, though at stage A Danny pronounced the vowel of *cheese* as [ɪ], [ʃɪg]. Similarly, notice that at stage A he pronounced *dustcart* as [kak], and by stage B this has become [dʊskɑt].

(ii) *Sound sequences*
Sound segments combine in various ways to form words, and we describe the sequences as combinations of consonants and vowels. If we look again at the mother's utterances in the stage A extracts, we can represent the individual words according to their sequences of consonants (C) and vowels (V) like this:

1
don't	[dont]	CVCC
want	[wɒnt]	CVCC
the	[ðə]	CV
egg	[ɛg]	VC
do	[du]	CV
you	[ju]	CV

2
what	[wɒt]	CVC
is	[ɪz]	VC
it	[ɪt]	VC
cold	[kold]	CVCC

3
cheese	[ʧiz]	CVC

4

what	[wɒt]	CVC
is	[ɪz]	VC
it	[ɪt]	VC
Dan	[dæn]	CVC
cart	[kat]	CVC
yes	[jɛs]	CVC
the	[ðə]	CV
dustcart	[dʊskɑt]	CVCCVC

So the mother can produce at least the following sequences: CV, VC, CVC, CVCC, CVCCVC. And if we analysed more of her speech, it would show her capable, as we would expect, of other types of sequence – all those in fact that belong to English pronunciation. Now examine Danny's sequences of vowel and consonant at stage A:

1

shell	[ʃaɪ] and [ʃu]	CV

2

cold	[kaʊ]	CV

3

cheese	[sɪg] and [ʃɪg]	CVC

4

dustcart	[kaːk]	CVC

On this evidence, Danny can only produce a limited range of sequences of sound segments at stage A. However, the rapid progress he makes in this aspect of language skill becomes immediately clear if you examine the sequences in the words he produces at stage B. Look in particular at his pronunciation of the word *alligator* in extract 4.

(iii) *Patterns of stress and pitch*

Little can be said about patterns of **stress placement** (which syllables carry more stress than others) at stage A, because at this stage Danny only produces utterances of one word, and each word is a monosyllable. So neither a syllable within a word, nor any particular word in a sequence of words, can receive more or less stress than any other. However, at stage C, the child's use of stress is clear as we see him using stress to foreground or emphasise particular words:

> D.   I got cold **bread** now

and applying stress to particular syllables in polysyllabic words:

> D.   I don't want to go to **Wa**tchett

But Danny's use of **pitch** to signal differences in meaning is quite clear from the start. Consider first how pitch is used by adult speakers. Say the sentence 'You're coming' first as if you were asking a question, and then as if you were answering a question. Most speakers will find that when asking the question, the pitch level at which they are speaking begins to rise on the first syllable of *coming*; when answering a question, the pitch level begins to fall on that syllable.

Now look at extract 4 from stage A:

M	what is it Dan?
D	[kàːk]
M	cart (.) yes (.) the dustcart

Here what the child says is marked as having a downward pitch movement, But what he is saying is, of course, an answer to a question from his mother. Danny is thus, even at this early stage of one-word utterances, using a pitch movement to mark his utterance as having the function of an answer, in much the same way as adults do.

Now extract 3 from stage A:

D	[síg]
M	m̀m
D	[ʃìg]
M	chéese?

In this extract the child is the first to speak. In fact he is asking for cheese, or in other words making a **request**. This time his utterance is marked as having an **upward** movement in pitch. So an upward pitch movement is associated for him with a request function. The mother, however, does not respond directly to the child's request, but queries what he has said, using what is in effect a **question**. Her utterance has upward pitch movement. Danny's response this time is an attempt to provide his mother with the information her question was intended to elicit, and so it is an **answer**. The same word is repeated, but with **downward** pitch movement. Thus Danny is using pitch movement in a systematic and meaningful way.

This description of Danny's skills in producing and sequencing segments of sound, and using stress and pitch, will give you some idea of the complexity of a child's task in learning how to pronounce the language. It is not complete, and you should try to apply the same systematic process of analysis to discover more for yourself.

6.3 Grammatical skills (cassette tape, section 17)

Children develop skills in pronunciation, of course, at the same time as they are developing knowledge of the use of words in different combinations to express meanings. This is what we refer to as a child's knowledge of the **grammar** of the language.

We shall look firstly at some examples of the speech of a linguistically advanced two-and-a-half-year old girl, Kirsty, and then at how Danny gradually developed the knowledge of the grammar that this girl had.

6.3.1 *Kirsty*

(i) *Sentence-types*
Children learn that when words are combined with others to form sequences, then these sequences must conform to particular patterns – that is, they develop an awareness of **sentence structure types** such as **declarative**, **interrogative**, **imperative**, for example:

I drop Katie's skirt in Tom's playpen	= declarative mood
did you find the card for Tom?	= interrogative mood
you speak in it (*i.e. the tape-recorder*)	= imperative mood

(ii) *Word-classes*

Children learn that words with quite different meanings can be used in similar ways. You can change the form of some words in the same way, or combine them with other words in the same way – that is, children develop an awareness of **word-classes** (or **parts of speech**) such as noun, verb, adjective.

(iii) *Grammatical roles*

Children learn that, independent of their meanings, words or groups of words have certain jobs to do in a sentence – that is, they become aware of **grammatical roles** such as **subject** and **predicate**, and within the predicate, the **predicator** (P) (or verb), **object** (O) or **complement** (C), and **adverbial** (A), for example:

S	*P*		*O*	
	auxiliary	*verb*	*modifier*	*noun/pronoun*
I	going to	iron	Katie's	coat
I	going to	do	Jane's	pants
I	going to	draw	my two little	girls
I	going to	have		'tatoes
Betty	going to	have		,orange
She	going to	have		juice
She	must	sit		(A) between my knees
You	must	wash		it
I	must	have		it

(iv) *Word-forms*

Children learn that they can alter meaning by using a variety of processes to change the form of words – for example, they become aware of the ways we use to show **tense** and **aspect** in the verb phrase of the predicator, and **number** in the noun phrase of the subject, object or complement, by adding inflections like *-ed*, *-ing*, and *-s*, for example:

	subject	*predicator*	*object/ complement*	*adverbial*
tense				
present				
(+ negative)	I	**don't** know		
past				
(+ negative)	I	**didn't** iron	it	
past	I	**did** hang	them	over
aspect				
perfective				
(+ negative)	I	**haven't** iron**ed**	that	
progressive	Tom	**'s** play**ing**		
	I	**'s** talk**ing**		to Tom
	they	**'re** sitt**ing**		together

number				
singular	Tom	would like	a *straw*	
plural	I	want	some *straws*	
singular	*he*	's got	a clean jumper	
plural	*they*	're falling down		a bit
singular	*this*	is	my *crayon*	
plural	*these*	are	my *crayons*	

(v) *Propositions and semantic roles*

When children use language they are making **meanings** by putting their thoughts – representations of actual, possible or desired situations – into words. We can refer to these word-based representations of situations as **propositions**.

In any situation there will be **participants** taking part in **processes**, for example, performing **actions** as **actors**, or causing things to happen as **agents**, having things done *to* them as the **affected** persons or *for* them as **beneficiaries**, finding themselves in particular sorts of relationship with one another and so on. And we often want to specify the **circumstances** in which these things are going on – to say *where, when, why* and *how* these processes are going on. A proposition, therefore, is concerned with expressing the **semantic roles** that people and things take on when they interact in a situation.

The smallest *grammatical* unit that can represent a proposition is a sentence consisting of one **clause**, as in the examples just given in sections (iii) and (iv), with the **grammatical roles** of subject, predicator, object(s)/complement and adverbial(s) (SPO/CA). Here are some examples of Kirsty's talk to illustrate the semantic roles played by the participants in the actions or processes:

	actor/ *agent*	*action* *(process)*	*affected*	*beneficiary*	*circumstances*
	I	drop	Katie's skirt		in Tom's playpen
did	you	find	the card	for Tom?	
	you	speak			

These semantic roles described in Kirsty's speech are only some of those that can be represented in a clause, but they represent the basic semantic relationships in a simple active clause in which the grammatical subject has the actor's role and the object the affected role. (cf. also section 9.2.2, Belfast Incident, sub-section (ii)b, which shows what happens to the semantic roles in passive clauses. There is a longer introduction in Dennis Freeborn, *A Course Book in English Grammar,* chapter 1 section 1.7. For a detailed description see, for example, Randoph Quirk *et al., A Comprehensive Grammar of the English Language*, chapter 10, pp. 740–54.) These short extracts from Kirsty's speech at two and a half show you how she is already competent in some of the basic features of English grammar.

6.3.2 *Danny*

We shall now look at the development of this grammatical knowledge in Danny's speech at the three stages we have already considered when examining his pronunciation.

Activity 6.2

For each stage:

(i) List the words which the child has inflected.
(ii) Indicate whether the inflected word is a *noun, adjective* or verb, and give the reasons for your classifications.
(iii) List the noun phrases (NPs) used by the child which involve the use of *determiners, adjectives* and other *modifiers,* in combination.
(iv) List examples of the child's use of *simple past tense* and *progressive aspect* in the verb phrase (VP).
(v) List examples of his use of the *negative* and of *interrogative mood.*
(vi) List examples of his use of *coordinated* and *subordinated* clauses.
(vii) List examples of words or phrases representing *agent, actor* or *affected roles* in a situation.
(viii) List examples of words or phrases representing the circumstances, i.e. the *where?, when?, why?* or *how?* of a situation

(Do not expect to find examples of all these features at every stage of the child's language development.)

Stage A

1 M do you want to open your egg?
      (3.0)
      the shell off
      don't want the egg shell do you?
   D [ʃaɪ ʃu] ugh
   M the shell's not nice
      only Mr Silly in your Silly book eats the shell doesn't he?
   D ugh {*laughs*}
2 M what is it ? cold?
   D [kaʊ]
   M is it ? put too much in ⌈ the ⌉
                              ⌊ D [sɪg]⌋

   M mm
   D [ʃɪg]
   M cheese?
   D cheese
   M well you eat your egg first and then you can have some cheese
3 M who's looking ⌈ who's looking⌉ through the camera
                    ⌊ D mum   ⌋

   D man
   M it's a man isn't it?
   D [gɔwən]
   M Gordon (.) that's right

Stage B

1 M that isn't a number ⌈it's a   ⌉
                          ⌊ D traffics⌋

	M	traffic
	D	go
	M	traffic lights (.) yes and it means go because it's on (.) what colour is it? when it says? when it means go?
	D	green
	M	green
2	M	what else can you see in there?
	D	more statue
	M	more statue
3	D	the big long lo long long train
	M	long crane
4	D	look (.) he went (winter) (.) (winterz)
	M	vintage yes (.) one two three vintage cars
	D	fast car vintage (.) fast car vintage
	M	fast car vintage
	D	fast car vintage
5	M	yeah well isn't (.) what's fallen out?
	D	fall out that man the man ⌈ down ⌉ ⌊ M mm ⌋ down
	D	down
6	M	what's he lifting? what's the crane lifting up?
	D	tractor
	M	oh it's another tractor isn't it?
7	M	what do you think it's doing if it's got brushes on the car? (0.5) what do you do with brushes?
	D	sweep (.) up
	M	sweep up
8	M	what do you think he's (.) putting water on the road for?
	D	piggy (0.5)
	M	splashing the piggy (.) what's the water doing?
	D	splash piggy
9	M	oh who's drawn on there then?
	D	Becca draw on there
	M	oh was it Rebecca?
	D	yes
10	M	who's that? (.) is that the daddy?
	D	no (.) Daddy sit (.) Daddy sit er er Danny sit (.) Daddy sit there
	M	he's sitting there is he? where's where where's the other family?
	D	look there's one
	M	there's some more family Danny (.) come on (.) there's the baby and a little girl (.) they're all going out to the seaside for the day (2.0) oh mustn't forget the Mummy (.) now who else is missing?
	D	(*******) Mummy sit there
	M	Mummy sit there
	D	no not sitting (**) that's Mummy's
	M	oh yes (.) Mummy's done it wrong (.) that's the little child (.) yes that's the Mummy (.) oh I'm silly (.) oh and there's the other one

Stage C

1	D	I doing like this all day
	M	come on (.) hurry up (.) I've eaten mine
	D	I do (.) I doing this all day look (.) I got a library book
	M	wha. which lib. what's your library book called?
	D	mister (**) and (**)
		that person er that dog
	M	that dog (.) do you know (.) can you remember what the dog's name is?
		(2.0)
		called Harry isn't he?
	D	Harry
	M	mm
2	D	I don't want to go to Watchett
	M	no (.) cos he's not there any more (.) they've moved
	D	I (.) we don't want go and see them
	M	don't you? but you'd like to go and see them in Liverpool wouldn't you?
	D	no I don't want (.) I want to go (.) when get bigger want to go on my own a a Watchett
	M	do you? you want to go on your own?
	D	not a bi. not a (.) when get bigger
	M	when you get bigger yes (.) you'll be able to do lots of things when you get bigger (.) you'll perhaps be able to ride on an aeroplane
	D	it's on (1.0) like on television
	M	mm (1.0) it showed you some children in the aeroplane on the television didn't it?

Commentary

Stage A

The most obvious feature of the child's talk here is that he speaks in single word utterances. The single words are, however, used to convey a variety of messages. In A(2), [kaʊ] = *cold* is used to label a quality. In A(3), *man* is used to label a sort of being to be found in the world, and [gɔwən] = *Gordon* is used to label a specific being in the child's world.

Can we then say that the child has sets of words for doing one sort of thing, like labelling persons? If we did, then we could use the terms from the description of English grammar, like adjective, noun, proper noun etc. But there are two problems if we do this:

(i) The child's 'single words' are not simply used as labels for things, qualities, people and actions. As well as this use, in A(1) [ʃaɪ ʃu] = *shell* is used as part of an expression of disgust. In A(2) [sɪg] and [ʃɪg] = *cheese* is used to express a request. Any one 'word' can be used for a variety of purposes by the child. On one occasion he may say [ʃɪg] to ask for some cheese, but on another simply to label it.

(ii) There is no way of distinguishing sets of words other than by the purpose for which they are used, and this, as we have seen, can vary with particular occasions of use. Adults and children know that *Gordon* belongs to a different set from *man*, because we can say *the man*, but can't say *the Gordon*. Similarly, we know that *cold* belongs to a different set from *cheese*, because we can say, for example, *colder*, but not *cheeser*. But Danny, at this stage, only uses words in isolation, and never alters their form.

At stage A, therefore, the child's language does not seem to involve any structural organisation.

Stage B

Stage B shows considerable development in the child's language. He is now combining words into sequences. Extracts 1–4 show that it now makes sense to talk of the child's awareness of different sets of words, even though he makes mistakes in classifying them.

In B(1) Danny applies a **plural marker** to the word *traffics*, which suggests that he knows something about the category **noun**.

In B(2) he does not apply the plural marker to the word *statue*, where the context would require it. This suggests that although he has begun to learn the difference between **count** and **non-count** nouns (e.g. *statues* and *traffic*), he has not yet mastered it.

In B(3), *long* is correctly placed in front of *train*; in B(4), *vintage* is wrongly placed after the noun *car*. This suggests that he has an emerging but not yet complete awareness of the category **adjective** and its place in the structure of the noun phrase.

B(5) shows an awareness of the **grammatical role** or function of the **subject** of a clause. In the question asked by Danny's mother, the word *what* is the subject of the clause.

In B(6), the word *what* in the question is the grammatical **object** in the clause. In B(7) and (8), the question is asking for an answer which supplies the **predicate** of the clause:

subject	predicate
brushes	sweep up
the water	splashes Piggy

B(9) and (10) show Danny using well-formed sentences, where everything that should be there is in place. In B(9), he is showing his understanding of **location** and uses a **prepositional phrase**, *on there* to show it. B(10) shows that he can distinguish different **mood** structures and use them:

declarative mood:	Daddy sit there	that's Mummy's
imperative mood:	look	

He can obviously understand **interrogative** structures as questions and answer them. He is beginning to use **progressive aspect** in the predicator:

no not sit*ting*

although he does not yet use the verb *be* as part of it, as in his mother's answer:

> no Mummy *isn't* sitt*ing* there

This clause also shows his understanding of the **negative** particle *not*.

Stage C

You can see clearly that stage C is the most adult-like of Danny's language, even though things that you would expect in adult speech are still missing.

C(1) and (2) show Danny using **determiners** – words that come first in a noun phrase and refer to definiteness and indefiniteness (like *a, the, this, some, each, much* and so on):

> *all* day   *a* library book   *that* dog   on *my* own

This allows Danny to be more specific in the references he makes.

He is again using progressive aspect in the verb phrase, and still hasn't learned to use the auxiliary verb *be*:

> I do*ing* this

He can use the negative, as before, and is now also using the auxiliary verb *do* with it:

> I *don't* want

Before this stage, he would have said 'I *no* want' or 'I *not* want'.

He is using more complex verb phrases, with **finite** and **non-finite** forms of the verb:

> I don't *want to go*

He can **inflect** an adjective to make the **comparative** form:

> when get *bigger*

He constructs prepositional phrases which are not to do with place or location:

> on my own

Perhaps the most significant development at stage C is Danny's use of **subordination**, when one clause is dependent on, or embedded in another clause. This modifies the meaning of whole sentence structures:

> *subordinate adverbial clause*   *main clause*
>
> [[when get bigger]   want to go on my own a Watchett]

This rather detailed description of what Danny 'knows' about the grammar of English helps to explain what was meant in the third paragraph of this chapter: 'If we consider just what goes on when children learn their first language, we can begin to appreciate the true nature and complexity of the skills which they have.'

We all know the grammar of English in the sense of *implicit knowledge* because we are all fluent speakers of the language. This little study of Danny's speech may help you to know the grammar in a more explicit way also.

6.4 Discourse and conversation skills (cassette tape, section 18)

Children learn and use their knowledge of the pronunciation and grammar of the language in the course of conversation. But to participate in conversation in a way that appears to be competent and natural requires skills that go beyond the ability to produce well-articulated grammatical sequences of words. These skills are referred to as **conversation** or **discourse** skills. They underly a child's ability to engage and then hold the attention of those she is speaking to by:

● taking turns at speaking in ways which produce smoothly flowing conversations,
● saying things which follow on from, or fit in with what others in the conversation are saying, and
● constructing utterances in ways which successfully achieve what the child intends, in relation to the other speakers in the conversation.

We can again examine Danny's language at different stages of his development to find out the extent to which he has learned these skills.

6.4.1 *Turn-taking*

Look again at stage A, extract (2) in section 6.3.2. There is a clear pattern here of alternating speakers, and so there is some form of **turn-taking**. However, if we look more closely we can see that the taking of turns differs from that in conversations of speakers who are more linguistically mature.

The sequence starts with a question directed to Danny. Before Danny's response the mother provides what is in effect the appropriate content for Danny's turn. Danny then takes the turn, using the material his mother has already provided for him, that is, the word *cold*. It is quite common in conversations between children and adults at this stage to find the mother consciously avoiding gaps in the conversation. She will deal with likely 'non-responses' by incorporating into her own turn material that would be an appropriate response for the child. The mother's next speaking turn is not completed before the child begins to speak:

> M   is it ? put too much in ⎡ the ⎤
> ⎣ D [sɪg]⎦
>
> M   mm

The child here starts to speak at a point when the mother's utterance is grammatically incomplete. She has produced only the preposition *in* of what is to be a prepositional phrase. One of the ways of timing the beginning of a speaking turn is to listen for points of grammatical completeness in the other speaker's turn. This is what Danny seems to fail to do.

The following illustration from Kirsty's speech at two and a half illustrates well that children can quite quickly come to monitor for grammatical completeness:

> M   no he doesn't have that milk in the packets any more he drinks the same milk as you doesn't he?
> K   mm
> M   out of a
> K   cup
> M   and the milkman brings it in a

K	house
M	yes he brings it to the house

Notice here that the child is monitoring the mother's speech sufficiently closely to be able to provide a word of just the right grammatical class to make the mother's utterance complete.

Children also become aware that gaps between turns are to be avoided, and that if they do occur, then something might be wrong – that is, the gap takes on some sort of meaning. Consider the following exchange between a mother and a three-year-old:

C	I'm gonna buy eight yoghurt
M	eight?
C	yeah
	(1.0)
	is that a lot?

Here the mother queries the child's first utterance by repeating part of what he said, and he confirms the mother's repetition. Normally at this point you would expect the mother to continue the topic in some way, or at the very least to say something. But for a full second, which is a long time in conversation, she says nothing. The child then continues with a question, 'is that a lot?' which implies that he interprets the mother's silence as suggesting that something was wrong with his original assertion.

We can see from these examples that as they learn to organise their turn-taking in conversation, children are able to avoid gaps between turns and overlapping of turns.

6.4.2 Coherence, or fitting-in

Conversation, of course, involves more than just taking turns at speaking. What is said must fit in with what has gone before, and its relevance must be apparent to each speaker. In the very early stages of language development it is rare for talk to be focused on a topic for more than three or four speaking turns. The child simply doesn't have the linguistic resources to do this. We can see something of the resources involved in maintaining talk over several turns by considering the following extract:

Mother and Stephanie

M	do you know how old you'll be?
S	well (.) how old
M	well how old are you now?
S	[fri]
M	so next birthday you'll be?
	(2.0)
S	four
M	four
S	yes (.) I like being four don't we?
M	do you like being four?
S	yes (.) bu.(.h) but w. after when Geoffrey's [bin] four how old will he be?
M	what do you think?
S	five
M	yes

S	and then how old?
M	and then he'll be six
S	and then how old will me?
M	and then you'll be five won't you?
S	and then it won't be our birthday(s) will it?
	(1.0)
	and it will be [stev] won't it?
M	mm
S	we we're have plenty of birthdays aren't we?
M	I hope so
S	but Father Christmas brung bringded our toys didn't he?
M	mm
	(1.0)
	he doesn't bring you toys on your birthday does he?
S	but after our birthday(s) (.) gonna (.) Christmas going to come but he but he won't eat a (.h) he (.) tart (.) he'll just leave one
M	one tart
S	yes (.) you've made one
M	did we leave him a tart last Christmas?
S	yes
	(2.0)
M	do you like tarts?
S	mm
	(1.0)
	but (.) but once (.) we couldn't eat some could we?
M	why not?
S	that's why they were (.) a bit stiff couldn't we?
M	a bit stiff
S	yes
M	oh
S	yes but you said they were didn't you?
M	oh I see

Here both mother and child contribute to the creation of coherent discourse through the use of (i) question–answer routines, (ii) continuers, (iii) lexical repetition, (iv) deixis and (v) question tags.

(i) *Question – answer routines*

These ensure topic responses and can be maintained over as many turns as you like, since any question (Q) can have another question as a response rather than an answer (A). On this basis the first six turns can be analysed as:

M	Q	do you know how old you'll be?
S	Q	well (.) how old?
M	Q	well how old are you now?
S	A	[fri]
M	Q	so next birthday you'll be?
		(2.0)
S	A	four

(ii) *Continuers*

These serve to treat what is to be said in some current speaking turn as following on in some logical way from what has been said in a previous turn. Often the logical link is signalled by some grammatical device:

S	**and then**	how old?
M	**and then**	he'll be six
S	**and then**	how old will me?
M	**and then**	you'll be five won't you?
S	**and then**	it won't be our birthday(s) will it?
		(1.0)
	and	it will be [stev] won't it?
M		mm
S		we we're have plenty of birthdays aren't we?
M		I hope so
S	**but**	Father Christmas brung bringded our toys didn't he?
M		mm
		(1.0)
		he doesn't bring you toys on your birthday does he?
S	**but**	after our birthday(s) (.) gonna (.) Christmas going to come

The items in bold type are clear indications that the turns they preface are 'on-topic' continuations.

(iii) *Lexical repetition*

This is a most basic method of linking turns and there are many examples in the extract, for example:

M	so next birthday you'll be?
	(2.0)
S	**four**
M	**four**
S	yes (.) I like being **four** don't we?
M	do you like being **four**?

(iv) *Deixis*

Deixis literally means *pointing*, and refers to the way in which speakers can use certain words to point to, rather than name, things already mentioned in a conversation. We use pronouns in this way. For example:

S	but **Father Christmas** brung bringded our toys didn't <u>he</u>?
M	mm
	(1.0)
	<u>he</u> doesn't bring you toys on your birthday does <u>he</u>?
S	. but after our birthday(s) (.) gonna (.) **Christmas** going to come but <u>he</u> but <u>he</u> won't eat a (.h) <u>he</u> (.) tart (.) <u>he</u>'ll just leave one

The relevance of the mother's turn and the child's second turn to her own first turn is maintained by the **deictic** use of the pronoun *he* to refer to Father Christmas.

(v) *Question tags*

Question tags do not necessarily function as requests for information, but have as a primary role the establishment of an obligation to **respond**. This can be done in other ways, for example, the use of terms of address as in, 'I like being four **mum**'. It would be odd not to respond to this. However, both speakers here use question tags as a way of ensuring 'listener response':

S	we we're have plenty of birthdays **aren't we**?
M	I hope so

6.4.3 *Response to other speaker's needs*

(i) *What they want to know*

Children become increasingly sensitive to the different ways in which messages need to be constructed. In the early stages children don't have the resources to adjust their messages to take account of their listener's needs and expectations. But look at the following extract from Danny's speech at his stage 3. He is responding to a question, and we can see him adjusting the way he refers to something in order to make his answer more specific, and so provide a better chance of satisfying the presumed 'informational needs' of his mother, that is, what she wants to know:

M	wha. which lib. what's your library book called?
D	mister (**) and (**)
	that person er that dog

(ii) *Politeness*

Children also learn to take account of such things as the need for politeness in constructing their requests:

C	want a bic bic
M	paːrdon?
	(1.5)
C	I would like a bic bic
M	that's better
C	please

The ways of showing politeness in requests are of course many, and range from the use of lexical items like *please* to complex syntactic constructions like *I was wondering if you would mind awfully if ..., Do you think you might possibly ...?*

Whilst all children have much in common, there will always be interesting differences between them in the way that they speak at any stage of development. Their pronunciation, grammar and ability to use language in conversation will be the special product of each child's experience of language. Any investigation you do of any child's language will be your own original research.

7. Variety and style in spoken English – I: grammar and vocabulary

If we consider the range of situations in which language is used, the many kinds of people with whom we communicate, and the different purposes for which we talk or write, the task of describing all the varieties of English usage proves very daunting. To create some kind of order in studying variety in language use, a framework of concepts is taken from **linguistics** (the systematic study of language).

Think of the English language as a system that we have all learned and carry around in our minds. Whenever we talk or write, we have to make choices from this system, which gives us a number of alternatives at each linguistic level, including choices of words from our **vocabulary** (or **lexis**), and different ways of putting these words together in 'strings' called **sentences**.

Our sentences must obey the rules that are followed by everyone who speaks English. Dialects of a language share the same rules except for a small number which differ slightly. The words must be in the right order to be **grammatical**, but again there is enough flexibility to allow a lot of choice.

Our vocabulary and grammar must be in the right **style**, or **appropriate** to the context, as well as grammatically correct. Usually we fall into the right style without really knowing what makes it right, but we do make mistakes. We can also use the wrong style deliberately if we want to, perhaps when we want to be funny, or possibly to annoy.

What follows, in the next chapters on variety and style, is a selected series of texts – spoken and written – which are clearly distinctive varieties of English. They are chosen partly because they are familiar and important varieties, and partly because they contrast with each other. The commentaries try to show, as explicitly as possible, how to make a descriptive analysis of a text.

The terminology from linguistics is used, as in the preceding chapters, to identify those features of the texts that distinguish them from other varieties. You cannot easily describe a flower garden without naming the flowers.

Sometimes the most prominent features of style are those that are the most frequent – there seem to be a lot of them. The problem is how to judge at what point the number of features is 'more frequent' than usual. Nevertheless, we do recognise stylistic features as being typical or unusual, from our everyday experience as speakers of English.

7.1 Bedtime stories (cassette tape, section 19)

Here are a few minutes taken from a narrative spoken by a five-year-old girl, and shared with another girl of the same age. They were both in the reception class of a York infants' school, and were talking to an adult for about an hour altogether, on all kinds of topics that came into their minds. The subject of 'bedtime' occupied them for a long time.

The transcription is into ordinary spelling, and does not attempt to show intonation, stress or regional accent.

Susan's narrative (part 1)

my Mummy's got (.) two pillows (.) one on top and one
underneath (.) and then she's got em (.) my Dad's got two (.) one
(.) and er he puts his head under the pillow because there's a em
(.) a sla. a slat (.) and he puts his head under the pillow and then
he goes to sleep (.) he covers hisself up and my Mummy chucks   5
the em (.) covers down the side here (.) and em sometimes I don't
have my bed chucked in but I like (.) and then er (.) sometimes
Alan won't go to bed because (.) sometimes when we put him to
bed and I go to bed he cries (.) and he thought ooh this is a good
idea he gets out of bed and walks (.) walks back into the room (.) 10
[*giggles*] cos he's in a bed like me now he used to go in his carry-
cot (.) but when we was going to get another one I slept in the
carry-cot (.) [*giggles*] and then (.) we've got another we've got a
bed now (.) and then every night when we put him to bed (.) he
gets up and goes into the room somet.(.) sometimes he walks (.) if 15
you put him to bed (.) and then he walks (.) and I thought ooh I'll
go back (.) daren't go in the room (.) then he tries again (.) so (.)
I'll go back (.) he'll never go in the room (.) so (.) my Mum's
heard him going trip trap in his bare feet because he can't put his
(.) blue slippers on yet they're like mine (.) em and then (.) and   20
then (.) she said 'come on in' and then when he gets into the room
my Mum says he's a naughty boy because he (.) I go to bed
before him you see because er (.) I want to go to bed and
sometimes when I'm tired I go (.) I don't go to bed (.) one time I
went when it was (.) half past nine (.) and it was nearly half past   25
ten when I went to bed (.)

Activity 7.1

List and describe some of the normal non-fluency features of the girl's speech
(see chapter 5).

(These features do not identify the special characteristics of Susan's language
use. But it it useful to examine them and to consider their function.)

Activity 7.2

Examine the transcript for non-standard vocabulary and grammar (see chapter 3).

If you do this systematically, some distinguishing features will become evident, which will help you to confirm Susan's language as (i) dialectal, and (ii) a child's.

Activity 7.3

Edit the text by leaving out the non-fluency features. Then write it out clause by clause, and group the clauses into clause-complexes (spoken 'sentences'). The criteria for grouping the clauses are:

(i)   **prosodic** – the meaning conveyed by intonation, stress and pauses;
(ii) **grammatical** – the meaning conveyed by the relationship between clauses, phrases and words; and
(iii) **semantic** – the meaning of words and the topics she chooses to talk about.

To show how this can be done, here is the beginning of the clause/clause-complex analysis. Column (a) = coordinating conjunctions (ccj); column (b) = subordinating conjunctions (scj); column (c) = initial adverbials (adverbials that precede the subject, and so are **thematic** in the clause).

	a *ccj*	b *scj*	c *theme*	
1				my Mummy's got two pillows, one on top and one underneath
2	and		then	she's got [*unfinished*]
3				my Dad's got one
4	and			he puts his head under the pillow
5		because		there's a slat
6	and			he puts his head under the pillow
7	and		then	he goes to sleep
8				he covers hisself up
9	and			my Mummy chucks the covers down the side here
10	and		sometimes	I don't have my bed chucked in
11	but			I like [*unfinished*]
12	and		then	Alan won't go to bed sometimes
13		because	[*unfinished*]	
14			sometimes	he cries
15		when		we put him to bed
16	and	Ø		I go to bed

a	b	c
ccj	*scj*	*theme*

	a	b	c
17	and		he thought
18			ooh this is a good idea
19			he gets out of bed
20	and		Ø walks back into the room
21	cos		he's in a bed like me now
22			he used to go in his carry-cot
23	but		I slept in the carry-cot
24		when	we was going to get another one

Commentary

(i) *Non-standard forms*

What is of most interest in Susan's talk is the frequency of non-standard English forms, and aspects of her language use which appear typical of a child. We shall identify and discuss these in some detail. (The initial figures refer to the lines of the transcription on p. 123.)

3–4   *because there's a slat* – she uses *because* or *cos* several times, some of them without any real causal relation being implied. Here she does not convey her full meaning, but assumes that her listener can infer the connection between the slat and Dad putting his head under the pillow.

5   *hisself* – dialectal (cf. chapter 3)

5   *chucks* – dialectal, or family usage?

6   *down the side here* – by using *here*, she is not yet distancing what she describes from the immediate context. She is not talking beside Dad's bed. Our vocabulary and grammar provide the means of 'pointing' to time, place and people (**deixis** and **deictic** features, see chapter 6). But deictic features can only be understood if the listener knows the context.

9   *and he thought* – notice her tendency to use both present and past tenses in her narrative, not always consistently related.

10   *the room* – means specifically what elsewhere would be called *the living room*.

12   *we was going to get* - dialectal past tense of *be*.

19–20 This sequence is typical of much of her narrative in its apparent lack of relevance. She links ideas connected in her mind by experience, but she has yet to learn to explain the connection to a listener. The reference to the colour of Alan's slippers, and the fact that they are like hers, shows the importance to her of facts which older children and adults would either explain in more detail, or omit.

(ii) *Clauses and clause-complexes*

The criteria (prosodic, grammatical and semantic) for dividing the transcript into clause-complexes are sometimes contradictory. For example, if *and* often occurs at the beginning of a spoken sentence but after a pause, then the convention of written English – that two clauses joined by *and* generally belong inside the same sentence – may not apply.

Pauses are not always reliable in marking the division between sentences, and occur for a number of different reasons within the clauses and phrases.

To try to identify a spoken sentence we have therefore to rely on a combination of clues from meaning (for example, we expect a sentence to express one topic), grammar and prosodic features. Even then, a decision will sometimes have to be an arbitrary choice, and we will not agree with each other's analysis. The idea of *sentence* in spoken English, as we have seen in chapter 5, is 'fuzzy'.

(iii) *The structure of a five-year-old child's language:*

The structure of Susan's language and the relationship between the clauses, which are the successive **propositions** or statements she is making, show some interesting features.

● *Linkage* – notice the expected frequency of *and* as a **continuer**, often followed by the adverb *then* to show sequencing.
● *Subordination* – **subordinate clauses** make **complex sentences**, and Susan uses *when* to indicate time, *because* to indicate a reason, and *if* to express a condition. These are **subordinating conjunctions**. She uses *so*, a **conjunct**, to show a result.

These all represent her developing understanding of how things happen, even though it is still limited in expression. In the talk not transcribed here she also uses *till*, but only once in an hour's conversation. Some common conjunctions which she did not use are: *while, after, before, although*.

So you can see that she still has some way to go in her **productive** use of language. It is likely, however, that she would understand these conjunctions in someone else's speech, in her **receptive** use of language. In assessing a variety or style of English we have to take into account what is not there, as much as what is.

● *Theme* – one quite frequent feature of her talk is the placing of an **adverbial** of time, usually *sometimes*, at the beginning of a clause, where it becomes prominent. This placing of an item at the front of a clause is called **theme**. The adverbial is **thematic** in the clause.
● *Verb phrase* – the **predicator** of a clause is always a verb or verb phrase (VP). VPs can be complex in adult language (e.g. I *might have been going to try to see...*), but in children's use of language they are still relatively simple. Complexity of the VP is a good measure of a developed use of English. The most complex of Susan's VPs in the short extracts used in this chapter are:

> *used to go* / *used to have* / *used to say* / *was going to get*

Elsewhere in the conversation she says:

> *I've been playing* / *I've been doing*

in which both the **perfective** (with *have*) and the **progressive** (with *be*) are combined. We also find combinations such as:

I *went out skipping*	I *try to put*
I *want to go*	We *went to fetch*
he *helps to build*	he *started to go to sleep*

and other series of predicators, linked to the other as if in a chain. This kind of structure is called **catenative**, which means 'connected like links in a chain'.

The following examples of catenatives are slightly different. The subject of the second verb is not the same as the subject of the first, and so comes between them:

We	*wouldn't like*	it	*to trot around*
My Mum's	*heard*	him	*going*
He	*had*	his foot	*bended*
my Mummy	*will let*	him	*come*

The distinctive style of Susan's language can therefore be partly identified with her use of non-standard English, both dialectal and immature, and partly described in terms of simpler forms of sentence and clause structure. The topics she chose to talk about were, naturally, related to her immediate experiences, and so determine the vocabulary she uses.

Activity 7.4

Identify what is non-standard in the following sentences, and then group the utterances into sets containing the same features. (These sentences are taken from the complete conversation between the two children and the teacher.)

More examples of non-standard forms in the children's language

1. Alan was kicking me. He had his foot bended like this.
2. When we was came to a corner ...
3. If I switch my blanket off there's got a switch and you switch it up.
4. When he came home from work he give me a new one.
5. My Dad went to work last morning.
6. He's drawed on thingy at window – he's drawed on it – all with my red pen what I got for Christmas.
7. One time I put a pillow that way and sleeped on it.
8. I always had a thingy what you had to not talk with it in your mouth. (*In answer to a question, What sort of thing happens in hospital?*)
9. My Dad said when he gets a load of money, because they haven't got many money you see yet and so when they've got a load of money they're going to get a big boiler.
10. I didn't like going in Uncle Ronnie's car because it steams up but it doesn't now.

Activity 7.5

No reference has so far been made to Susan's regional accent. Listen again to the tape-recording, and describe some of the marked features of her pronunciation, using the methods described in chapter 4.

Activity 7.6

(i) Listen to section 20 of the tape-recording, which continues Susan's narrative.

(ii) Comment on and explain these items from her talk:
   (a) the use of *my* in the phrase *my Alan*.
   (b) the function of *the* in *in the bed*.
   (c) *through the lino*.
   (d) *he never go*.
   (e) *a blanket what popped in a plug* and *the thingy what makes the engine warm had broke down*.
   (f) the sequence from *I used to have a blanket* to *but it wasn't now*.
   (g) *we went to fetch the round ring on the car so the policeman could see it*.
   (h) the incident with the tractor.
   (i) *red and blue grandma*.

Susan's narrative (part 2)

my Alan sometimes sleeps in the bed if he don't want to go in his
his own bed (.) [*coughs*] (.) my Mum won't (.) well we want (.)
my Mummy will let him come in his (.) my bed (.) but (.) last last
night em my Daddy tried to put him in bed (.) oh no (.) he goes
through the lino back into the room (.) oh no (.) he never go in my   5
bed (.) last time (.) my Mummy put him in my bed and er he
never (.) he never em (.) he (.) he wanted to come out (.) cos he (.)
cos he doesn't like sleeping in my bed because (.) I've got (.) I
used to have a (.) a blanket what popped in a plug and we've put
it (.) in Alan's now because my Mummy's sleeping in the big   10
bedroom now (.) and er they used to say it was going to be mine
but it wasn't now

and em (.) my Dad knows this one (.) he's called Bricky and er he
goes to do bricks and er (.) and then he (.) and then he helped to   15
(.) build it and Bricky's got another boy (.) and er sometimes (.)

but last week when we went out (.) em we went to (.) fetch the
round ring on the car so the policeman would see it and er we
couldn't because it was open at half past one and er my Daddy   20
only came home nearly at tea-time and then em (.) and then when
we got [*coughs*] got some catkins (.) em (.) it was nearly (.) we
was there and we stopped (.) my Dad switched (.) thingy up and
then he had a look at (.) well the thingy what makes the engine
warm (.) had broke down but em my Daddy wouldn't (.)   25

when he was came to a corner when we was going to go (.)
straight or not em (.) he went straight past and my Mummy (.) she
didn't like going straight past because they didn't (.) my Daddy
didn't know there was a (.) straight field where the tractor could   30

come straight and then straight and go through the field but em he
didn't look very far and then he turned (.)

it took us to grandma's but (.) we was going to go to blue
grandma's you see and em (.) we didn't go but we went to the   35
shop near my red grandma's (.) and then when we came back
from the shop we went to red grandma's (.) then blue grandma's
[*teacher*: who's red grandma and blue grandma?]
em (.) my blue grandma didn't want a blue door but she's got a
blue door (.) she had a red one before (.) and my red (.) and my   40
red grandma *had* a red door (.) they both had a red door (.) and
now they've both got (.) a blue door
[*teacher*: how do you know which is which?]
because er (.) we can tell (.) we can tell because they're (.) they
don't live in the both street you see   45

7.2   Unscripted commentary

7.2.1   *Goal!* (cassette tape, section 21)

Broadcasters on television and radio sometimes use scripts – texts that are written to
be read aloud – but may also have to speak off the cuff. One of the commonest
examples of this technique is **unscripted commentary**. The commentator describes
and comments upon an event as it is taking place.

The big difference between TV and radio commentary is obvious – the TV viewer
can see what's going on, but the radio listener cannot, and the radio commentator has
to provide everything that is necessary for our understanding and enjoyment of the
event in words. Some commentators talk continuously, even on television.

Although commentators have individual styles, they have a great deal in common
in their use of English, which is why unscripted commentary can be described as a
variety of spoken English. The example which follows consists of the same short
period of an international soccer match between England and Belgium, described by
television and radio commentators.

Radio commentary

and again it's Wilkins high across the area looking for Keegan
Keegan gets the header in (.) not enough power (.) Ceulemans
fortunately for Belgium is there to clear (.) not very far though (.)
Sansom comes forward a yard in from the near touchline the
England left (.) long ball from Sansom high across the area Pfaff   5
is there (.) punches the ball away (.) not very far but effectively
(1.0)
and Cools the (.) Belgian captain picks it up in space (.) far side
from us the Belgian left (.) he's tackled fiercely though (.) and he
loses the ball to Coppel (.) to Brooking (.) tall Brooking (.) of   10
West Ham (.) touches the ball on (.) Wilkins (.) good ball too to
Brooking (.) Brooking got four red-shirted Belgians around him

(.) turns the ball back to Keegan (.) England's captain (.) Keegan
holds (.) still holds then starts to move forward slowly (.) goes
away from van Moer's tackle (.) another tackle comes in on   15
Keegan though (.) and in any case it's (.) a a (.) a foul tackle this
time (.) plus a handball I think (.) so it's a free kick to England (.)
this is halfway inside the Belgian half (.) England nil Belgium nil
(.) the opening game (.) of this group for both these sides (.) and
again (.) cries of 'England' ringing round the stadium Wilkins takes   20
the free kick short to Brooking (.) five yards outside the Belgian
penalty area (.) good running by Brooking (.) down to the bye-line
(.) cuts the ball back (.) Meeuws is there to head the ball away (.)
not very far Wilkins trying to get the shot in Wilkins going forward
a chance for Wilkins here (.) and Wilkins (.) has scored for   25
England (.) oh a most intelligent goal (.) by Ray Wilkins ...

Television commentary

Wilkins
(2.0)
Keegan up
(6.0)
to Sansom   5
(2.0)
goalkeeper's coming and Johnson's up there with him (.) and it was
a reasonably good punch by er Pfaff he found one of his own
players and got the danger cleared
(3.0)   10
Coppel (.) so tenacious in the tackle (.) Brooking
(2.0)
Wilkins
(2.0)
Brooking   15
(2.0)
Keegan
(7.0)
and Keegan trying to take two of them on and a handball I suspect
against van der Elst   20
(4.0)
Phil Thompson this time has made his way forward for the free kick
on the far side
(2.0)
Watson has stayed back   25
(5.0)
Wilkins to Brooking
(7.0)
away by Meeuws (1.0) van der Elst (.) Wilkins (.) well done by Ray
Wilkins can he finish it? (1.0) oh I say (1.0) Ray Wilkins scores for   30
England and a cooler goal you couldn't wish to see look at that (.)
he lobbed it over the defence and then over the goal-keeper ...

(i) *Vocabulary*

The following lists of words from the commentaries are related to soccer football, but not all of them are exclusive to soccer. Set phrases, or **collocations**, are included, since they often link two or more common words together to provide a technical term. For example, the words *free* and *kick* have many uses in ordinary speech and writing, but put together as *free kick* in the context of a soccer match they form a lexical item with a special meaning. We use the term **lexical item** to refer to single words also.

Activity 7.7

(i)   How far are the following lexical items confined to the vocabulary of soccer, and how far do they belong to other sports or activities?

(ii)   Which of them have different meanings in other contexts of use? Try putting them into sentences where their meaning is changed.

For example: I found a bird with a broken left *wing*.
                        The offside front *wing* of my car was dented.

You will find it very helpful to use a dictionary.

goal	the left	holds	long ball
left wing	full back	come up	robbed
possession	Belgian half	brought down	free kick
defender	referee	tackle	the area
offside	off the ball	penalty area	white line
header	to clear	touchline	punches
away in space	foul	handball	lobbed
bye-line	goal	linesman	goalkeeper

Notice how the naming of places and of people is also 'context bound'. *West Ham* and *Southampton* do not refer to places but to football clubs with managers, players and fans. Keegan and Brooking were, at the time, national figures in the sporting pages of newspapers.

(ii) *Grammatical features*

If we first discover those typical features that the two transcriptions have in common, we can then compare other examples of unscripted commentary to see whether we have identified a variety which has its own rules.

It is usual to take Standard English as the norm for comparison. Remember that it is a written standard, and that the idea of 'appropriateness' is essential in judging a variety of language in its context of use.

The problem of identifying what a sentence is in spoken English has already been discussed (chapter 5). Unscripted commentary has its own kind of **clause** structure. The beginning of the radio commentary is set out below to show the structure of its clauses more clearly. A clause that makes a statement (a **declarative** clause) will contain a **subject** (S) (usually a noun phrase, NP), and a **predicator** (P – always a verb phrase, VP), and, depending upon its meaning, one or more **objects** (O) or

complements (C), and one or more **adverbials** (A). Column (a) contains coordinators, column (b) subordinators, and column (c) linking adverbs (**adjuncts**) or thematic adverbials.

	ccj	scj	theme	S	P	O/C	A
1	and		again	it	's	Wilkins	high
							across the area
2					looking for	Keegan	
3				Keegan	gets	the header	in
4				Ø	Ø not	enough power	
5				Ceulemans	is		there
					to clear		fortunately
							for Belgium
6				Ø	Ø not		very far though

Activity 7.8

(i) Complete the clause analysis of the radio commentary.
(ii) Describe what is unusual about the grammatical structure.

Commentary on the clause analysis

1 *Deletion of clause elements*
When you try to fit the clauses of the commentary into the SPOA pattern, you find that elements are frequently not there, yet the meaning is perfectly clear in spite of this. Are these clauses really incomplete? Should we think of commentary as having its own grammar?

We can derive the incomplete clauses of the commentary from complete ones which might be spoken in different circumstances. For example:

> and again it's Wilkins high across the area looking for Keegan

could be expanded into the statement,

> and again it's Wilkins *who kicks/passes the ball* high across the *penalty* area, looking for Keegan

where *looking for Keegan* means *aiming for* or something like it.
    Frequently the commentator makes a statement like,

> not enough power   not very far though
> long ball from Sansom   good ball too to Brooking

These can all be expanded into complete sentences by adding *That was/ is...* or *There was/ is....* We can say that some clause elements have been **deleted**. The commentator presents an action, pointing to its existence as a fact. He states the fact without the preliminary **existential *there***. It has become conventional for this style to be used in most unscripted commentary.

You can compare it with the headlines of newspapers (cf. chapter 8), in which **grammatical**, or **function words** are deleted because of restricted space.

Activity 7.9

Fill in some of the **deletions** in the two commentaries so that they make acceptable Standard English clauses. Note what you have to add or alter.

2 *Tense in the predicator*
Present tense Commentators describe what is going on as they speak. Therefore they tend to use the **simple present tense** a lot:

> Keegan *gets* the header in
> he *loses* the ball to Coppel

Activity 7.10

List some other examples of the simple present tense.

Other tenses It may seem obvious that we should use the present tense for actions that are taking place in the present time, but in fact we rarely use it in ordinary conversation. We are more likely to use the **present progressive tense**, of which there are some examples in the commentaries:

> Wilkins *(is) trying* to get the shot in

When referring back to an incident that has taken place, then a commentator will use the **simple past tense**:

> he *found* one of his own players

or perhaps the **present perfect tense**:

> Watson *has stayed* back

Occasionally the commentator may have to refer to something about to happen, and so will use the **modal auxiliary verb** *will*, or *be going to* to express the future:

> so again England *will try*

Activity 7.11

List the VPs (verb phrases) and find out which tense is the most frequently used.

3 *Omission of* be *from the predicator*
One word is often omitted in unscripted commentary. Here are some examples:

> cries of 'England' Ø ringing round the stadium
> Wilkins Ø going forward

The deleted word is the verb *be*, and whether it is the **main verb** or an **auxiliary** in the verb phrase of the predicator, it is often left out.

Activity 7.12 —————————————————————

List the clauses containing the verb *be* in the predicator, and those in which *be* is deleted. (Remember that the verb *be* has several forms – *am, is, are, was, were*, etc.)

---

4 *Subject and object noun phrases*
As part of the job of providing interesting comment and information, the commentator will do more than just name a player, for example:

> Cools the Belgian captain
> Keegan England's captain

in which the **proper noun**, the name of the player, is followed by an identifying NP (noun phrase) in **apposition** to it, or:

> tall Brooking of West Ham

where the name of the player is the **head word** of an expanded NP, with **modifiers**. Most of the subject NPs in the commentaries are proper nouns, with or without modifiers.

5 *Adverbials*
The high frequency of **adverbials** is another marked feature of this style. It arises from the purpose of commentary in describing when, where and how events are taking place, because it is one of the main functions of adverbs and adverbials to provide information about **time, place** and **manner**.

6 *Theme*
This is mentioned because it was a marked feature of Susan's talk in *Bedtime Stories*. In the unscripted commentary texts, however, adverbials are rarely brought to the front of the clause. Can you suggest a reason?

7 *Coordination of clauses*
The relative infrequency of *and* as a clause coordinator or continuer is in contrast with Susan's talk, and so with ordinary conversational usage.

8 *Subordination*
In the two transcripts, there are no subordinate **adverbial clauses**, that is, clauses beginning with conjunctions like *because, when* or *as*, though we have noted the frequency of adverbials within the clause. Why is this?

(iii) *Fluency*
Listening to broadcast commentary, you will find very few examples of the normal non-fluency that we expect to accompany conversational narrative. Hesitations, self-corrections, false starts, incomplete utterances and fillers are rarely heard. This suggests that unscripted commentary is an acquired skill, and that though it sounds spontaneous, it has to be learned and practised.

It would be difficult to find another variety of spoken English that resembles it in style: a series of simple declarative clauses, with few coordinators, frequent deletion, a high proportion of adverbials and an unusual degree of fluency in delivery.

It does not follow, of course, that all other radio and television commentaries will fall into this stylistic pattern in exactly the same way. In order that you can begin to find out for yourself, here are extracts from other commentaries for analysis and discussion:

7.2.2 *Trooping the Colour* (radio commentary – cassette tape, section 22)

Part of a full commentary of the ceremony is transcribed and set out below, showing initial linking words in the first three columns, as before, separately from the main text. Adverbs like *then* and *now* do not have to come first. Their **unmarked** position is clause-final, that is, at the end. If they do come first, then they are in the **marked** position which we have called **theme.** For example:

> *marked position*: *(thematic)*   *now* the Queen rides round
> *unmarked position*:   the Queen rides round *now*

Activity 7.13

Listen to the tape-recording and complete the transcription.

Activity 7.14

What is the frequency, in this commentary, of (i) thematic adverbials and (ii) deletion? Explain the reasons for what you discover.

Activity 7.15

Compare the prosodic features of the commentator's speech – intonation (pitch, loudness, tempo) and stress – with those of the football commentator.

Trooping the Colour

1	now	the royal procession having completed the inspection
		the Queen rides back towards us here to the saluting base
		led by the Brigade-Major and those four brilliant Life
		Guards
2		the Queen somehow looking regal graceful and military 5
		all at the same time
3		the next order will be the one word 'Troop' from
		Colonel Golson
	not perhaps	the most difficult of the one hundred and thirteen words
		of command believe it or not which he has to remember 10
4	but	it sets off a whole chain of events including the actual
		Trooping itself
5	first	the massed bands of all five Guards regiments march and
		counter-march in slow

	and	quick time	15
		three hundred and eighty of the finest military musicians	
		in the world	
		nineteen ranks of twenty	
		a stunning square down there to the left of musical	
		military skill	20
		formidable in size sound experience and showmanship	
6	at their heads	five drum-majors	
		coats of gold lace	
		gold maces in their hands	

7.2.3 *Snooker match*

The following short extract from the commentary on a televised snooker match suggests that deletion does not depend upon the speed and excitement of an event. Snooker is not a fast game, and there are lengthy periods of silence in the commentary.

Activity 7.16 —————————————————————————

(i)   Identify the places of deleted elements and suggest words to fill them in.
(ii) Comment on any difficulties which the vocabulary might present to anyone knowing nothing about the game of snooker
(iii) Discuss possible reasons why the commentator does not use complete sentences, although he has plenty of time.

Snooker commentary
(Pauses are marked in seconds in brackets – e.g. (7.0) is seven seconds)

1 and obviously Steve can't squeeze between the brown and the blue
   (1.0)
   so just looking to try and possibly come off the side cushion (.) and
   rest against this red on the back cushion
   (24.0)   5
2 no it looks as though he's coming round the angles very [*unfinished*]
   (6.0)
   I think he was trying to snick off one of those two reds and go back
   to baulk but a very risky shot to play and he's been rather fortunate
   the white has finished up tight on the cushion   10
   (7.0)
3 eleven points in it then
   (55.0)
4 can cut this red into the right-hand centre pocket (.) just put a little
   screw on the white ball to hold it for the black and just needs good   15
   position on the black to clinch this game
   (50.0)
5 and that's a good one
   (2.0)
   yes just the black and the last red to leave Steve needing snookers   20

7.3 Television interviews

An **interview** is conducted through language and its accompanying paralinguistic features of gesture, facial and bodily expression. The choices of language use will depend upon the subject and nature of the interview, of course, and you will be able to list a number of situations that are normally conducted as interviews between two people, or sets of people. For example:

- doctor and patient;
- employer and applicant for a job;
- opinion poll researcher and member of the public;
- policeman and visitor bringing lost property to a police station;
- detective and someone 'helping the police with their enquiries';
- college lecturer and potential student;
- radio or television interviewer and politician or other public figure.

The essential structure of an interview consists of the interviewer asking questions, and the interviewee responding with answers, and therefore would seem at first to be a simple procedure. But there are many ways of asking questions, and of answering or failing to answer questions. The study of the techniques of both interviewing and being interviewed is a serious topic which is of particular importance in business and industry and in the academic world. It is intended to produce 'the right people for the job' in industry, and to sort out students best able to follow a course of study in colleges and universities.

A proper study of interviews and interviewing would fill a book, so here we must limit ourselves to a selective look at aspects of a specific variety of interview, that of a politician on television. We shall focus principally on the subject of the chapter, the choices of vocabulary and grammar, rather than other very important and interesting features of the purpose and methods of televised political interviews.

7.3.1 *How we ask questions*

Grammar books will tell you that to make a statement we use the **declarative mood**, to ask a question, the **interrogative mood**, and to give an order, the **imperative mood** (see section 6.3.1 for examples in a child's speech). This can be illustrated from televised political interviews:

Declarative mood
The subject (S) comes before the predicator (P):

S	P	O/C	A
you	discuss	matters	in Cabinet
you	don't call	Cabinet ministers	to heel
700,000 new jobs	is	an excellent record	
many many women	want	part-time jobs	

Interrogative mood
(i) If the question appears to seek the answer 'yes' or 'no', that part of the predicator functioning as the operator-verb (op-v) comes before the subject. If there is a single

main verb, then the auxiliary verb *do* is introduced as the operator-verb. This is called a **yes/no question**:

op-v	S	P	O/C	A
can	the country	afford	this damaging steel strike?	
are	you	prepared to withhold	some of our contributions?	
does	your law	limit	it	enough?

(ii) If the question asks *who/?which?/what?/when?/why?/who?/*or *how?*, the *wh-*word comes first:

wh-	op-v *or main verb*	S	P	O/C
why	does	the Government	refuse to pay?	
when	will	that	be?	
what	is	your estimate?		

(iii) A declarative statement can be turned into a question by the addition of an interrogative **tag**. For example:

				tag	
	S	P	C	P	S
it won't be a fine because of course	it	's not	criminal law	is	it?

Imperative mood

The base form of the verb is used, without a subject (unless *you* is inserted), and proves to be very rare in televised political interviews. In fact there are no occurrences in the three hours of interviews used as data for this section, so the following examples are made up:

P	O/C	A
tell	me	
try to remember	the reason	
be	honest	with me
don't	evade	the question

Why are most of these examples unlikely to be used by a television interviewer?

The three moods and what they do are not, however, in a simple one-to-one relationship. The terms *declarative, interrogative* and *imperative* are used to describe the grammatical structures of SP(CA), PS(CA) and P(CA) respectively. The terms *statement, question* and *command* are used to describe the **discourse function** of an utterance. Consequently, although declarative sentences tend to be used to make statements, interrogatives to ask questions and imperatives to make commands, they may not do so in a particular context of situation.

For example, a **question** seeking a **response** may be put by using a declarative sentence,

	S	P	C
so	you	're	still dead set against any idea of an incomes policy?

138

rather than an interrogative,

> P   S   C
> are you still dead set against any idea of an incomes policy?

7.3.2 *The interviewer's questions in televised political interviews*

Politeness

The attitude of an interviewer to a public figure is sometimes one of polite deference, perhaps marked by an introduction to a question with the form *may I?* or a similar **modal verb** which has the effect of 'softening' the question, as in:

> **may I put to you though the view Prime Minister which has been widely expressed that** flexibility by the Government in dealing with this dispute now would be wisdom rather than weakness?

The interviewer's yes/no interrogative *may I put to you?* is not expecting the answer *yes you may put it to me*, or *no you may not put it to me*. It is a polite introductory formula to the yes/no question,

> would flexibility by the Government in dealing with this dispute now be wisdom rather than weakness?

Notice also the polite use of the title *Prime Minister* by the interviewer, rather than addressing her as *Mrs Thatcher*.

Challenging

During the development of televised interviews of politicians from the 1960s to the 1990s, the method of interviewers changed. Instead of simply asking questions to enable the politician to respond, they themselves became involved in the exchange by challenging the politicians' answers, raising controversy and acting in some respects as an adversary rather than a neutral interviewer. Some of the evidence for this 'adversarial' approach to interviewing is marked by the grammatical structure of their questions.

(i) *but ...* The use of *but* to introduce a question or response implies some form of disagreement or doubt over the preceding response. For example:

> **but** does your law limit it enough?
> **but** the proposals don't give a right for an injunction against a union.

(ii) *negatives* The same sense of disagreement or challenge can be implied by asking a negative question. For example:

> **is there not a** danger in practice that these reforms could lead to a judicial quagmire?

suggests that the interviewer thinks that there is a danger.

(iii) *Modal verbs* The use of *may I?* as a polite introduction has been pointed out. Modal verbs are also used in questions, suggesting possibility and probability rather than fact, and sometimes indicating the interviewer's point of view, as in the following question, which is also negative in form:

might there not be cases of trade unionists ending up in gaol for defying a judge's order?

which suggests *I think there might be, don't you?*

Activity 7.17

Read the following series of questions, taken from three TV interviews with Mrs Thatcher in the 1980s by different interviewers.

(i)   For each question:
        (a) Identify the mood as declarative, *wh*-interrogative, *yes/no* interrogative or tag.
        (b) Discuss the effect of uses of introductory words like *but* or *well*, negatives and/or modals, and any other features that seem to indicate the interviewer's own point of view.
(ii)   How many of the questions support the view that TV interviewers adopt an adversarial role in questioning a politician? What is your evidence?

1. but we haven't yet got to the stage where a union can be sued or have an injunction against it (.)
    and if you can't do that under these proposals and you can't get at its funds (.) has not Mr Prior laboured and brought forth a mouse?
2. may we turn to Mr Prior's proposals for a new law to curb the abuse of trade Union power? is it correct first Prime Minister that you wanted a short quick bill to outlaw secondary strikes?
3. but would not the extra cost to the taxpayer required to settle it be much less than the cost of letting it drag on and on?
4. because you said before the election (.) as Prime Minister I could not waste time on having any internal argument (.) now you're telling me that you love having them
5. but if you're alarmed at the level of pay settlements what is the right level? the level which the country can afford?
6. did your talks this morning with Chancellor Schmidt help you with regard to getting back this thousand million or so of our contribution to the EEC budget?
7. but the proposals don't give a right for an injunction against a union (.) it gives a right for an injunction against a trade unionist but not against the union itself
8. but do you think that you and your ministers care sufficiently about the unemployed? (.) do you think the way in which the problem is being addressed actually shows a knowledge of everyday life among everyday people?
    unemployed? (.) do you think the way in which the problem is being addressed actually shows a knowledge of everyday life among everyday people?
9. but have you not said (.) in the past five minutes (.) that most of the pits in South Wales (.) a number of pits in Scotland (.) some in Yorkshire (.) and the pits in Kent (.) will have to be shut down?
10. so you did actually say to Mr Heseltine that he could go away and see what he could do?

11. but the point is about uneconomic pits (.) what is an uneconomic pit?
12. you want to shut them down?
13. now you say that (.) but the international community has given the thumbs down to that (.) it's given the thumbs down to your running of the economy
14. you em said in the House of Commons (.) that there were a number of matters in the whole business that could have been handled better (.) when you said that were you thinking of the way other people did things or were you also talking about yourself?
15. but would you float off Land Rover separately is the point
16. you once said (.) Mrs Thatcher (.) that in politics it was easier to walk up than down (.) and much more difficult (.) to walk down (.) gracefully (.) how would you know (.) when the moment had come to walk down?

7.3.3 *The interviewee's responses and answers to questions*

The following commentary describes some of the more prominent grammatical and lexical features to be found in a long TV interview of Mrs Margaret Thatcher, who was then Prime Minister, in February 1986. Whether or not they are the same features in all other TV interviews would be a matter for further research.

Using pronouns
The personal pronouns – *I, you, he, she, it,*(singular) and *we, you, they* (plural), and the possessive pronouns *my, your, his, her, its* and *our, your, their* – are used to refer to people and things that have already been named or to which we can point. The use of some pronouns is not as obvious and straightforward, however, as this grammatical definition suggests, because they are important markers of the **relationship** between one speaker and another. In a TV interview, the politician is aware of the viewing audience watching in their homes, who take part in the relationships set up in the broadcast by pronouns like *I, we* and *you*.

I and *you*   The pronoun *I* is used by a speaker to refer to herself/himself. One use of *you* in an interview is to refer to the other speaker (I = interviewer; T = Mrs Thatcher):

   I   **you** said in the House of Commons ...
      I suppose what people are surprised at is ...
   T   **I** notice **you** leant forward as if it was a catch question ...

The use of *you* to address the other speaker also occurs in **comment clauses** like *as you will recall*, which function like parentheses or interpolations. Typical examples in the interview being examined are:

   T   and although **AS YOU SAY** (.) we're not back to the volume we were (.) in 1979 ...
   T   no I don't (.) first we're getting the job creation up (.)
      AS I'VE ALREADY INDICATED ...
   I   you've often talked about this 700,000 jobs (.) in fact (.) the vast majority (.) **AS YOU KNOW** (.) of those jobs are not full-time jobs like the jobs that were lost but part-time jobs

I   our (.) competitive position against other countries **AS YOU'VE COMPLAINED** and other people have pointed out (.) is already being eroded by the wage increases and salary increases people are taking

In the interview, both Mrs Thatcher and the interviewer used this kind of comment clause to each other as follows:

T	I
as you know (8)	as you know (5)
as you will recall (3)	as you've complained (1)
you'll remember (2)	
as you say (1)	
as I've indicated (1)	

Activity 7.18

Discuss how comment clauses like *as you know* and *as you will recall* affect what a speaker is saying. Why do we use them?

The use of the comment clause *you know* as a kind of **filler** is very common in spoken English, and in many speakers can become an almost meaningless insertion, similar to *sort of* and *like*. It is used several times in the interview, for example in:

T   coal industry (.) **YOU KNOW** (.) is not manufacturing ...
T   it isn't (.) **YOU KNOW** (.) ...

This function of *you know* as a filler is different from its normal grammatical function as a **reporting** verb, as in,

T   you know what it is if the people take lower paid jobs ...

It can emphasise what is being said, and also challenge the other speaker.

But the use of *you* in an interview is not restricted to addressing the other speaker, and is regularly used in all kinds of speech situations as an **impersonal** pronoun, referring to people in general. In a political broadcast, *you* generally includes the viewing audience.

Activity 7.19

(i)   Who is being referred to as *you* in the following extracts from Mrs Thatcher's responses in the interview?
(ii)   Are the referents of *you* impersonal and general, or can they be more closely identified? Is the TV viewer also addressed as *you*? What effect might this have?

1.   well **you** don't call Cabinet ministers to heel (.) **you** discuss matters in Cabinet
2.   I had had (.) as **you** do have when **you** have sensitive commercial matters on a particular company (.) **you** tend to get together only the ministers who need to know (.) because they are commercially sensitive (.) and **you** don't go more widely ...

3.   but **you** know (.) if **you** want an assured future (.) **you**'ve got to be successful (.) if **you** want an assured future for the people who are working in it (.) **you**'ve got to be successful ...
4.   **you** had strikes (.) **you** had the Winter of Discontent (.) **you** had a government unprepared to tackle the industrial problems ...

We   *We* may refer to the interviewer and politician, *you and I*, together in the studio. But this use is in fact rare, because their talk is not restricted to themselves as a pair of individuals. Much more typical is, for example,

T   **I** feel that **we** owe quite a debt to the people who are in the bottom half (.) **we** have taken in my view (.) too high a proportion of their income in tax

The *we* must refer to others, and possibly two different others – to the general public in *we owe quite a debt,* and to the Government in *we have taken.* But the reference is not precise, and so there may be ambiguity and vagueness of reference to a general *we* which may include the viewers watching the programme. We can call this a **collective** use of *we,* which sometimes assumes that the viewing audience – the general public – is in agreement with the speaker.

Activity 7.20

Read the following responses by Mrs Thatcher which contain the first-person plural pronouns *we/our,* and discuss who is probably being referred to by the pronouns. How many different references can you identify?

1.   I thought **our** policy would prevail in the end ...
2.   **We** had to go to a full Economic Committee of the Cabinet to make the decision (.) and **we** did
3.   it was part of the argument when **we** went into the Common Market ...
4.   it's heart-breaking to go to the Middle East and see the Japanese substitute for Land Rover (.) because **we** haven't been able to make enough ...
5.   so **we** had a go in the last Budget at stepping up those programmes (.) but in the end **we** simply have got to get more creation of wealth .....
6.   in fact **we** had a lot of hidden unemployment (.)
     steel industry had not been tackled (.)
     we've tackled it ...

They   The third-person plural pronouns *they/them/their* are normally used after a specific person or object as been named, and so there is less likelihood of ambiguity of reference than when using *we* or *you* in a general sense. Some obvious examples are:

there are **twenty-one members of Cabinet** (.)
on one issue if **they** all speak two minutes (.) that's forty-two minutes ....
many many women want part-time jobs (.) it suits **them**
it's a matter for **Westland's board and Westland shareholders** to determine **their** own future

One   The **impersonal pronoun** *one* is rarely used by most speakers, and tends to be regarded as formal and rather old-fashioned. Mrs Thatcher uses it three times only in an hour's interview, so it appears to be an unintentional substitute for her more normal use of *I*, *you* or *we*:

Activity 7.21

Substitute the most suitable alternative pronoun for *one* in the three occurrences.

1.   should I have asserted authority earlier? (.) **one** tried to by agreement ...
2.   we've got to act together and **one** many many times at Question Time said over and over again .
3.   and so that's something which **one** has to consider (.) if you're really passionately keen as most of us are (.) to have cars made here ...

TV interviews, like commentary, are unscripted, and will therefore show common features of spoken language in contrast with written, scripted dialogue. The occasionally haphazard use of pronouns is one such feature.

Activity 7.22

Discuss the use of the pronouns in the following extract from the interview. Do the changes of pronoun materially affect the meaning?

> we have discussion (.) we have internal discussion (.) very very lively discussion (.) that's the way I work because we always talk things through (.) we never never never come to a conclusion without having all views represented and discussed (.) I mean that's one reason why you have it in Cabinet committee (.) that is the way I work and that's the way we reach our conclusions

Style and structure

(a) *Clause-complexes*   TV interviews are no doubt carefully prepared by both interviewer and interviewee, but the interviewee's responses are unscripted, and this will therefore be reflected in the style and structure of the responses. There is a tendency for clauses to follow each other in a looser relationship of clause-complexes than we would expect in the sentences of a written script, linked by *and, and then, but, or* (see sections 5.3. and 7.1) and clauses may be inserted like parentheses. For example:

T	er well we made several efforts to em (.) h restore collective responsibility (.)
and	indeed you'll remember
that	on the Thursday afternoon after Cabinet on December 19th I reasserted it once again hh
but	somehow because of this other emotional thing it was extremely

difficult h
and   then as you know we went into recess and had a very very difficult time
       h
and   we had to restore collective responsibility on January 9th h
       then not merely as a principle (.)
but   say look (.) all right (.) we agree the principle h
but   it's how it's applied that matters h
and   because it's very sensitive because Westland is near to making a
       decision h
       we really must keep out (.)
and   that unfortunately was when Michael Heseltine resigned

Activity 7.23

Turn the extract into a form that would be acceptable as an example of written English.

(b) *Rhetoric – parallelism and repetition*   The influence of public and Parliamentary speech-making can also be detected in some of the **rhetorical** features of a political interviewee's responses. Devices like **parallelism** with repeated vocabulary and grammatical patterns occur (see also section 9.1) as in this extract from Mrs Thatcher's interview:

well   I hope so (.)
          I never had any question in my own mind
but   let me be let me be perfectly clear
          WE WERE ELECTED TO DO the difficult things
          YES
          WE WERE ELECTED TO TAKE some very tough decisions
          YES
          people know that mid-term popularity does sink (.)
when   you come (.) to an election (.)
          they still want a government
          WHICH KNOWS the direction in which it is going
          WHICH HONOURS inititative
          WHICH DOES NOT   WANT BRITAIN to be defeatist
but   **WANTS A BRITAIN** to take pride in
                                 our achievements
because   we have in fact got a system
          WHICH   ENABLES them to take advantage of the opportunities
and   **WHICH   PRODUCES** business which can compete the world
          over
and   **WHICH   HAS** a legal system and justice which   **STILL** we
                                                               took the
          world over
and   **STILL** is
                                                               highly honoured

This extract comes towards the end of the interview, and reads more like the peroration of a speech than informal spoken language.

Parallelism contains **repetition** of the whole or part of clauses and phrases. The repetition of words and phrases for emphasis is also a common feature of speech, as in,

> and we had a **very very** difficult time ...
> well (.) **very very** quickly (.) as you will recall ...
> it was a tragedy (.) **that should not have occurred** (.) **that should not have occurred** (.) **that should not have occurred** (.) ...
> we **never never never** come to a conclusion without having all views represented and discussed ...
> but what we have got is **much much** more flourishing than it was in 1979 ...

(c) *Colloquial and informal* A TV political interview is watched in the home by a large audience, and the style of spoken language adopted by an interviewee will therefore tend to be informal rather than formal, and is likely to contain a high proportion of colloquial words and phrases.

We must not overgeneralise from the limited data being used, and some of the style and vocabulary used by Mrs Thatcher is part of her **idiolect** – the language use typical of an individual person. But there is a lot of evidence of her use of colloquial and informal language.

People We find in this interview, for example, a frequent use of the word *people* to refer generally to others where a more precise descriptive noun might have been used:

> where there are questions which **people** wish again to come to Cabinet ...
> but often we report from Cabinet committees to Cabinet so that **people** know precisely what has been decided ...

Here the noun *ministers* would fit. In some instances, *people* is probably the most suitable word, for example when referring to *the British people*,

> it's the right course for Britain (.) so many other governments are following it (.) but it's a course to make Britain proud (.) because **her people** take advantage of their opportunities (.) they don't just put up placards to government and say more for us (.) they say we have a responsibility (.) by our own efforts (.) for our own future (.) and for our neighbours and for our community

but the word occurs over fifty times in the interview, and seems to be a marker of the speaker's style.

Get It is probable that we have all been recommended not to use the verb *get*, or to be very selective in its use. It is, however, very common in spoken English, and no less so in Mrs Thatcher's 1986 TV interview, in which we find *get, getting* and *got/ got to* over forty times. For example:

> 350,000 or 400,000 people **get** new jobs every month ...
> it 's the Germans and the Japanese who'll **get** the orders and the jobs ...

we've **got to** act together ...
those talks had scarcely **got** anywhere ...
and really are **getting** demoralised ...
because I believe we've **got** now (.) we're **getting** responsible management ...

Things The word *thing(s)* is commonly used to make a general reference, as in,

it would have been **the wise thing** to do ...
I was very much concerned with how **things** were going ...

and there is nothing to remark about this usage even in a formal context. But there are instances in the interview of the use of the word *thing* which would be marked as colloquial, including:

whether he could put a bid together or explore the possibility I think was **the official thing** ...
but somehow because of **this other emotional thing** it was extremely difficult

Look A characteristic feature of Mrs Thatcher's language in interviews was her use of *look* to begin a turn or an utterance. In the interview we are examining it was used in this way twelve times, sometimes to reinforce her own statement of policy or fact, as in,

and we had to restore collective responsibility on January 9th (.) then not merely as a principle (.) but say **LOOK** (.) all right (.) we agree the principle (.) but it's how it's applied that matters

or quoting what she had said or should have said to another person,

you discuss them in the Economic Committe of the Cabinet (.) you say now **LOOK** (.) we've got to act together
I think what you're really saying is should I have said to him **LOOK** (.) either you're even-handed or else you go

or quoting what someone else said

well very very quickly as you will recall (.) the Attorney-General came round to see the Cabinet Secretary and said **LOOK** what's happened?

or what they might say,

I hope we don't have bad by-election results (.) I hope we have people saying **LOOK** (.) they know where they're going (.) she won't veer to the right or left (.) she'll go steadily forward

or replying directly to the interviewer

LOOK (.) no one wants more than I do for British Leyland to get more than 4% of the European market (.) to be able to stand on its own two feet (.) and not to have to come to the taxpayer
no no it's not enough (.) but **LOOK** inward investment we were talking about a moment ago has created (.) a 100,000 jobs (.) that's very good

Activity 7.24

What in your opinion is the function and effect of this use of *Look!*?

Other examples   Here are a few other examples of vocabulary which you will probably agree are marked as informal:

> but Austin Rover ... ought to be in the league with **the big boys** (.) **the big boys** like General Motors ...
> there's been **a fantastic amount ...**
> you can't just wait for **the bobby** on the beat ...
> they're **wishy-washy** ...

7.3.4   *Television interviews used for political propaganda*

Politicians take part in televised interviews in order to present their party's policies to the public, so they need to learn the art of trying to 'set the agenda' themselves, making their responses statements of their party's collective view. Research has shown that politicians' answers in TV and radio interviews tend to contain a greater proportion of evasions than those of other interviewees in other situations. Both interviewer and politician may challenge the other so that the interview takes on some of the aspects of a **debate**.

In section 7.3 we have focused almost exclusively on linguistic features of the interviewer's and interviewee's speech. Other important aspects not discussed concern the interaction of the two speakers, which you could look at after having read chapter 8, and the social/political significance of such interviews, which this book does not try to examine directly.

A daily newspaper, published on the day after the interview we have been examining, contained these remarks:

> If there is indeed to be a leadership struggle, moreover, then "so be it".
>
> But if you were looking for one word to remember from the session it would surely be "incidentally". Because on the economy or unemployment or the future cohesions of her Government she so often felt "incidentally" obliged to rattle through a set piece of statistics or pat phrases which bore no relation whatsoever to the question she'd been asked ...

The first comment identifies a personal feature of Mrs Thatcher's spoken idiolect, which can be illustrated by these extracts from the interview:

> T   I think he became too personally involved in that particular solution (.) **so be it**
> I   if somebody were to challenge you ... would you fight?
> T   well (.) if they do **so be it** (.) **so be it** (.) and I shall fight

The second comment turns out to be misleading and exaggerated (though it clearly reflects the writer's impressions of the Mrs Thatcher's handling of the interview), because she in fact used *incidentally* only twice:

> **incidentally** (.) you referred to it as a crisis (.) it wasn't a crisis of
> the kind that Falklands was ...
> the coal industry had not been tackled (.) coal industry **incidentally**
> is not manufacturing ...

Whether or not she answered the questions could only be decided from a detailed analysis of a transcript of the whole broadcast. Here to conclude this chapter is a transcription of an extract.

Activity 7.25

Use the transcription to discuss or analyse any of the features of speech and discourse described in this or the next chapter. (In a short extract you will not find examples of all of them.)

Transcription of part of a television interview, February 1986

I	let's just look at society (.) more generally (.)	
	not at jobs particularly though I think perhaps that's part of it h	
	are you concerned that that when people look <u>back</u> on the	
	Thatcher years (.)	
	they will say there was a <u>bad</u> side (.)	5
	we have <u>bad</u> memories (.) as well as (.) <u>good</u> memories to set	
	alongside it h em	
	memories of rising crime (.) memories of violence on picket	
	lines (.)	
	memories of (.) disruption in schools	10
	the very (.) opposite of the kind of <u>vir</u>tues that Thatcherism (.)	
	was meant to stand for?	
T	hh I think that they know (.) that <u>some</u> of those things (.)	
	are the <u>price</u> you <u>had</u> to <u>pay</u> (.) for <u>ha:l</u>ting (.) the de<u>cline</u> into	
	which <u>Brit</u>ain had <u>fallen</u> .h.h	15
	re<u>mem</u>ber the circumstances under which we took over (.)	
	as I said industries <u>over-manned</u> (.) <u>full</u> of restrictive practices (.)	
	the Trade Unions had <u>prac</u>tically <u>taken</u> <u>over</u> <u>Brit</u>ain hh	
	the opinion polls which I <u>used</u> to look at on this particular	
	factor h	20
	said they thought the Trade Union leaders had more power than	
	the Government hh	
	you had <u>strikes</u> (.) you had the <u>Winter</u> of <u>Discontent</u> h	
	you had a government <u>un</u>prepared to <u>tackle</u> the industrial	
	problems (.)	25
	they'd to <u>have</u> over-manning to let it continue h	
	they <u>didn't</u> <u>like</u> to <u>make</u> the un<u>pop</u>ular difficult decision h	
	so we <u>were</u> in decline .h Britain <u>was</u> defeatist	

it was becoming ungovernable (.) yes we <u>had</u> to tackle those (.)
<u>steel</u> (.) is now in profit h we're tackling <u>coal</u> h   30
we <u>had</u> to alter the Trade Union legislation (.) we <u>did</u> h
it has brought about a <u>transformation</u> h
and we did it by putting back <u>faith</u> in the <u>or</u>dinary Trade Union
member h
and not in their Trade Union <u>bos</u>ses h   35
because we weren't going to have the ordinary Trade Union
members <u>shoved</u> <u>around</u>
(.) by some of their bosses who wanted <u>power</u> (.)

⌈ to <u>them</u>⌉ and not to their members
⌊ I but ⌋   40

⌈ (.) (.) now I could go on (.) (.) and I've brought a <u>transformation</u> (.)⌉
⌊ I I I was talking about (.) yes now I was (.) I was asking you about) ⌋

⌈ T (.) <u>and</u> (.) . yes we <u>had</u> to go through (.) that coal strike⌉ (.) it
⌊ I yes (.) the pain is just what I'm talking about ⌋
was <u>not</u> <u>our</u> <u>fault</u> (.) h   45
that <u>many</u> of the mi- the the <u>striking</u> miners h <u>they</u> were (.) the picket
lines were against the <u>working</u> <u>miners</u>⌈ (.) ⌉ not against the
                                              ⌊ I but ⌋

Government⌈ against the workers ⌉ h
          ⌊ I do you (.) do you also⌋   50
I think people <u>realise</u> h <u>that</u> <u>had</u> to be gone through and they're
<u>grate</u>ful ...

8. Variety and style in spoken English – II: conversation

8.1 Conversation analysis

Ordinary conversation is perhaps the most important variety of social language use, and the most basic, in the sense that in infancy we are motivated to learn the language or languages we hear around us just so that we can interact with other people. And, of course, we continue to use language in daily conversational interaction with others throughout our lives. Many of us, it is true, might spend some of our time using the written medium to complete forms or produce notes, letters, reports, essays, articles or books, but for all of us, most of our time is spent talking to others. (See David Langford, *Analysing Talk*, ch. 1, for a fuller discussion of spoken and writen language use.)

Conversation analysis has become an important branch of language study. Its aim is to discover the rules and regularities that govern how we talk to one another and to show how our more or less subconscious knowledge of these rules and regularities helps us to make sense of each other.

Conversation analysts are particularly interested in three aspects of talk:

- how participants use the various resources of spoken language, e.g. pitch, stress, pause, tempo, vocabulary and grammar, in their production of conversation;
- how participants manage conversation as a kind of activity that must simultaneously involve the separate, but interlocking, behaviours of several speakers;
- how participants manage conversation to achieve their own particular purposes.

Most of us think of *conversation* as the thing that is going on when two or more people talk to each other, on an equal footing, about people they know, things they have been experiencing or doing, their plans for the future and so on. When talk about these matters has some underlying professional purpose or context, e.g. a police interrogation, a job interview, a media interview or chat show, we would not regard what is going on as ordinary conversation. Furthermore, when we produce a piece of talk with a well-defined purpose such as asking someone to call in at the chemist's, asking for directions in the street, or complaining about someone's behaviour towards us, we would not usually call such talk *conversation*.

Nevertheless, conversation analysts do regard such forms of talk as *conversational*, in the technical sense that the talk involves **participants** in the reciprocating roles of **speaker** and **listener**, and is **spontaneous** rather than scripted or planned. Thus the conversation analyst is interested in any talk that involves people who, at various points in the talk, will be both speaker and listener, and who will be spontaneously constructing what they have to say.

Of course, some instances of conversation will be more constrained than others. Compare, for example, the talk of the classroom and talk over lunch. Or compare the talk of an interview with a careers adviser, and the talk of a chat about the future with friends.

The two conversations examined in chapter 5, where the differences between speech and writing were discussed, are not typical of what we think of as normal everyday conversation. They were specially set up and recorded, and constrained in the particular way that the father took on a *directing* role, asking questions and generally keeping the talk going. To get the least constrained and fully spontaneous conversation, the speakers need to be quite uninhibited and unaware of the tape-recorder. This situation is never easy to record, and indeed the problem of how to record fully spontaneous conversation has been called 'the observer's paradox':

> ...the aim of linguistic research in the community must be to find out how people talk when they are not being systematically observed; yet we can only obtain this data by systematic observation.
>
> (William Labov, *The Study of Language in its Social Context,* 1970)

To record a conversation when speakers are unaware is not acceptable, so you should always obtain permission to record someone's speech. Even if you do, a satisfactory recording of conversation, for purposes of study, is difficult to achieve. A BBC television series in the 1970s came close to overcoming the observer's paradox by filming and recording a working-class family's daily activities over a long period, with the cameras and microphones set up in their home and following them around wherever they went. The members of the family became so used to the presence of cameras that they produced what appeared to be completely normal behaviour and speech – so normal that some viewers objected to the language used from time to time.

We shall use three extracts of recorded conversation from the series to illustrate how the participants deal with the three aspects of talk listed above (p. 151)

1 *Tom B. and Mrs W.* (cassette tape section 23)

(Tom has been living with Mrs W's daughter Marion, and Mrs W asks him when he intends to get married.)

T   ↑Everybody else↑ has been talking about marriage
   (1.0)
   but ↑I'm↑ the one that's getting married
   (.)
   we <u>will</u> get married like you know
   (.)
   ↓we intend↓ (.) /tu::/ get married and that but not just yet
   (.)
   ⎡I mean   ⎤
MW ⎣see <u>I</u>'m not⎦ ↑don't↑ get me wrong

T ↑I'm↑ not interfering [↑I'm↑ just wondering what you] think
                          [oh no (.) oh yeah   ]
about why (.) <u>why</u> you don't want to get [<u>married</u>] I mean you're <u>both</u> over
                                               [T °mm°   ]
eighteen ↑<u>nothing</u>↑ [I can do] but I ↑<u>don't</u>↑ like seeing Marion hurt
                     [T °mm°]
(0.5)

T I don't want to get married just yet and that like you know
(0.5)
and I think to myself [we-   ]   [T°mm   ]
MW   [well ↑I think↑] you'd find she [wants to be]
married before she moves into that flat
T ↑Oh↑ I think <u>she::</u> does yeah
MW well ↑don't↑ you consider her at all I mean::
(0.5)
T Oh yeah but I - I don't want to get married just yet
(1.0)
T [you see]   [I mean] a few
   [MW yeah] well ↑what do you call just yet↑ h.h. [I mean]
more ↑<u>months</u>↑ at least I mean I'm not going to rush into marriage in seven
weeks' time
(.)
it's as simple as that
(.)
mean I mean Ma- ↑Ma↑rion either takes it or she leaves it
(.)
I'm ↑not↑ getting marr [ied just yet]
MW   [↑what↑   ] if she leaves it?
T well it's (.) <u>that's</u> it then ↑isn't it↑

2 *Heather and Mrs W.* (cassette tape section 24)

(The mother and daughter are talking about a married sister, Karen, who had been living in the house with her husband and child, and who has now moved into her own flat.)

H ↑the first day↑ she moved out she had to come round here
(6.0)
MW your father and I were talking this morning wh- (.) and ↑we said↑ that
when ↑you::↑ (.) get married (.) and have a home of your own: (.)
↑you're↑ going to be nice and strong:: (.) you'll be able to ↑co:pe↑ on
your ↑own↑ you'll=
H =I will
MW You'll k [eep the place ↑really spotless↑]
           [H I will I'll make my friends   ]
MW [and you'll]
   [H I'll make]
MW make=
H =friends

MW   well we said all this because you're a very strong character::
(.)

H   all ⌈ right   ⌉
          ⌊ MW ↑Karen isn't↑⌋

H   But Mum wha- ↑what would she do if none of us lived in Reading an ↑
or if she had to get a house out of Reading ↑what↑ <u>would</u> she do::
⌈ you tell me that   ⌉
⌊ MW she would have ⌋ (.) she would have to

man ⌈ age ⌉   ⌈MW Ye:s ⌉   ⌈ But   ⌉
      ⌊H <u>Ex</u> ⌋<u>actly</u> (.) so why don't ⌊ she star ⌋ t trying to ⌊ now:: ⌋

MW   the poi ⌈ nt is she's ↑not such a strong::↑   ⌉ character
            ⌊H But no she can't because you sympathise with her⌋

H   hhh ↑it's not the <u>point</u>↑ she's as str- ↑she↑ <u>stronger</u> that what she
makes out I'll tell you that now:

MW   well ↑may↑be ⌈ ::   ⌉ ⌈ maybe   ⌉
                      ⌊H Sh ⌋ e's a ⌊ lot stronger⌋ ↑cos↑ otherwise I would
have drived her mad when she <u>lived</u> here but no she's a lot stronger
than what she makes out to you lot I'll tell you now:

MW   well I'm just trying to help her get ⌈ (.) acc⌉ limatised (.)
                                   ⌊H yeah ⌋

MW   hh so ↑therefore ↑=
H   =Exactly you helped her=
MW   I've tried to ⌈ do it ↑grad↑ually::   ⌉
                ⌊H you ↑helped↑ her when she ⌋ come <u>here</u> you helped
her when she come here hh then you had to help her in doing <u>other</u>
things when she was here hh then you ↑helped↑ her in summat <u>else</u>
then summat <u>else</u> then summat <u>else</u> hh now she's gone you're
helping her in summat <u>else</u> ↑again↑=

MW   =well I'm ⌈ MW jus-⌉
             ⌊H hh   ⌋ ↑ then↑ it'd be <u>summ</u>at else and <u>summ</u>at <u>else</u>
and <u>summ</u>at <u>else</u>
(.)

H   but in the long run you ain't going to help 'cos she's going to be lo::st
(0.5)

MW   ↑well↑ then:: ↑↑then I've done all I can haven't
⌈ I I've got the satisfaction of knowing I've   ⌉
⌊ H <u>Exact</u>ly now you needn't bother any more ⌋

MW   tried
H   you <u>have</u> tried
(.)

H   ↑<u>you've</u>↑ tried more than anyone⌈ could   ⌉try=
                              ⌊MW Right⌋

MW   =so now I'm grad⌈ ually trying to break her   ⌉off of coming up so often=
                    ⌊H Now you should give up ⌋

H   =Exactly because you might as well give ↑u::p↑
MW   well why have ↑why↑ should I give up

H   Because:: you ain't ↑helping↑ [her no more   ]
                                               MW DID I GIVE UP ON YOU

H   Don't bother:: ↑I↑ don't need your help though
        (0.5)

MW   [No but as I say it's ↑nice↑ to have ↑people there↑]
        [H That's the trouble with you lot you're too   soft on her
        (.)
        the <u>more::</u> you lot are like that the <u>worse</u> she's going to be::
        (1.0)
        it's Karen all ↑over↑ if she know she got it coming cushy she ain't
        got to <u>bother</u> have she::

3 *Tom, Marion and the Minister* (cassette tape section 25)

(Tom has at last agreed on a wedding date, and he and Marion go to the minister of the church where they want to be married.)

(a)   *First extract*

Mi   I've been <u>watching:</u> (.) you know /ði/ [(1.0)   ] programme
                                [Ma AHUH]

    [on T   ] V
    [T The programme]
    [(1.0)] I'm <u>not</u> <u>preach</u>ing at you (.) ↑but↑ as a minister of
    [T mm]
    [/ði/   ] chur:ch that erm (.) ↑I↑ naturally h <u>stand</u> for the
    [T mm ye:s]
    <u>Christ</u>ian <u>doc</u>trine of <u>marriage</u> [(1.0)] and erm (.) you <u>are::</u> sincere in
                                     [mm]
    that you want /tu:/ <u>marry</u> (.) <u>Marion</u> [(1.0)   ] and really make a
                                    [T mm yeah]
    <u>go</u> of it (.) that is s [o   ] isn't it=
                   [T oh]

T   =↑Oh↑ <u>that</u> is so [yeah we] ↑I mean↑ we <u>definitely</u> <u>do</u> intend to: (.)
                      [Mi Ye:s]
    h <u>make</u> a go of it and that

Mi   Ye:s
    (0.5)

T   I [mean   ] we are d- (.) ↑we've ↑been intending to get married for
      [Mi Good]
    a lo-(.) ↑quite↑ a <u>while</u> now like [you know   ]
                             [Mi That's right]
    (0.5)

Mi   Ye:s
    (.)
    you'll <u>re</u>member for many a day:: (.) the <u>vows</u> that you've <u>made</u> to
    each other (0.5) because i- although it's a <u>simple</u> <u>ser</u>vice it's a
    pro↑<u>found</u>↑ service=

```
T       =mm=
Ma      =mm
```

(b)   *Second extract*

```
Mi      Had you thought of the organ
        (.)
        er
        (.)
```

```
Ma      er⌈ m          ⌉                    ⌈Ma Not⌉ really
          ⌊Mi Have⌋ you:: looked that far ahead yet ⌊or    ⌋
        actually I::'⌈ve      ⌉ erm
                     ⌊Mi No⌋
        (.)
```

```
Mi      Normally these days we don't sing *The Voice that Breath'd o'er Eden*
T       [laughs]
Ma      [laughs]
Mi      er you know neither do we sing *Rescue the Perishing*
T       I was just about to suggest that you would really want one because as
        you say it sort of puts the finishing touches to ⌈it     ⌉
                                                         ⌊Mi that⌋ 's right=
```

```
Ma      =Well y- ⌈it'd    ⌉ be dead without it wouldn't it
                 ⌊Mi Yeah⌋
Mi      Ye::s=
Ma      =mm=
Mi      =Yes ↑Good↑
        (2.0)
Mi      Now is there any question you'd like to (.) bring to me
T       See:: ↑when↑ we fir- ↑at↑ first we thought you know:: me and
        Marion started living together and that ⌈(.)   ⌉ we thought that
                                                ⌊Mi mm⌋
        might have had the effect on the Church like you know
        (.)
        hh I mean=
Mi      =Look Tom (.) if only people would remember (.) we're not here to
        prejudge any ⌈body ⌉
                     ⌊T mm⌋
Mi      I am not=
T       = mm no
Mi      and (.) I:: (.) I say this that ↑if I can perform this ser::vice↑ ⌈to   ⌉ get
                                                                          ⌊T mm⌋
        you to do /ði/ (.) honour ⌈able thing        ⌉ you ⌈know     ⌉
                                  ⌊T honourable thing⌋     ⌊T which is⌋marriage
        then:: you can face the world ⌈and  ⌉ you say:: (.) she belongs to me
                                      ⌊T mm⌋
        ⌈(.)  ⌉ I belong ⌈to her⌉
        ⌊T mm⌋           ⌊T mm  ⌋
        ↑it's↑ as simple as that
```

8.2 Managing the resources of spoken language

8.2.1 *Loudness*

Activity 8.1

Listen to each extract and pay particular attention to the loudness with which the talk is produced. In which extracts is the talk loudest, and why?

Discussion

We tend to speak loudly usually for one or both of two reasons, either because of the physical circumstances in which we are speaking, or because of our emotional state when speaking.

Relevant physical circumstances could include the following:

- we want to speak when others are already doing so;
- we are speaking to a large group;
- we are speaking where there is a lot of noise;
- the person we are talking to is hard of hearing, or is assumed to have other difficulties in processing spoken language.

One emotional state often associated with a loud voice is, of course, anger. And we are much more likely to display our anger when we are talking to someone towards whom we feel equal or superior in status.

In the three extracts you will have noticed that the use of loud voices is much in evidence in the conversations between Tom and Mrs W, and between Mrs W and her daughter. The use of loud voice is almost entirely absent from the conversation with the minister. This is no doubt because of the relationship between the participants, and because there are points of dispute in the first two extracts, but not in the third.

8.2.2 *Tempo*

Activity 8.2

Listen to each extract and select one fragment of talk where the tempo or speed of the speaker noticeably quickens, and one fragment where the tempo noticeably slows down. Suggest reasons for the changes in tempo.

Discussion

There are several instances of abrupt changes of tempo in the extracts; here are just two examples for illustration. There is an abrupt slow-down in tempo in extract 1 as Mrs W says,

Fragment 1   but I ↑<u>don't</u>↑ like seeing Marion hurt

It seems likely that this is, for Mrs W, the main message of her speaking turn, and by slowing down and enunciating more carefully, she can draw particular attention to it.

In Extract 2 we find Mrs W doing just the opposite, and suddenly producing talk at a considerably quicker pace. This occurs when she says in a loud voice,

Fragment 2 ...
H   Because:: you ain't ↑helping↑ [her no more   ]
⇒   [MW DID I GIVE UP] ON YOU

The crucial thing here is that what Mrs W wants to say is spoken whilst her daughter is still talking. Mrs W speaks in a faster tempo in order to slip it into the ongoing flow of her daughter's talk.

8.2.3 *Stress*

Activity 8.3 _____

In each of the extracts you will find that particular words, or parts of words, are made prominent because they receive extra stress (indicated by underlining in the transcription). Stressing a word indicates some sort of contrast.
    Study the following fragment from extract 1, and suggest what contrast is intended, and how this contributes to the meaning of what is said.

====================================

Fragment 3
T   ↑Oh↑ I think she:: does yeah

Discussion

The intended contrast here seems to be between the person referred to as *she* – Marion, and the person who refers to himself as *I* – Tom. We can infer from the basic sentence *I think that she does* the fact that Marion (*she*) wants to get married soon, and we infer from the stress on *she* the added meaning that this is something that Tom (*I*) does not want. What effect would changing the stress to *I*, *think* or *does* have?

8.2.4 *Pauses*

Activity 8.4 _____

In the following fragments from extracts 1 and 2 you will see that the speakers incorporate pauses into their talk.
    Comment on the functions that the pauses have in each fragment.

====================================

Fragment 4
T   ↑Everybody else↑ has been talking about marriage
     (1.0)
     but ↑I'm↑ the one that's getting married
     (.)
     we will get married like you know

Fragment 5

MW   your father and I were talking this morning wh-
(.)
and ↑we said↑ that when ↑you::↑
(.)
get married
(.)
and have a home of your own:
(.)
↑you're↑ going to be nice and strong:: (.)

Discussion

The essential thing to notice here is that in fragment 4 each segment separated by a pause is a complete clause, and could stand alone in its context as a message. This is not so in fragment 5. Here the pauses occur following a cut-off, a subordinate clause or a coordinate clause within the subordinate clause. The pauses therefore do not enclose potentially independent messages, but are rather a way of marking grammatical structure at the level of clause or clause-complex.

So while in Fragment 4 the pauses function to signal *information* structure, in fragment 5 they function to signal *grammatical* structure.

8.2.5 Context

Activity 8.5 ⎯⎯⎯⎯⎯⎯⎯⎯⎯⎯⎯⎯⎯⎯⎯⎯⎯⎯⎯

The choices of vocabulary and grammar that we make in conversation are highly dependent on the context. Similarly, our interpretation of what others say must be equally dependent upon context.

Examine the following fragment from extract 2 and comment on the ways in which interpretation is dependent on context.

Fragment 6

H   But Mum wha- ↑what would she do if none of us lived in Reading an-↑ or if
       she had to get a house out of Reading ↑what↑ <u>would</u> she do::
       ⎡ you tell me that   ⎤
       ⎣ MW she would have ⎦ (.) she would have to man ⎡ age   ⎤
                                                        ⎣ H <u>Ex</u> ⎦ <u>actly</u> (.)

H   so why don't ⎡ she star ⎤ t trying to now::
                     ⎣ MW Ye:s ⎦

Discussion

H's turn is produced as some sort of **objection** in reply to something MW has said. We know that it is a **reply** because of the choice of *but*, which signals a particular kind of connection to what has just been said. The meaning of *Mum* is, of course, provided by the context of the conversation and the relationship between the speaker and addressee.

The turn also contains a number of pronouns whose meanings, or **referents**, can only be determined through a knowledge of the context. *You* and *me* refer to the addressee (MW) and speaker (H) in this particular conversation. *Us* refers to the family group relevant to the speaker and addressee. *She* is the individual (Karen) referred to earlier in the conversation.

The turn is used to put a question about *what* the individual referred to as *she* would *do* in certain circumstances. Individuals can *do* all sorts of things, so what do *what* and *do* mean here? The most obvious sort of *doing* referred to is Karen's coping with independent living – which is the topic of the conversation. So the aspect of context relevant to interpretation up to this point is the whole topic of conversation.

MW's turn contains the word *she* and a verb phrase which includes the **modal auxiliary verb** *would*. Both the word *she* and the structure of the verb phrase *would have to manage* have been taken over from H's prior turn – *what would she do*. It is therefore H's prior turn which provides the context for the interpretation of MW's turn.

In the final turn of the fragment H starts with the word *Exactly*. This can only be interpreted by referring to the whole of what MW has just said, since it is in effect produced as an **agreement** to the whole content of that turn. H then goes on to use the word *so*, which links what is about to be said to what has just been said by MW. H then produces a clause with an incomplete verb phrase, *start trying to ...* . This can be interpreted only if we supply the word *manage* contained in the prior speaker's turn. The word *now*, of course, can only be interpreted by reference to the actual moment of speaking.

We can see from this discussion just how dependent on context the interpretation of individual words and structures can be.

The **social roles** that participants bring to a conversation are also important in determining their choices of vocabulary and grammar. Notice, for example, in extract 3 how the minister asks the couple if they have any questions.

8.3   The management of multi-party talk

8.3.1   *The listener role*

Activity 8.6

Comment on what the following fragment from extract 3 tells us about how we listen to each other in conversation.

Fragment 7
Mi   and (.) I:: (.) I say this that ↑if I can perform this ser::vice↑ ⌈ to ⌉ get
                                                          ⌊*T* mm⌋

       you to do /ði/ (.) honour ⌈ able thing   ⌉
                                 ⌊*T* honourable thing ⌋

Discussion

The minister is doing most of the talking in this fragment, so we can say he is in the **speaker role**, whilst Tom is in the **listener role**. Although Tom is in the listener role, he does in fact have something to say, and he makes a contribution on two occasions while the minister is still talking. His contributions **overlap** with the minister's talk. Nevertheless Tom does not have a lot to say, and he is not trying to take over the speaker role from the minister. What is interesting is *what* he says and *where* he says it.

He says *mm* at precisely the point where the minister has completed a clause. *mm* is a very minimal response, and because it is so minimal it cannot represent an attempt to take over the speaker role. So what Tom says is timed to coincide with the completion of a clause and to show that he is happy to continue in the listener role. This suggests that when we listen we are attentive to points of grammatical completion and we tend to display that attentiveness.

Tom's second contribution is slightly in overlap with the minister's talk, but you will have noticed that the phrase it is in overlap with completes a clause. Again the contribution is minimal, just one two-word phrase, *honourable thing*. What is particularly interesting here is that the two words complete a noun phrase with the structure *determiner + adjective + noun*. The minister in his talk up to the point of overlap has produced the determiner *the* and part of the adjective *honourable* of the complete noun phrase:

det		*adjective*
/ðɪ/	(.)	honour-

Tom in effect supplies the elements of structure that he can perceive to be missing at that point. Furthermore he produces just those words which the minister produces. Thus, in being attentive as a listener, Tom is actually **anticipating** in fairly precise terms what the minister needs to say to complete the components of his talk.

This suggests that as listeners we anticipate what is coming next, and so provide some basis for knowing when we may take on the speaker role.

8.3.2 *The speaker role*

Activity 8.7 ─────────────────

In the following fragment from extract 2 we can see that H is trying to get the speaker role. How does she do this, and what does the way in which she does it tell us about what she assumes her rights to the speaker role to be?

═══════════════════════════════════════

Fragment 8
MW   well I'm just trying to help her get [(.)   acc] limatised
                                          [*H* yeah]

        (.)
MW   hh so ↑therefore ↑=
H   =Exactly you helped her=
MW   I've tried to [do it ↑grad↑ually::   ]
                    [*H* you ↑helped↑ her when she] come <u>here</u> you helped her
        when she come here hh ...

Discussion

H says *yeah* at a point where MW's turn is not fully complete, and from what is said subsequently it is likely that the *yeah* is produced as some sort of acknowledgement of MW's claim about trying to *help* her daughter. Following a pause MW then continues with *so therefore*, thus explicitly linking what she is about to say with what she has just said. What is about to be said is thus being treated as a straightforward **continuation** of her turn. H's *yeah* is not being treated as in any way grounds for MW to give up the speaker role.

However, before MW can proceed with her continuation, H jumps in with her *Exactly you helped her*. MW nevertheless presses on without any suggestion that what H has started to say gives her any right to the speaker role. But part way through MW's further continuation, H again comes in with *You ↑helped ↑her when she come here*. Part of this is said in overlap with what MW is saying, and part following MW's apparent completion of her turn. H, however, then repeats what she has just said, which was partly in overlap with MW's talk.

So we can see here that despite H's efforts to get the speaker role, MW continues, and H effectively acknowledges that this is her right by repeating what she knows she should not have been trying to say whilst MW was still talking.

This suggests that the listener recognises that she has a right to the speaker role only when the speaker's turn is properly finished, and when she is prepared to give it up.

8.4 The management of conversation to achieve particular purposes

Activity 8.8 ─────────────────────────────

In the following fragment from extract 1, decide whether MW is trying to get Tom to:

(i) provide information on his attitude to marriage, or
(ii) be warned about his behaviour towards her daughter, or
(iii) give an excuse for his reluctance to marry.

───

Fragment 9

MW   see I'm not)) ↑don't↑ get me wrong
          ↑I'm↑ not interfering [↑I'm↑ just wondering what you] think about why (.)
T   oh no (.) oh yeah
MW   why you don't want to get [married] I mean you're both over eighteen
                                                    T °mm°
          ↑nothing↑ [I can do] but I ↑don't↑ like seeing Marion hurt
                          T °mm°

Discussion

There is a sense in which MW is trying to get information, give a warning and get an excuse. What is interesting is the way in which MW constructs her talk to achieve these different purposes. MW wants information, but denies that she has any right to it:

↑don't↑ get me wrong ↑I'm↑ not interfering you're <u>both</u> over eighteen ↑<u>nothing</u>↑ I can do

In seeking information she does not use a direct interrogative form such as *Why won't you marry?* Rather she prefaces it with the **distancing** clause,

↑I↑'m just wondering

and she is seeking information in the form of an excuse, as an answer to,

<u>why</u> you don't want to get <u>married</u>

Whilst on the one hand MW's rights have been denied by Tom, they are asserted again in,

I ↑<u>don't</u>↑ like seeing Marion hurt

What is left unsaid is who the agent of Marion's hurt would be – the clear **implication** is that it would be Tom – and what might be the consequences of Marion's being hurt, given that MW would not like it. One implication is that they might be dire for Tom.

These few illustrations, which show how the investigation of conversation can reveal its organisation, should suggest ways of extending this kind of analysis to the rest of the extracts, and indeed to any conversation that you might record and transcribe yourself.

9. Variety in written English – I: reporting the news

'Here is the news. First, the headlines ...' For many people, 'the news' is an important part of daily life, both on radio and television, and in the newspaper delivered to the home or picked up in the newsagent's or supermarket. But 'the news' is not the simple truth about events, waiting out there to be passed on to the rest of the country. It is a 'commodity', something manufactured by journalists and writers. Its material is language, and if we think of language as a **system** or **network of choices**, we can see that the choices of vocabulary and grammar made by journalists are what determine our understanding of an event which is reported as 'the news'.

It is therefore most important that we should be aware of the way in which our knowledge of what goes on is constructed out of our reading of the news. The study of language can help us to be critical, sometimes even sceptical, about what we are told.

9.1 What the headlines say

Newspaper headlines have a familiar and conventional linguistic structure not unlike telegrams in their brevity. Here we shall discuss their function in press reports, and in particular how they present the ideology of the newspaper. By *ideology* is meant the system of beliefs about society which underlie the reporting of news.

The wording of a headline is affected by at least three things: (i) the ideas to be expressed, (ii) the technology of printing and (iii) the kind of reader associated with a particular paper. We expect a different selection of news items and kinds of photograph in the tabloid papers, compared with the broadsheets, as well as differences of typography and style. These differences will be expressed in the headlines also.

A newspaper editor's description of the function of headlines, and how they should be written, is presented in the book *News Headlines*, which is part of the series *Editing and Design*, by Harold Evans. The series was written as a training manual for journalists.

Harold Evans' three criteria for good headline writing are **simplicity**, **informality** and **impact**. The headline, he says, should be a clear signal, swiftly readable, economical in reading time and space, and its style in proportion to the news it reports. In other words, there is a test of acceptability relevant to good headline English as well as to other styles of writing.

Activity 9.1

(i) Collect a series of headlines from two or more different daily newspapers, and evaluate them according to the three criteria of simplicity, informality and impact.
(ii) Are there differences between the headline styles of tabloid and broadsheet newspapers?
(iii) What are the linguistic features of headlines by which you identify the three criteria?

Read these three quotations from *News Headlines,* and then go on to answer the questions which follow in Activity 9.2:

(a) A single consistent style emphasises the journalistic effort of the newspaper to produce some semblance of comprehensible order from the disordered world.

(b) The headline must tell the news. Many who do not read the story none the less retain an impression from scanning the headlines.

(c) All good headlines follow certain rules, in what they say and how they say it. What they say is the single most urgent newspoint, as the newspaper sees it, accurately, intelligibly, and impartially. Accuracy and impartiality are the most important basic constituents.

Activity 9.2

(i) What does Harold Evans mean by his opposition of *order* in the newspaper and *disorder* in the world?
(ii) Scan the headlines of two different newspapers and consider what impressions you get of the worlds they present.
(iii) Harold Evans condemns 'selective perception' and 'the odious practice of using loaded words'. If it is the job of a newspaper to *interpret* and *explain* the news, as well as to report it, is it in fact possible for it to avoid selective perception and be impartial?

(You should return to question (iii) again after you have finished the chapter.)

Obvious selective perception, or bias, can be seen when a newspaper does not report a particular event that other papers do report, or when certain features of an event are reported and not others. But choices have to be made because space is limited, just as, in radio and television news, time is limited. Compare the selection of items that appear in a two-minute news flash compared with a thirty-minute broadcast, for example. These choices, though important, are not linguistic matters. This study is confined to language use – how the news that *is* chosen for reporting is presented.

The claim of impartiality in news reporting will be tested in this section by closely analysing some headlines, and in section 9.2 by examining extracts from complete reports. We shall show that the vocabulary and grammar of headlines and news reports combine to reveal a distinctive point of view, which implies at least some partiality or bias.

9.1.1 Reactions to Government proposals

Here are two sets of headlines, taken from two daily newspapers in 1980, reporting the same events relating to Government proposals for British Rail, the Post Office and the generation of electricity.

Newspaper A

FOUR BR COMPANIES TO BE SOLD OFF

Imports influx feared as Post Office profits are creamed off

JOSEPH CUTS OFF PHONE MONOPOLY

HOWELL TO ALLOW FIRMS TO SELL POWER

Newspaper B

LOOTERS LET LOOSE ON BRITISH RAIL ASSETS

'Power for profit' plan

TORIES GRAB 2 INDUSTRIES FOR THE CITY

Activity 9.3

Examine the vocabulary and structure of the headlines and assess the views and sympathies of paper A and paper B. (The papers are labelled A and B, because if they were named, your judgement might be affected by your knowledge of the paper's political views, rather than by the linguistic evidence.)
Discuss them, or make your own assessment, before going on to read the analytical commentary.

Commentary

FOUR BR COMPANIES TO BE SOLD OFF

This appears at first to be impartial, a plain statement of an intended course of action. It is a **passive clause**, and the **agent** is not included, that is, the person or institution by whom the companies are to be sold off. But the *Concise Oxford Dictionary* defines *to sell off* as *to clear out stock at reduced prices*, which is not the same as *to sell*. There is therefore an implied attitude of disapproval in A's use of *to sell off*.

LOOTERS LET LOOSE ON BRITISH RAIL ASSETS

The primary meaning of *to loot* is *to plunder in time of war or civil disorder*. It implies force, and possessions taken illegally.

To let loose is a verb applied to releasing or unchaining, typically a hunting-dog or pack, and has **connotative** or **associative** meanings suggesting fierceness, wildness, an attack on a prey.

Assets means *property which has value,* and which could be used to meet debts, for example. The obviously unfavourable connotations or associations of this headline are focused on those institutions, companies and individuals who might buy British Rail assets if they were given the opportunity. By likening them to looters preying on BR, the headline questions the morality of the proposal.

Imports influx feared as Post Office profits are creamed off

JOSEPH CUTS OFF PHONE MONOPOLY

This is a combination of main headline and overline (or strapline). The overline is an additional explanatory comment on the main headline.

Sir Keith Joseph was the Conservative Secretary for Industry. The use of surname only is usual in headlines, though in a text it would contrast in formality and politeness with *Sir Keith*, or the full name with title.

The use of *cuts off*, a term from the vocabulary of the public utilities in relation to customers who don't pay their bills, is obviously deliberate. (Some newspapers are known for their use of punning in headlines and news reports.) The headline refers to *monopoly* – the exclusive possession of the right to trade in some commodity – but does not seem to approve or disapprove, and so appears impartial.

But the overline is more explicit. *To cream off* is to take away the richest part, and here may indicate disapproval which the text of the report might confirm or not.

HOWELL TO ALLOW FIRMS TO SELL POWER

Mr David Howell was Secretary for Energy. The government's policy included the privatisation of the whole or parts of previously nationalised industries. This headline refers to proposals that would allow private companies to generate and sell electricity, and appears neutral in its attitude.

'Power for profit' plan

TORIES GRAB 2 INDUSTRIES FOR THE CITY

One headline with overline covers both proposals. The word *profit* carries connotations of either approval or disapproval in relation to trade and industry, depending on the point of view of the speaker/writer and of the listener/reader, and whether they consider the making of private profit an acceptable activity or not.

The word *Tory* goes back to the later seventeenth century, and like other terms that were originally impolite, has now become acceptable for *Conservative* by Conservatives. But it retains connotations of disapproval when used by non-Conservatives. (Compare the use of the word *Socialist* in some newspapers to describe the Labour party.)

So the connotative meanings of words are relative to the speaker and listener, and slight differences may carry significant overtones of meaning. The same words can be either favourable or unfavourable in their meanings, depending upon who is writing and reading them.

This headline is markedly loaded against the government's proposals:

grab   *to seize suddenly, snatch at*, implying selfish motives and impolite actions.

the City   *the City of London*, the phrase representing the international financial centre made up of the banks and companies whose main offices and work are in the City of London.

for the City   implies that the government is making proposals for selling nationalised industries on behalf of, for the profit of, traders in the City, and not for disinterested motives.

The language of newspaper B implies a model of society different from that of paper A.

Activity 9.4

Discuss the connotative meanings, for different speakers and listeners, of: *Communist, Red, Conservative, comrade, Fascist, extremist, reactionary, solidarity, democratic, left-wing, right-wing, bully-boy, capitalist, law and order.*

Activity 9.5

Take a report on the same event from two newspapers, preferably of opposing views, and find words and phrases with marked contrasting connotative meanings.

9.1.2 *Events at British Leyland*

Activity 9.6

Examine the differences in the reporting of news in the following pairs of headlines, from the same newspapers A and B. They describe a series of events over a period of three weeks in November 1980 at a BL (British Leyland) car factory.

Industrial strikes were staple items of news at that time, but disputes at British Leyland were given specially extensive coverage. Sir Michael Edwardes was chairman of BL.

(i) 4 November

(A)   <u>Company decides to put its</u>   (B)
           <u>case directly to workers</u>   <u>Stewards reject final offer</u>

Stewards call for all-out BL strike

Edwardes' bid to break BL strike vote

(ii) 7 November

(A) **Edwardes tells BL unions that strike would bring closure**

(B) **Leyland at crunch as pay talks fail**

(iii) 19 November

(A) **BL unions end strike threat as 1,600 jobs are lost at Talbot**

(B) **Don't mistake our anger, says Leyland convenor**

(iv) 22 November

(A) <u>**Police at Longbridge as anger mounts over 500 lay offs**</u>

Trouble flares as BL workers demonstrate

(B) **Metro fury as workers laid off at drop of hat**

Commentary

(i) *4 November*
Both newspapers have headlines with overlines, but the content of A's headline is in B's overline, and vice versa. This shows an interesting contrast in the assessment of the major item of news.

(A)   <u>**Company decides to put its case directly to workers**</u>
     Stewards call for all-out BL strike

The union shop stewards in the BL factory are the **initiators** of the action of calling a strike. In grammatical terms, *stewards* is the **subject** of the clause and also its **theme**, coming first.

Since shop stewards are the intermediaries between the company and the workers, there are obvious implications in the use of *directly* in the overline. The stewards are to be by-passed and normal procedures not followed.

Notice the identification of three **participants** in the **verbal processes** of *calling for* and *deciding to put a case to*: (a) the company, (b) the unions and (c) the workers.

(B)

<u>**Stewards reject final offer**</u>

Edwardes' bid to break BL strike vote

The **initiator** of the action, or the attempted action, *bid*, is here the chairman of BL. The strike has not yet taken place, but a vote in favour of a strike has been obtained. To *break a strike* is to use some kind of force to end it, so that the the strikers are unsuccessful.

The word *break* has strong historical associations for trade unionists, linked with past actions by governments and employers in using the police and the armed forces as *strike-breakers*. To use it in relation to a vote is to evoke these associations of violent confrontation.

The overline implies the participation of BL management, even though the phrase *by the company* does not appear. The offer, we infer, was not good enough. Notice that *stewards* is the subject and so the theme of the headline, so the stewards are presented as the initiators of the action, and focus of interest.

(ii) *7 November*

(A)

Edwardes tells BL unions
that strike would bring closure

A few days later, and the company has put its case directly to the workers.

The chairman is the initiator, but again of a verbal process, *tells*. To some extent, the headline dissociates him from responsibility for the results of a strike. The **modal auxiliary verb** *would*, like other modals in English, is ambiguously vague. In *strike would bring closure*, *closure*, the **object** of *bring* (= *cause*), is presented as a direct result of *strike*, the **subject** of the clause, so that it is the strikers who are said to initiate the action of 'causing the closure of the company'. But only the chairman and board of directors of a company have power to close it, so the headline omits the essential fact of the chairman's responsibility.

The modal verb *would* has a 'softening' effect on the underlying implications of what is really a *threat*. One of its meanings suggests 'possibility' only. But what the chairman meant was almost certainly:

Edwardes will close BL if workers strike

What does this suggest about the newspaper's attitude?

Notice also how the grammar of the newspaper headline uses nouns, not verbs, for actions. In fact, it is people who strike, and close things. Turning an action into a 'thing', using nouns for verbs, is called **nominalisation**, and is an often-used device which allows you not to make individual men and women responsible for causing things to happen.

The version 'Edwardes will close BL if workers strike' replaces the nouns of the original headline (*strike* and *closure*) with verbs (*strike* and *close* – the word *strike* can be a noun or a verb). 'Strike would bring closure' relieves the chairman of any blame.

(B) # Leyland at crunch as pay talks fail

The colloquial *at crunch* implies a decisive event which is imminent, but the headline itself does not make clear what the event – whether to strike or not – might be. The *as*-clause suggests both time (*when*) and reason (*because*). The noun *talks* is the subject of the verb *fail*, but this is shorthand for 'management and unions fail to agree'. This paper does not headline Sir Michael Edwardes' statement/threat.

(iii) *19 November*

(A) # BL unions end strike threat as 1,600 jobs are lost at Talbot

The strike did not happen, and a majority of the workers in BL voted to accept the pay offer of the management. The representatives who were negotiating (the unions) had to accept this vote, and are reported as initiating the action which ended the threat.

The loss of jobs in the Talbot car manufacturing firm's factory is headlined as a significant event in relation to BL. *as 1,600 jobs are lost at Talbot* is a subordinate clause and implies both cause and simultaneous action. (Subordinate clauses in headlines are rare, but that when they do occur, they are almost always *as*-clauses.)

(B) # Don't mistake our anger, says Leyland convenor

A reader must know several things to understand this headline: (i) knowledge of the series of events conveyed by the one word *Leyland*, and (ii) of the structure of trade unions, and the role of a *convenor* – a senior official who *convenes* meetings of the shop stewards, and (iii) knowledge that the strike is already off, so that the anger of the convenor can be understood as directed against the manner in which the settlement was reached.

Paper B, in headlining the fact that the strike was not amicably settled, is supporting the convenor's point of view.

(iv) *22 November*

(A) ### Police at Longbridge as anger mounts over 500 lay offs
Trouble flares as BL workers demonstrate

Overline and main headline combine to cover several aspects of events that occurred only a few days later.

The subject and theme of the first part of the overline is *Police*. The use of the police is considered to be of primary importance. The reason is implied in the *as*-clause, with the attribution of *anger* as a result of (*over*) 500 workers being laid off.

The police are not called in because people are angry, however, but because they are acting in a way that is interpreted as being in breach of the law, like a disturbance of the peace, or damage to persons and property. So the headlining of the use of the police has important implications.

Trouble flares is similar in its meaning to *anger mounts*, a stage later, the effect of a cause.

To demonstrate, is used as an **intransitive verb**, meaning *to make a public protest*. A public demonstration is legal, but the headline implies a series of events, with cause and effect inferred by the reader from the word order. In conveying information, the first word or phrase in a clause (the theme), and the last (where new information tends to be put), are important. So if we take the first and last words in the overline and headline, and rearrange them in their chronological order, we get: (1) *lay-offs* – (2) *demonstrate* – (3) *trouble* – (4) *police* or, *the managers laid off a number of workers who then demonstrated and caused trouble which led to someone calling in the police*.

This summarizes paper A's interpretation of the events. But it is the *police* and *trouble* which are made the most prominent as the themes of the overline and headline, not the *lay-offs* and the *demonstration*. Whose side does the paper take, whether intentionally or not?

(B) Metro fury as workers laid off at drop of hat

B's headline includes A's *anger* as *fury*, which is somewhat stronger, but does not mention *police*, *demonstration* or *trouble*. It adds the information that the workers were engaged on production of the Metro car, and comments adversely against management, by implication, in the colloquial phrase *at (the) drop of (a) hat*.

These analyses and commentaries do not imply that all headlines can be dissected for clear evidence of point of view or bias. But examining headlines from two or more papers will sometimes reveal conflicting interpretations of events. Consistent interpretations within each paper make up their contrasting ideologies.

Activity 9.7

Analyse the following groups of headlines, which report the same items of news in the two newspapers from which the preceding examples have been taken.

(i) (A) **Civil Service unions likely to protest at attempt to limit pay**
6pc limit stays but MPs win big rise

(B) **Unions see red at rise for Soames**
£27,825 for me, peanuts for you

(ii) (A) **£500m package aimed at cutting jobless by 216,000**
Measures a boost to Tory morale
Government package to help youngsters

(B) **One year on low pay then sack**
Thatcher peanuts plan for youth
Hypocrisy and blackmail

(C) (a third newspaper)
First aid for jobless
MAGGIE'S £700M BOOST FOR JOBS

9.1.3 *Headlines – the lighter side*

Sub-editors prepare journalists' copy for printing and add headlines. They sometimes make a headline prominent by devising a play on words, usually with items of news that are less serious. For example,

The left-wing journal that put Labour right

superimposes the meaning of *Left* and *Right* in politics on that of *to put someone right*, in the sense of *to correct*, as well as commenting on the changed policies of the Labour party, *moving to the Right*.

Wine bar lifts its wine bar

is a pun in which *wine bar* has the two meanings of *premises where wine is served* and *the prohibition on serving wine* (in this case, the serving of wine from South Africa).

Activity 9.8

Discuss the following headlines, identify the word-play and suggest the news which each of them was reporting:

1 BRICKMAKERS CEMENT THEIR DEAL
2. BEWARE THE VIBES OF GLOOM
3. BECK'S FIZZ TOO LATE
    (Beck was the name of a German yacht captain in a sailing race)
4. ALLIED SKITTLED AS THE TOUGH TIMES STRIKE BOWLING
    (Allied Leisure runs ten-pin bowling and night clubs)
5. NO CANNES DO
6. FIT OF PEEK
7. LEICESTER LOSE THEIR LUSTRE
8. ERM WILL LEAVE US WITH POUNDING HEADACHE
    (ERM stands for Exchange Rate Mechanism)
9. TRADITIONAL TURKEY FARMERS GIVE EC THE BIRD
    (EC is the European Community)
10. ROVERS THE PASS MASTERS
    (Blackburn Rovers, the football team)
11. RETAILERS DREAMING OF A GLOOMY CHRISTMAS
12. SADDLERS SET OUT TO HARNESS SKILLS
13. THE NEW ETHOS SWEEPS THROUGH LINCOLN STREETS
    (News about street-cleaning in Lincoln)
14. A MINISTER BITTEN, BUT NEVER SHY
    (A Government minister is here referred to)
15. TRICK OR TREATY?

Sometimes intentionally, sometimes not, headlines can also be **ambiguous**, having two possible meanings. Ambiguity can occur for several reasons, two of which are:

(i)   A word can have more than one meaning. For example, the verb *grilled* could mean either *cooked under a grill*, or *interrogated*, which produces the **lexical ambiguity** of,

Gas rig men grilled by villagers

(ii)   The same word can function as more than one part of speech. For example, *split* can be either a verb (*to split*) or a noun (*a split*), with related meanings; *looms* can be the plural of the noun *a loom* or the present tense of the verb *to loom*, and these words have quite different meanings. This leads to **grammatical** as well as lexical ambiguity, as in,

Evangelicals split looms

which has the structure either,

S		P	
NP		VP	
m		h	
Evangelicals		split	looms

which is its intended meaning – *a split between the Evangelicals is looming*, or,

S	P	O
NP	VP	NP
Evangelicals	split	looms

which has the nonsensical meaning of *the Evangelicals are splitting looms*.

Activity 9.9

Identify the ambiguity in the following headlines

1.   DO YOU WANT A WOMAN VICAR?
2.   DOCTORS REVIEW BODY
3.   SHEEP RUSTLING IN HILLS
4.   MINE EXPLODED
5.   QUEEN SEES DANCER TAKE TEN CURTAINS
6.   POLICE FIND CONSTABLE DRAWING IN ATTIC
7.   BIG CUTS TO BE MADE AT HOSPITAL
8.   DINNER LADIES TO GET CHOP
9.   ACTRESS IMPROVING
10   IRA BOMB GUTS FACTORY
11   SCHOOLGIRL SUSPENDED BY HEAD
12   STAR'S BROKEN LEG HITS BOX OFFICE
13   BEDS MOVE
14   COUNCILLORS WALK OUT OVER TYPISTS
15   BRITISH GIRL HAS TO SCRATCH
16   SPOTTED MEN STEALING SALMON

(*These examples from Fritz Spiegl's 'Keep taking the Tabloids', Pan Books 1983*)

9.2   News reporting

9.2.1   *Style*

The style of newspaper reporting in the nineteenth century was very formal in both vocabulary and grammar. This tradition still holds to some extent for the 'quality' (broadsheet) newspapers today, but they themselves were affected by the changes in size, layout and style brought about by the popular newspapers in 'tabloid' form. Too often, people condemn the popularisation of daily newspapers without bothering to assess the good and bad in them. An interesting commentary on tabloid style is contained in *Daily Mirror Style* by Keith Waterhouse. He describes good popular newspaper style in this way:

> It is a plain, straightforward, well-ordered narrative, completely without gimmicks. There are no fancy words, and no needless words...The material is arranged chronologically, with the briefest of introductions. No attempt is made to tempt the reader with window-dressing or with lurid shock-drama labels...

These criteria apply to both serious writing about serious matters and to the reporting of ephemeral news in a light mood.

Activity 9.10

Here is a short, typical example of a very minor piece of news, to be forgotten almost as soon as read. What are the features of its style that make it clearly a piece of popular reporting?

SUMMER SPOONFUL 'RIP-OFF'

Tennis fans were charged £1 for half a dozen strawberries with cream at Wimbledon yesterday.

But at 16p a mouthful, many fans boycotted them.

Seasoned Wimbledon-goer Kay Demetriou, 17, took her own punnet of 20 strawberries bought for 28p at a greengrocers up the road.

Said Kay, from Streatham, South London: 'I've been ripped off here before.

'I decided it wasn't going to happen this year.'

Commentary

The layout, adopted by all the tabloid newspapers, is one sentence to each paragraph, occasionally two, so that each successive topic is presented very economically.

Sentence structure is also simple, with little use of subordination except a **qualifying clause** (*bought for...*) and **reported clauses** following *said*.

Marked grammatical features lie within the clause. In sentence 2, the adverbial *at 16p a mouthful* comes first as theme, after *but*, which links it to sentence 1.

Seasoned Wimbledon-goer Kay Demetriou, 17, is a compressed noun phrase, with descriptive **pre-modifiers** before the name, and the figure for her age in **apposition** to it.

Notice the inversion of *Said Kay,* and the descriptive **post-modifier** following it.

Vocabulary is informal, sometimes colloquial, e.g. *rip-off.*

Activity 9.11

Make your own commentary on the following news report, describing the marked features of the language which are typical of popular journalistic style.

M-WAY SHOCK BY WHIZZKID

Drivers on a motorway were startled by the machine whizzing along with them.

For six-year-old Robert Flynn decided to take his diddy BMX bike on the M57 near Wolverhampton for a test run. And with legs moving like pistons, he tried to keep up with the traffic.

Stunned

Driving in the opposite direction was quick-thinking Dave Hodgetts, who shot off the motorway at the next junction and zoomed back to overtake Robert.

"I was stunned," said Dave, of Brookside, Telford, Shrops.

"The lad's little legs were racing away and he looked really deter-mined."

Dave stopped Robert and called the police because he was worried about the risk of an accident.

Soon afterwards a real speed machine drew up – a police Jaguar. And Robert was treated to a ride home to Hedgrow Walk, Wolverhampton.

He was let off with a lecture – and warned not to ride too fast.

9.2.2 *Ideology and bias*

We now return to the major topic of this chapter, already introduced in the discussion of headlines – the question of impartiality and selective perception in news reporting.

Activity 9.12

(i)   Read the two reports printed on pp. 179–80 under the title of 'Sheffield incident'.
(ii)   By reading the headlines only, what impression of the incident do you obtain from each paper?

Activity 9.13

Look for answers to these questions in each report:
(i)   Identify the 'single most urgent news point, as the paper sees it' and give the evidence for your conclusion.
(ii)   Look at the connotations of important lexical items. For example, what is the effect, on your perception of the events, of the italicised words or phrases in the following extracts? Try substituting alternative words, and assess the difference:

    1   big Thatcher *nosh*   (A, headline)
    2   The People's March for Jobs 83 banner *stood proud*   (A, para. 4)
    3   the banners which *festooned* the forecourt   (A, para. 5)
    4   the evening went *peacefully*   (A, para. 6)
    5   the *drama* happened   (B, para. 3)
    6   the Prime Minister *braved* 3,000 protestors   (B, para. 3)
    7   speakers...*tried to speak* to the crowd   (B, para. 11)
    8   *missiles* were thrown   (B, para. 9)

Can you find any other words which have definite connotations?

Activity 9.14

Rewriting the text in certain ways can be helpful, for example, setting out the actions of each participant separately. This reveals both how the participants are *named* and what they are said to have *done*.
    What is the important difference between the two reports shown by the following rewriting of the actions of the police horse?

(The sign Ø indicates a participant reference which has been grammatically deleted from the text.)

	participant	*action*	
(A)	a police horse	bolted	into the police car
	the horse	fell	over the boot of the car
	Ø	breaking	the rear window
	= *3 references*		
(B)	a police horse	bolted	
	it	threw	its woman rider
	Ø	crashed	into...a police car

participant	action	
(its face)	smashing	a window
her mount	frightened	(by a missile)
the animal	bolted	past a line of police
he	tried to get round	the...car
he	slipped	
Ø	unseated	WPC Wilson
Ø	snapped	his bridle
the horse	smashed into	the back of the Jaguar
Ø	dashing off	

= 12 references

Activity 9.15

Write out similar analyses for (i) the rider, (ii) the police, (iii) the diners, (iv) Mrs Thatcher, and then comment on the significant differences you find between them.

Activity 9.16

Perhaps the most important contrast between the two reports lies in their interpretation of the crowd's behaviour.

Use the following summary to comment on each paper's attitude towards the composition of the crowd and its behaviour.

(A)	5,000 people	demonstrated	(colourfully)
		opposed	Mrs Thatcher's policies
		packed	the forecourt of the Cathedral
		stood	for one minute's silence
		booed & hissed	the diners
		(brought)	banners
		played music	
(B)	3,000 protestors	demonstrated	(noisily)
		protested	
		threw	eggs & flour
		aimed	missile at WPC
		caused trouble	for WPC
		made noise	
		threw	missiles
		drowned out	speeches of their own speakers
		shouted	'Maggie out'

The *people/protestors* are named or **classified** as follows:

(A) **people of Sheffield:**
the Sheffield unemployed
trade unionists
peace activists and Asian people

trade unions and local groups:
NUR, TGWU, NUPE
Bangladeshi community
Asian youth movement
Sheffield street band
Caribbean group

(B) crowd of trade unionists and city council leaders like NUM President Arthur
Scargill and city council leader David Blunkett
supporters
crowd

Activity 9.17

Now make a summary of the principal differences between the two newspaper
reports, using the selection of events in each paper, and the language used to
describe each selection as the basis of your commentary.

1 SHEFFIELD INCIDENT – April 1983

(The paragraphs are numbered for easy reference.)
Report (A)

Boos for big Thatcher nosh

1 In a colourful demonstration, the people of Sheffield showed Mrs Thatcher the strength of the opposition to her policies last night as she arrived at the Master Cutlers' annual feast.

2 About 5,000 people packed the forecourt of the Sheffield Cathedral opposite the Cutlers' Hall from 5.30 until 7.30 when they stood for one minute's silence for the millions unemployed.

3 As the diners arrived by luxury coach bejewelled and in formal evening wear, the Sheffield unemployed, trade unionists, peace activists, and Asian people, booed and hissed.

4 The People's March for Jobs '83 banner stood proud in the centre of the sea of banners from trade unions and local groups.

5 Among the banners which festooned the forecourt were those from the Sheffield NUR, TGWU, NUPE, South Yorkshire ASTMS, NALGO, Sheffield Peace Movement, the Sheffield Bangladeshi community and the Asian youth movement.

6 Over a thousand police were

brought on to protect Thatcher from the crowds, but the evening went peacefully with music from the celebrated Sheffield Street Band and a Caribbean group.

7   Earlier, a police horse bolted into a police car heading the Premier's cavalcade. The rider slid off as the horse fell over the boot of the car, breaking the rear window.

Report (B)

Police horse bolts in Maggie demo

1   **A POLICE horse bolted at the height of a noisy demonstration against Mrs Thatcher last night.**

2   It threw its woman rider and crashed into the rear of a police car, its face smashing a window.

3   The drama happened as the Prime Minister braved 3,000 protestors to attend the Annual Cutlers' Feast in Sheffield.

4   As she stepped from her black Jaguar, eggs, flour and apples were thrown from the crowd of trade unionists and city council leaders.

5   But one missile, aimed near Jane Wilson, South Yorkshire Police's only woman horse rider, frightened her mount, a five-year-old gelding called Fusilier. The animal bolted past a line of police and Press.

6   As he tried to get round the back of Mrs Thatcher's car, he slipped, unseated WPC Wilson and snapped his bridle.

Missiles

7   The horse smashed into the back of the Jaguar before dashing off down the road with helmeted WPC Wilson chasing.

8   A senior officer said: 'Jane was obviously having trouble before the Prime Minister arrived because of the crowd.

9   'She was doing her best under difficult circumstances but as the Prime Minister arrived the crowd's noise reached a crescendo and missiles were thrown.'

10   Mrs Thatcher was hustled inside the Cutlers Hall and did not see the incident 25 feet away.

11   The city council had provided scaffolding for a stage where speakers like NUM President Arthur Scargill and city council leader David Blunkett tried to speak to the crowd, almost outnumbered by police.

12   Speeches were drowned out by their own supporters with shouts of 'Maggie out.'

13   Police said 13 people had been arrested, including a juvenile and a girl. Two were for assault, three for throwing eggs and the rest for breach of the peace.

Commentary

The two reports are contrasted in several ways. Newspaper A headlines the crowd response and refers disparagingly to the event that the Prime Minister was attending by using the colloquial word *nosh* for *feast*. Of seven paragraphs, only the last reports the bolting of a police horse.

The bolting of the horse is not only the topic of the headline of B, but also the subject of seven of the thirteen paragraphs.

If you have made a close study of the text in the way suggested, you will probably agree that paper A describes the whole event as primarily a peaceful and colourful anti-government demonstration, and contrasts the situation of the unemployed with that of those attending the feast by implication.

Paper B describes the demonstration as a noisy and potentially violent occasion by concentrating upon the personal drama of the police horse and woman rider. There are also inconsistencies in B's text.

In describing an event that it defines as news, a newspaper's choice of vocabulary and grammatical structures will give evidence of attitudes to participants and actions that are not impartial – in other words, there is selective perception.

2 BELFAST INCIDENT – July 1981

Two reports of an incident which took place during and after a funeral in Belfast, Northern Ireland offer interesting differences.

Activity 9.18

Assess the point of view of each report from a first reading.

Report (A)

Army swoop on funeral rifleman

1   Savage street fighting broke out in Republican West Belfast yesterday after an Army snatch squad moved in to arrest and disarm three uniformed and masked Provisional IRA men minutes after they had fired a volley of shots over the coffin of Joseph McDonnell, the Maze hunger striker who died on Wednesday after 61 days without food.

2   At least four men and a woman were arrested. A number of rifles were recovered.

3   The three armed men, acting under orders from a Gaelic-speaking officer, emerged from the crowd as the huge funeral procession made its way down the Falls Road towards the Mill Town cemetery.

4   They aimed the volley over the tricolour draped coffin of Mr McDonnell which was flanked on either side by other IRA men in masks and uniforms.

5   On orders from the officer, they fired the volley and attempted to disappear, aided

by other mourners who held out opened umbrellas to hide them from photographers and television crews.

6   Moving through a funnel which opened up in the crowd, the men made for a house nearby, presumably to change from uniforms into civilian clothing.

7   At that point, an army squad, backed up by a large number of other soldiers and police who had been hiding behind a row of houses, moved in to attempt to arrest them.

8   The house the men made for had probably been pinpointed by Army surveillance helicopters, which constantly circled the funeral procession.

9   Scores of youths broke off from the funeral procession which continued towards the cemetery and made a determined attempt to prevent the soldiers from reaching the house.

10   At least five pistol or rifle shots were heard, but it is not clear where they came from. As the youths tore up paving stones and bombarded the Army with a fusillade of missiles, the soldiers kept them at bay by firing a constant barrage of rubber bullets.

11   The police said that when the Army squad broke into the house they were confronted by armed men. Two of the men were shot and one was detained and taken to hospital, where his condition was described last

12   The other gunman, although wounded, escaped. The search for him is continuing. A woman in the house was arrested and in a follow-up operation four other men were also arrested.

13   In the house the Army found three Garrand rifles, combat jackets, hoods and gloves.

14   As the battle raged, women and children screamed. Some mothers threw their children on to the ground and lay on top of them. Other people who had been lining the funeral route took sanctuary in a church.

15   The police denied that the security forces had fired rubber bullets indiscriminately.

Report (B)

Troops fire plastic bullets into mourners

1   British troops fired a hail of plastic bullets into mourners at the massive funeral of Long Kesh hunger striker Joe McDonnell yesterday – and within minutes much of West Belfast was in uproar.

2   Thousands came for the funeral of the hunger striker, the fifth to die, but after the IRA colour party had fired the now traditional volley of shots over his flag-draped coffin, the troops stormed in.

3   An army statement later claimed that five of the men involved in the firing party had been captured along with several of the weapons after shots had been fired in a house.

4   Armoured cars ferried troops into a pitched battle as plastic bullets were replied to with stones.

Activity 9.19

Answer the following questions:

(i) Few people read two daily newspapers. What impression of the incident is likely to be given to readers of each paper from the headlines only?

(ii) Discuss the choice of vocabulary in the following selected paired extracts, and what the choices tell us about the papers' point of view towards the events.

(iii) Find other paired extracts and analyse their differences.

	Paper A	Paper B
1	*the soldiers*	*British troops*

What does the use of British in (B) imply? Do you find the use of the word *troops* more, or less favourable than *soldiers*, or do they mean much the same?

2	*kept them at bay by firing*	*fired*

What are the associative meanings of the phrase *kept them at bay*?

3	*scores of youths*	*mourners*

If you attend a funeral, you are a *mourner,* for the time being, whether you are young or old. What is the purpose here of identifying the participants in different ways?

4	*Joseph McDonnell* *Mr McDonnell*	*Joe McDonnell*

Joe, a diminutive, is a more informal mode of address than *Joseph* or *Mr.* What is its effect on a reader?

5	*hunger striker who died on Wednesday after 61 days without food*	*hunger striker, the fifth to die*

Two choices of additional information. Are their implications different?

6	*three uniformed and masked Provisional IRA men* *three armed men* *Gaelic-speaking officer*	*IRA colour party* *firing party*

Contrast the two descriptions, with special reference to the connotations of *uniformed* and *colour/firing party.* If the officer spoke Gaelic, why did paper A report the fact?

7	*volley of shots*	*now traditional volley of shots*

Consider the implications of the added *now traditional* in paper B.

8	*paving stones* *a fusillade of missiles*	*stones*

Are the differences important?

Paper A	Paper B
9 *armed men, gunman*	*five of the men*

Would you refer to a soldier as a *gunman*? If not, what does the word mean?

| 10   *arrested* | *captured* |

What is the significant difference between the two?

Commentary

The two interpretations of the funeral incident are obviously controversial in their difference. It raises the question of the possibility of neutral reporting. Our choice of language seems to give away our attitude whether we want it to or not.

(i) *The headlines:*
Each paper has chosen a different aspect of the sequence of events to sum up the whole:

Army swoop on funeral riflemen (A)

Troops fire plastic bullets into mourners (B)

Consider first the choice of vocabulary.

- *Army* v. *Troops* – a **collective** noun standing for the official presence of soldiers in Northern Ireland (*Army*), against a **plural** noun for soldiers as individuals who perform actions (*troops*).
- *swoop on* v. *fire plastic bullets* – the first a **metaphor** suggesting the image of a bird of prey, a sudden attack to seize and carry off; the second a **literal** statement implying the use of firearms by men.
- *funeral riflemen* v. *into mourners* – the stated objective of the Army's plan, *men who fired rifles at a funeral,* contrasts with the object of attack, *mourners,* in B's headline, which describes a later incident, but headlines it as the major event.

(ii) *The reports:*
(a) Vocabulary   In Activity 9.19 you have already examined significant vocabulary – those words and phrases from both reports which have more or less the same reference to the events and the participants. The differences observed in the headlines are consistently found in the reports also.

Notice that the first two paragraphs of A are a summary of the principal events of the incident, and some of its items are repeated in the later paragraphs. As a summary, these two paragraphs are directly comparable with the shorter report in B.

By now you will agree that newspaper A is sympathetic to the Army and the task assigned to it in Northern Ireland by the Government, and that B is sympathetic towards the IRA.

(b) Grammatical structure; active and passive clauses   When we describe actions and events, we perceive something going on which involves one or more participants. For example, in *the three armed men ... attempted to disappear,* the three men, acting as a group, are **actors** performing an **action**. They do the

disappearing. The clause might have been simply, *They disappeared.* This kind of clause is called **intransitive**.

Some actions involve two sets of participants, firstly the **actor** who performs it (or the **agent** who causes it to happen), and secondly those who are **affected** by the action. X (the actor/agent) does something to Y (affected). For example,

actor/agent (S)	action (P)	affected (O)
an Army squad	arrest and disarm	three IRA men
British troops	fired	plastic bullets
the youths	bombarded	the Army

These clauses are called **transitive**.

The clause structures relate the actor/agent to the action and the affected person or thing by means of the **word order** represented by SPO – the **subject** is followed by the **predicator** (or **verb**), which is followed by the **object**. Change the order, and the meaning is changed. *The Army arrested three IRA men* does not mean the same as *Three IRA men arrested the Army.*

This SPO structure has the grammatical feature called **active voice**, and can be changed into what is called the **passive voice** very easily. Notice how the actor and the affected participants change places in the clause:

affected (S)	action (P)	actor/agent (A)
three IRA men	were arrested and disarmed	by an Army squad
plastic bullets	were fired	by British troops
the Army	was bombarded	by the youths

Activity 9.20

What are the rules for changing an active clause into a passive clause? Try to answer this from the evidence of the clauses just quoted, but refer to a descriptive grammar also to confirm what you discover.

Now an interesting thing about using the passive form of a transitive clause is that you can leave out the *by*-phrase, which says who the actor/agent was, and the clause remains grammatical. You have omitted some information, of course, but that does not affect the grammatical acceptability of the clause. This can be very useful.

So the clauses could have been written:

Three IRA men were arrested and disarmed.
Plastic bullets were fired.
The Army was bombarded.

The grammatical subject of a clause is important because it comes before the predicator and is usually the theme of the clause also. We may tend to think of the subject of a clause as the actor, even when the clause is passive, because of its prominence.

It is possible, therefore, to imply that the participant who is *affected* by an action (the object in an active clause), is actually partly responsible for the action in a passive clause, when it is the subject. This is especially so if the actor/agent in the *by*-phrase in the passive, is omitted.

Activity 9.21

(i) Write down a list of the passive forms actually used in report A, and answer these questions from your list:

   Who arrested the four men and the woman and recovered the rifles?
   Who flanked the coffin?
   Who aided the IRA men?
   Who backed up the Army squad?
   Who pinpointed the house?
   Who heard the pistol and rifle shots?
   Who confronted the Army squad?
   Who shot two of the men?
   Who detained one?
   Who took the man to hospital?
   Who described his condition as serious?

(ii) In each case, say whether the evidence is in the **agentive phrase** – that is, the *by*-phrase – or whether this phrase is deleted and you have to infer it from the context.

Commentary

It is possible that we become less aware of people's responsibility for causing things to happen to others if they are not named, and using a passive clause is one way of not naming. This does not imply that the use of the passive always hides essential information, but it may do. For example, we do not need to know who described the shot man's condition as serious in report A, but we would be interested to know who shot him. Saying *two of the men were shot* is not as complete a statement as *the Army squad shot two of the men.*

Activity 9.22

(i) Write down the passive clauses in report B and answer these questions:
   Who captured the five men? Who fired the shots?
   Who replied to plastic bullets with stones?

(ii) Comment on why you can or cannot answer the questions, when there are no agentive phrases.

Commentary

There is also in newspaper B another clear example of the way in which you can avoid naming an actor/agent, and so diminish his or her responsibility for an action, by using the passive voice in a clause and omitting the agentive phrase.

If we try to convert the passive clause *plastic bullets were replied to with stones* into its active form, we cannot supply the subject:

X replied to plastic bullets with stones.

X must presumably be some of the crowd of mourners, but they are not identified in B, as they are in A, as *youths*.

Whether consciously done or not, it is clear that B has avoided naming those who *replied* (or *threw, bombarded, hurled, lobbed, flung, flipped, chucked*?) the *stones* (or *paving stones, missiles*?) at the soldiers who fired plastic bullets. This clause also implies quite clearly, without actually saying so, that the Army fired at the mourners first, in the use of the verb *were replied to*. A *reply* always *follows*.

Therefore it is possible to play down the role of certain actors by using the passive and so not naming them – and this goes unnoticed by most readers. You cannot do this in an active clause, because the actor is also the grammatical subject, and this you cannot omit.

(c) *Grammatical structure; using transformations*   To analyse the reports in detail, another useful technique is to 'transform' the varieties of sentence and clause structure of the text into basic 'underlying' structures with the same pattern:

1 actor/agent / 2 action / 3 affected person or thing

as in a simple SPO active clause like *the youths / threw / stones*, where the surface structure matches the underlying structure.

But in *plastic bullets were replied to with stones*, the surface structure leaves out much of the underlying structure, which contains several **propositions**, but none of the participants or actions in brackets are named in the news report

actor/agent	action	affected
1 *(soldiers)*	*(caused):*	
2 **plastic bullets**	*(hit)*	*(people)*
3 *(people)*	*(threw)*	**stones**
	= replied	

Only the words in bold type appear in the report, so it is clear that the surface structure leaves out a great deal, and that a reader may not notice the real implications and so not ask, 'Who acted first?' and 'Who threw stones?'

Activity 9.23

Work through the reports, or take selected parts of them, and reduce the surface forms to their basic patterns of actor/action/affected. (In some cases, there will be no affected or second participant.)

   Take each of the four participant groups (the Army, the IRA men, the crowd of mourners, and the youths) in turn, and see how the reports differ in the attribution of responsibility for action. Then answer these questions:

(i)   Is there any significant difference between the two reports in their attribution of action to the Army?

(ii)   Do the more detailed references to IRA action in (A) affect your understanding of what happened?

(iii)   Contrast the actions attributed to the mourners in (A) and (B).

With practice you will be able to scan a text and discover its important features without setting it out in such detail, but the methods illustrated help to make sure that you do not miss anything important.

You should now be able to say something positive about selective reporting in newspapers *from the evidence of the texts*, without knowing which papers they are.

Activity 9.24

Compare and contrast the following texts, which are extracts from the reports of an incident in the North Yorkshire town of Selby in July 1984 during the national miner's strike of 1984–5. The texts are from two different newspapers, A and B. Use the methods demonstrated in the chapter to examine:

(i)   the connotations of the vocabulary used to name the participants and actions;
(ii) the style of presentation.

Relate the vocabulary and style to the interpretation of the events likely to be given to the readers of each paper.
(The Selby coalfield was still under development, and contractors were busy in construction work at the mines in the area. Mr Arthur Scargill was President of the National Union of Mineworkers.)

The Seige of Selby – July 1984

Newspaper A – headlines, first set, front page

Scargill's storm-troops terrify a town
THE SIEGE OF SELBY
Shoppers' fury over the mobs

Second set, page 2

Town's rule of terror
FLYING PICKETS BLOCKADE
BRIDGE IN DAWN SWOOP

1   A town put under mob rule by Arthur Scargill's flying pickets last night demanded: "This must never happen again."

2   The military style operation in the quiet market town of Selby involved 4,000 strikers. It left police helpless as five-mile traffic jams rapidly built up.

3   This is how a town centre shopkeeper – still too afraid to give his name – last night summed up the siege of Selby:

4   "It was nothing more than the rule of the mob. People were terrified. Now many are angry and insisting that this must not be allowed to happen again."

5   While the storm-troop batt-alions were blockading Selby, Mr Scargill and Coal Board boss Ian MacGregor were meeting in London in a bid to end the bitter 17-week strike.

6   It was dawn when nearly 600 miners took over the narrow Selby toll bridge on the A19 which is the only way over the River Ouse without making a 10-mile detour through narrow lanes.

7   With the town now sealed off, more than 500 pickets rampaged through the streets. They terrified shopkeepers and housewives and overturned a contractor's van.

8   Said an elderly shopkeeper: "A mob of at least 500 came down High Street jeering and chanting. It was bedlam."

9   It was some hours before Selby returned to normal. Pickets later claimed that they had blockaded the town to stop contractors' and materials getting through to the pits. But police said: "This was just another attempt at mob rule."

Injured

10   Ten police and four pickets were hurt and there were four arrests.

11   Many militant miners fear the new Selby coalfield because of its rich reserves, high efficiency and low production costs.

12   They cannot forget that the 4,000 miners who will be em-ployed at Selby will be able to turn out the same amount of coal as 20,000 men today.

Newspaper B – small headlines, page 3

<u>Pickets move on to market town</u>
Selby's arranged marriage strained

1   Selby, the market town that is going through an arranged marriage with the mining community, yesterday experienced at first hand the effects of the miners' dispute.

2   Reports of rampaging miners and of the town being under siege were greatly exaggerated. But the incidents around Selby will probably do the miners little good in a town that will be of increasing importance to them in the years to come.

3   When normality returned

yesterday, 10 policemen had been slightly hurt, one of whom was detained in hospital, three pickets had been taken to hospital but later discharged and a construction worker had been slightly hurt. Two police vans and a construction workers' van were overturned.

4   The local difficulty began shortly before 6.45 am when about 3,000 miners converged on Selby and avoided police efforts to stop them.

5   The miners have been trying to persuade construction work-

ers not to cross picket lines.

6   The miners did not stop the construction workers going in and this obviously caused some frustration. Two police vans were overturned.

7   Miners later temporarily blockaded the main toll bridge into Selby. Their peaceful protest drew residents' grumbles about being delayed for more than two hours.

8   As they dispersed, a group of miners spotted a rented van being used to take construction workers to the pits. The van had been held up in the traffic queue.

9   According to local residents, men surrounded the van and began banging on the side. They overturned it with the men inside.

In the following tables, the actions reported in the newspapers are reduced to their underlying **propositions** in a kind of 'deconstruction' of the reports. Those who did something, or caused something to happen (the **actors** and **agents**) are listed in the first column; what they did (the **process**) is in the second column; those who had something done to them (the **affected**) are in the fourth column. The third column (**attribute**), for qualities or feelings attributed to participants, is only needed for two propositions in these texts.

An action that is **reported**, following verbs like *said, claimed, summed up,* or phrases like *according to*, etc., is marked by the sign <">. This implies that the paper is not asserting that the statement is true.

The different ways of naming, or **classifying** the participants are ignored in the table, and one word is chosen to represent each of the main participants, *miners* and *police*.

The table should help you to identify more quickly just what each paper alleged that the miners and the police actually did, and how many times the two participants were referred to.

Newspaper B is a little more difficult to analyse than A, because it is an ironic commentary on what papers like A had already published about the incident.

Analysis of actional and verbal processes – what happened?

Newspaper A

Actor/agent	Process	Attribute	Affected
Headlines			
miners	terrify		Selby
miners	(be)siege		Selby
shoppers	be furious		at miners
miners	rule		Selby
miners	terrorise		Selby
miners	blockade		Selby bridge
miners	swoop		

	Actor/agent	Process	Attribute	Affected
	Text			
1	miners	rule		Selby
2	miners/military	operate		in Selby
	police		helpless	
	traffic	jams		
3	shopkeeper		afraid	
	shopkeeper	say:		
4	" miners	rule		Selby
	" miners	terrify		Selby people
5	miners	blockade		Selby
	Scargill & MacGregor	meet		
6	miners	take over		Selby bridge
7	miners	seal off		Selby
	miners	rampage		
	miners	terrify		Selby shopkeepers & housewives
	miners	overturn		van
8	shopkeeper	say:		
	" miners	came down		
	" miners	jeer		
	" miners	chant		
	" miners	cause bedlam		
9	miners	say:		
	" miners for	blockade		Selby
	" miners	prevent getting through		contractors & materials
	police	say:		
	" miners	attempt to rule		Selby
10	?miners	hurt		10 police
	?police	hurt		4 miners
	police	arrest		4 miners

Newspaper B

	Actor/agent	Process	Attribute	Affected
	Headlines			
1	miners	move on to		Selby
	Text			
2	Ø?	exaggerate:		
	Ø?	report:		
	" miners	rampage		
	" miners	(be)siege		Selby
3	miners	hurt		10 policemen
	Ø?	detain in hospital		1 policeman
	Ø?	take to hospital		3 miners
	Ø?	discharge from hospital		3 miners
	miners	hurt		worker
	miners	overturn		2 police vans & 1 van
4	miners	converge on Selby		
	miners	avoid police		
5	miners	try to persuade		workers
6	miners	did NOT persuade		workers
	miners		frustrated	
	miners	overturn		2 police vans
7	miners	blockade		Selby bridge
	miners	protest peacefully		
	Selby residents	grumble		
	miners	delay		Selby residents
8	miners	disperse		
	miners	spot		van
9	Selby residents	say:		
	" miners	surround		van
	" miners	bang on		van
	" miners	overturn		van
	" workers	be inside		van

The attitude of each newspaper towards the events in Selby is now made clearer. The language used in A's headline *The Siege of Selby*, is consistent with its assertions about the violent aggressiveness of the miners' behaviour. It is a kind of *warfare*:

terrify	besiege	rule	terrorise	blockade	swoop
blockade	take over	seal off	rampage	overturn	cause bedlam

The words describing their 'verbal behaviour', *jeer* and *chant* are consistent with this point of view also, whereas the miners' actions are interpreted quite differently in newspaper B, apart from their *hurting* police and a worker, and *banging on* and *overturning* a van. Their movements are not aggressive when they *move on to* or *converge on* Selby. Although they *blockade* the bridge, *they try to persuade* workers and *protest peacefully*. At worst, they *delay* the residents of Selby, and finally *disperse*. This does not describe the actions of a *rampaging mob*.

Activity 9.25

Study the following extracts from newspaper reports of incidents which took place in June 1986 and comment on the use of language in presenting what happened. Can you identify any of the newspaper reports as tabloid or broadsheet in style? What evidence do you use to decide?

The Peace Convoy – June 1986

Summary of the events from a newspaper report:

> The hippy convoy which had been camped at Stoney Cross in the New Forest was dispersing around the country yesterday after police and social service officials jointly broke up the group.

Text A – a daily newspaper report (with large accompanying photograph)

SO WHERE DOES HE GO NOW?
Innocent on the road of rejection

HUNCHED against the wind in the security of a borrowed blanket, the child stumbled across the land that had briefly been his home.

The boy looked bewildered against the background of the three unmoved policemen.

Confusion

The man with him, a ragged symbol of the hippies, plunged his hands into the empty pockets of his tattered jeans and the stones on the ground bit into his feet. His bedding hung over his arm.

The child burrowed deeper in to the blanket and stared back with innocent confusion at the towering impassive policemen. Little emotion flickered from their eyes.

The only friendship, the only token of parting affection, the only hint of kindness to a child came from a free-running dog. An old Labrador sniffed the child amiably and licked gently.

The Child and The Man With Nowhere to Go looked at one another with despair. He plunged his hands even more deeply into his pockets - and the three of them set off together.

A confused child, a ragged, hope-crushed man and a friendly old dog.

All on the Road of Rejection.

Text B – report in a weekly newspaper

Police 'victory' over hippies

For almost three weeks British newspapers and television screens have been full of reports, commentaries and even "research" articles on a rather unusual subject – the struggle between a group of homeless and aimless people denoted in the press here by the vague term "hippies", and the British authorities.

The reason for the confrontation was the intention by representatives of this group to hold their traditional song festival in the Stonehenge area, where there is a concentration of structures dating back to the Neolithic era.

The hippies have been organising such festivals every year since 1977. Last year, however, the attempts to organise it came up against a ban by the authorities. On arriving there, the hippies were met by the police and bloody clashes ensued.

The same thing happened this year as well. Driven out of Stonehenge, the homeless people, many of them with small children, tried to set up camp on vacant land belonging to a local farmer.

A few days later, however, the Supreme Court issued an edict prohibiting them from staying there and the hippies, under pressure from the law and order forces, ended up on the road once again. About a week ago they made yet another attempt to set up camp – this time on a disused airfield near the village of Stoney Cross in Hampshire. Nor on this occasion, however, did they manage to hold out for longer than a week.

At dawn on June 9 about 500 policemen arrived in special vehicles, surrounded the camp and once and for all broke up the hippies' refuge. Reporting the successful completion of "Operation Dawn", as the police raid is bombastically named in official documents, the newspapers wrote that as result of it, 42 persons were arrested and the rest were "dispersed" and "sent home" – to homes which they simply do not have.

Of course, the government can ban and even break up song festivals set up by the hippies. But the root of the problem lies elsewhere.

The hippies are first and foremost homeless and deprived people who can find no place for themselves in contemporary British society, and the more unemployment grows and the other social problems intensify, as is happening at present, the more frequently will arise similar types of conflicts reflecting the overall sick state of contemporary Western society.

Text C – a Sunday newspaper columnist

NO HIPPY ENDING THEN

HOME SECRETARY Douglas Hurd describes the hippy "peace convoy" as "a band of medieval brigands".

But in the Middle Ages brigands did not have half so cushy a time as these bums, beggars, vandals, and thieves, with whom grovelling TV personalities like Frank Bough and Desmond Morris, both of whom should know better, choose to sympathise.

Medieval brigands would swiftly have found themselves set upon by the vassals and hounds of baron landlords, or by royal servants or by local freemen. They would have found their lives to be not only nasty and brutish, but decidedly short.

What is more, they would not have been followed around by clerks from the exchequer dishing out substantial sums of cash each Thursday to enable them to carry on marauding through the countryside.

The hippies claim, with arrant humbug, to be living "an alternative life style". The claim would by marginally less fraudulent if they had found an alternative to the dole we so foolishly give them, and they so eagerly take.

Text D – a daily newspaper

Peace convoy smashed
42 arrests as police seize vehicles in dawn swoop

AS DAWN broke on Stoney Cross in Hampshire's New Forest 500 police swooped on the peace convoy yesterday to break up their camp.

The police had come under cover of darkness in a huge armada of cars and vans to the site and moved in at about 4.45 am.

They were greeted with car horn hoots and warning shouts of "police on site" by alerted convoy members to waken many others who were blissfully unaware of the police invasion.

The police had code-named their massive exercise "operation day break".

Hampshire assistant chief constable John Wright in what must rate as the understatement of the year declared: "We are inviting the occupants of the site to leave."

The police then proceeded to arrest 42 members of the 300-strong peace convoy and impound over 100 vehicles deemed unroadworthy. ...

10. Variety in written English – II: style

PART 1 THE LANGUAGE OF LITERATURE

One of the defining features of literature is its special use of language. In many novels and short stories, in drama and especially in verse and poetry, language is itself **foregrounded** or 'made strange'. Its style is different from that of other everyday uses. It is said to **deviate** from ordinary language. By applying to literary texts the methods of analysis which have been demonstrated on other varieties of English, you can discover interesting facts about the many different ways in which language is used in literature, and these will help in your evaluation of a literary work.

10.1 The Preacher

The Bible is widely read as literature, and there has been much controversy over the relative merits of new translations of the Bible in comparison with the Authorised Version of 1611, which was for centuries the only version of the Bible available to be read and heard in the churches. What makes the Bible literature? What it says, or how it says it? Here are three versions of a verse from the Old Testament book Ecclesiastes.

Activity 10.1

Read the texts, and make your own judgement about their literary qualities before continuing with the commentary.

1. I returned, and saw under the sun, that the race is not to the swift, nor the battle to the strong, neither yet bread to the wise, nor yet riches to men of understanding, nor yet favour to men of skill; but time and chance happeneth to them all.

2. Objective consideration of contemporary phenomena compels the conclusion that success or failure in competitive activities exhibits no tendency to be commensurate with innate capacity, but that a considerable element of the unpredictable must invariably be taken into account.

3. Using your loaf won't fill your bread-bin, a mystery preacher warned in a pulpit blast yesterday.

  And punters will be pipped to know that though the horse they backed is first past the post – they won't pick up their winnings.

  HE-MEN have had it, according to the no-holds-barred sermon.

Commentary

Here are three contrasting styles of written English, versions of the same original Hebrew text. Keith Waterhouse concludes his book *Daily Mirror Style* with them.

Do they all say the same thing? You will agree that only the first, from the King James Bible, would be accepted as literary. The second is a **parody** of bureaucratic English, 'officialese', by George Orwell. The third is a **pastiche** written in the style of a tabloid newspaper by Keith Waterhouse himself, but not as an example of good journalism – 'That's not style. But it's what gets into newspapers.' So it is not content that makes a work literary.

The literary version was very much influenced by the language of earlier sixteenth century translations of the Bible, and so already formal and archaic by the early seventeenth century. Without a knowledge of ancient Hebrew, it is not possible to know how closely the translation follows the original text, but it would be reasonable to assume that it is as close to the Hebrew as could be achieved.

George Orwell wrote 'Politics and the English Language' in 1946. The parody was intended to illustrate what he called 'staleness of imagery' and 'lack of precision':

> The first contains forty-nine words but only sixty syllables, and all its words are those of everyday life. The second contains thirty-eight words of ninety syllables: eighteen of its words are from Latin roots, and one from Greek. The first sentence contains six vivid images, and only one phrase ('time and chance') that could be called vague. The second contains not a single fresh, arresting phrase, and in spite of its ninety syllables it gives only a shortened version of the meaning contained in the first.

One important difference between the two versions is that version 1 uses mostly **concrete nouns** (*sun, race, battle, bread, riches, men*) and simple descriptive adjectives used as nouns (*the swift, the strong, the wise*). The parody has **abstract nouns**, which are less direct in their reference (*considerations, phenomena, conclusion, success, failure* and so on).

Equally important in version 1 is the **parallelism** of the successive clauses and phrases, that is, the grammatical patterns repeat themselves, but with different words:

		the race	is not	to the swift
nor		the battle		to the strong
neither	yet	bread		to the wise
nor	yet	riches		to men of understanding
nor	yet	favour		to men of skill

This parallelism of structure is responsible for the strong **rhythm** of the verse when we read it aloud, or hear it read in imagination, as we must if we are to respond to its meaning. You can see that it is poetry. Orwell's parody is not, and the vagueness given to it by the polysyllabled Latinate words in meaning also provides a mushy lack of rhythm.

For these reasons, we can say that version 1 is literary, and version 2 is not. But what about version 3? It seems to have the concreteness of vocabulary of the first version (*loaf, bread-bin, preacher, pulpit, blast* and so on), and several of these are used as **metaphors**, not in their literal sense. Parts of it have some liveliness, a sort of 'falling rhythm',

I **using** your I **loaf** won't I **fill** your I **bread**-bin	/xx/x/x/x
I HE-MEN have I **had** it	/xx/x
I **first** I **past** the I **post**	//x/

but this is neither sustained nor very significant.

Keith Waterhouse imitates the practice of most of the tabloid press news reports in writing only one sentence in each paragraph, but its chief feature is the use of colloquial vocabulary and metaphor, which some critics would call *cliché* and reject as bad English without further analysis. On the other hand, you may enjoy this style for its outrageous linking of *using your loaf* ('using your understanding') with *fill your bread-bin* and its double meaning, which is both literal, and slang for *belly*.

The second sentence, in its version of 'the race is not to the swift', again uses colloquial words and phrases in a racy alternative. The third has the punch-line, and is consistently informal (*have had it* in the sense of *will fail*, and *no-holds-barred* as a pre-modifier to *sermon*).

This journalistic pastiche is clever and amusing because we respond to it not as journalism, but with the echoes of the Biblical version in our mind, and the absurd contrast makes it own effect. If you do not know the original, then any pastiche will be ineffective. Your reading of any text is strongly affected by what you think it is. The question as to whether it is literature is left for you to debate.

10.2 The Good Samaritan again

Activity 10.2 _____

Read the two versions of the parable of the Good Samaritan in chapter 2, and say whether you prefer either version for its literary qualities. Can you then say more precisely what those literary qualities are?

Activity 10.3

Then read the following version of the parable, discuss the differences in vocabulary and their effect, and comment on the style of this version in comparison with the first two. Answer these questions:

(i)   Is it a translation?
(ii)   Is it the same story?
(iii) Is it literature?

A man was going from his apartment in the project to his friend's house. While he was walking, a couple of muggers jumped him in a dark place. He didn't have very much, so they took his wallet and clothes and beat on him and stomped on him – they almost killed him.   5

Before long a hood came by, but he didn't give a care. Besides, the cops might ask him questions, so he beat it out of there. Next came a squeak – never gave the poor guy a second look. After a while a real cool square comes along. He sees the character, feels sorry for him. So he puts a couple of Band-aids on, gives him a   10
drink, and a lift in his car. The square even put him up in a room some place. Cost him two bucks too!

So who do you think the best guy was? Well, you got the message, bud. But you don't have to be a square to show love, and to be sorry for someone, and to help a guy. But get with it, man –   15
this is what God wants you to do.

10.3   Exercises in style

10.3.1   *From the French*

The French author Raymond Queneau wrote a book called *Exercices de Style*, which was published in 1947. In it, the same fragment of a story is told in ninety-nine different versions. It has been translated into English by Barbara Wright, and was published as *Exercises in Style* in 1958.

How can you tell the same story ninety-nine times? The translator has said:

In the same way as the story as such doesn't matter, the particular language it is written in doesn't matter as such... Queneau's tour-de-force lies in the fact that the simplicity and banality of the material he starts from gives birth to so much...

His purpose here, in the *Exercices*, is, I think, a profound exploration into the possibilities of language... He pushes language around in a multiplicity of directions to see what will happen.

To try to tell you the story in advance would only add another version to Queneau's. His first 'exercise', called *Notation*, is the best introduction, because it is written like a set of notes for a story – an outline of what happens.

The object of this study is to show how the linguistic features of the writing determine our recognition of the differences between the exercises. You should look at:

- The choice of **vocabulary** – why one word rather than another? What connotations do particular words bring with them? Do some words seem to stand out of their context? Do they form lexical sets?
- The **grammatical** choices – phrase, clause and sentence structures, word and phrase order.
- The kind of **discourse** which the text represents – who is the narrator? From whose point of view is it told? Is it monologue or dialogue?

Other questions will arise in particular exercises. It is easy enough to say in general terms what each one is about, but you must try to answer the question 'How do I know?' in detail.

Here are some of the ninety-nine variations, followed by descriptive commentaries. Read the texts and make descriptive analyses of the vocabulary, grammar and discourse features which make each text distinctive.

Activity 10.4

On *Notation*

(i)   Identify the characters.
(ii) Where does the action take place?
(iii) When does it happen?
(iv) What happens?
(v)   What do you learn about the characters?
(vi) Who is telling the story?

1   Notation

In the S bus, in the rush hour. A chap of about 26, felt hat with a cord instead of a ribbon, neck too long, as if someone's been having a tug-of-war with it. People getting off. The chap in question gets annoyed with one of the men standing next to him. He accuses him of jostling him every time anyone goes past. A snivelling tone which is meant to be aggressive. When he sees a vacant seat he throws himself on to it.

Two hours later, I meet him in the Cour de Rome, in front of the gare Saint-Lazare. He's with a friend who's saying: "You ought to get an extra button put on your overcoat." He shows him where (at the lapels) and why.

Activity 10.5

On *The Subjective Side*

(i) Who is telling the story?
(ii) The events are not told in the same order. Why?

cont.

(iii) Consider the effect on the narrative, and our impressions of the main character (which can only be inferred from the words on the page), if some of his words and phrases had been chosen differently. Substitute them for what he actually said, and discuss what difference of meaning follows:

my clothes	for	my attire
wearing	for	inaugurating
fashionable	for	sprightly
didn't criticize	for	didn't dare attack
complained to	for	roundly told off
a passenger	for	a vulgar type
jostling	for	ill-treating
uncomfortable	for	unspeakably foul
buses	for	omnibi
people	for	hoi polloi
travel on them	for	have to consent to use them

(iv) Do any features of the grammar reinforce your impressions of the character?

2 The Subjective Side

I was not displeased with my attire this day. I was inaugurating a new, rather sprightly hat, and an overcoat of which I thought most highly. Met X in front of the gare Saint-Lazare who tried to spoil my pleasure by trying to prove that this overcoat is cut too low at the lapel and that I ought to have an extra button on it. At least he didn't dare attack my head-gear.

A bit earlier I had roundly told off a vulgar type who was purposely ill-treating me every time anyone went by getting on or off. This happened in one of those unspeakably foul omnibi which fill up with hoi polloi precisely at those times when I have to consent to use them.

Activity 10.6

On *Telegraphic*

(i) Rewrite the text in normal prose.
(ii) What have you had to add to the text to do this?

3 Telegraphic

BUS CROWDED STOP YNGMAN LONGNECK PLAITEN-CIRCLED HAT APOSTROPHISES UNKNOWN PASSENGER UNAPPARENT REASON STOP QUERY FINGERS FEET HURT CONTACT HEEL ALLEGED PURPOSELY STOP YNGMAN ABANDONS DISCUSSION PROVACANT SEAT STOP 1400 HOURS PLACE ROME YNGMAN LISTENS SARTORIAL ADVICE FRIEND STOP MOVE BUTTON STOP SIGNED ARCTURUS

Commentary on *Notation*

The characters:
  a chap (call him C);
  a man(Y);
  a friend of C's (X);
  the narrator (N).

The place:
  in the S bus;
  in front of the Saint-Lazare railway station in the Cour de Rome, Paris.

The time:
  year and day unspecified; 'in the rush hour' and 'two hours later'.

The events:
  C accuses Y of jostling him while both are standing in a crowded bus. C takes
  a vacant seat;
  X tells C that C needs an extra button on his overcoat.

What else are we told?
  about C: C is about twenty-six, has a long neck, and wears a hat with a cord
  instead of a ribbon round it. We learn something about him from his accusation of
  Y, his 'snivelling tone' which is meant to be aggressive;
  about Y, X and N: Nothing.

This is obviously not a traditional story with a beginning, middle and end. Nothing happens that would seem to deserve mention. We are led to wonder what Queneau is going to make of it in the 98 following versions. The clue lies in the language, not in the story-line.

Vocabulary

Reference to the characters as *chap, man, friend* is informal and carries no other connotation.

Notice that C *accuses* Y; the narrator does not say that Y jostles C as a fact, so it may be C's sensitivity that is misplaced. This impression is reinforced by *snivelling*, which implies weakness. C's aggressive intentions are not successfully communicated.

C does not sit down, but *throws himself on to* a seat. This implies an emotional response - anger or petulance.

Grammar

Two features convey the sense of notes for a story:
● The **minor sentences** in the first paragraph, which lack one or other of the elements usually found in a clause, the subject NP or the predicator VP.
  In the S bus, in the rush hour – two **prepositional phrases** (PrepPs), functioning as **adverbials** of place.
  A chap of about 26 – an NP.
  felt hat ... ribbon – another NP.
  neck too long – the **linking verb** *be* is omitted, and the **possessive pronoun** *his* before the noun.

People getting off - the **auxiliary verb** *be* is omitted.

A snivellling tone ... aggressive - a complex NP with a qualifying **relative clause.**

- The use of the **simple present tense**, which is unusual in narrative:

gets annoyed	accuses	goes	is meant
sees	throws	meet	's (= is)
shows			

The only apparent exceptions are:

's been having   (present + perfective + progressive)
's saying   (present + progressive)

which are complex but still present in tense.

Discourse

It is **third-person** narrative, though the narrator appears to place himself within the events when he says, 'Two hours later, I meet him ...' But he does not interact with C and X, only observes them.

Commentary on *The Subjective Side*

The title is important. This is a subjective point of view, told in the first person by the character C, the 'chap of about 26' in *Notation*, and one of the character sketches.

Discourse

Notice that the order of events is reversed. The event of the day for C is the fact that he is wearing his new hat and overcoat, so this comes first. His meeting with X is related to this, and so the affair on the bus is less important.

The chronological order of events, whether fact (as in newspaper reporting) or fiction (as in novels or short stories), is often rearranged to give prominence to one of them. This is part of what we mean by **plot** in a novel. The amount of space used, as well as order, is also significant.

Our first impression of C in *Notation* is reinforced by his own words.

Vocabulary

If we think of our use of words as making a choice from a number of alternatives when we talk or write, then we can see how style can be viewed as *how* we say something, which is in addition to our primary choice of *what* to say, or whether to say it.

Grammar

A number of grammatical features combine to convey the impression of the narrator's voice – perhaps writing a diary? *Met X...* suggests this, though it is the only example of the omission of the subject *I*, but the impression is conveyed through the precise formality of the self-confessions that C is making, and the consistency in his character that is built up.

(i)   *I was not displeased with...* – a double negative which does convey the positive *'I was pleased with...* but with a suggestion of hesitancy or self-deprecation, perhaps.

(ii)   *of which I thought most highly* – partly the lexical choice of 'to think highly of' in relation to an overcoat, but also the formal style of *of which*, avoiding the preposition-at-the-end form of *which I thought most highly of.* Compare *which I liked a lot.*

(iii)   *tried to spoil, trying to prove, didn't dare attack, have to consent to use.* These **catenative** structures of two or more verbs linked by *to* (except with *dare*) also fill in C's character. *Try to* implies *didn't succeed*; *didn't dare* implies the superiority of C in his relationship with X; *have to* suggests reluctance, and *consent* condescension.

(iv)   A number of **adverbs** combine also to express C's point of view: *At least* functions as a **sentence adverbial** (or **disjunct**). '*roundly* told off' implies C's manner of telling as he imagines it, and '*purposely* ill-treating me' is C's interpretation of Y's behaviour. '*unspeakably* foul omnibi', or 'so foul that I can't speak of it' equally gives away C's attitude, and '*precisely* at those times' suggests the (to him) unfortunate concurrence of the rush-hour and his time-table.

The complete subjectivity of the fictional C's account of his day can be readily seen from this analysis of the lexical and grammatical choices which are the means of conveying the discourse.

Commentary on *Telegraphic*

Telegrams (which were discontinued in the 1980s) were charged by the word, so it was cheaper to leave out unessential words, and to compress as much information as possible into single words (making them up if necessary). This can be done by **compounding** and **abbreviating** and by the omission of **function words** which are necessary to construct a grammatical sentence in most other varieties of English. For example, 'YNGMAN LONGNECK' has two wo.ds, but 'a young man with a long neck' has seven. (Compare newspaper headlines in chapter 9 and spoken unscripted commentary in chapter 7.)

We can rewrite the telegram to include function words, and to expand compounds and abbreviations, which will also require some re-ordering of the words and changes of form:

> There is a CROWDED BUS. A YOUNG MAN with a LONG NECK and wearing a HAT which is ENCIRCLED by a PLAIT APOSTROPHISES a PASSENGER who is UNKNOWN to him for NO APPARENT REASON. It is ALLEGED that the passenger made CONTACT with his HEEL and it is possible that (= QUERY) the young man's FINGERS and FEET were HURT. The YOUNG MAN ABANDONS any DISCUSSION in order to (= PRO) sit in a VACANT SEAT. At 2 p.m. (= 1400 HOURS) in the PLACE de ROME the YOUNG MAN LISTENS to ADVICE about his overcoat (= SARTORIAL) from a FRIEND. He told him he should MOVE a BUTTON.

The function words in English (sometimes called **grammatical** words) are the **determiners, conjunctions, prepositions** and **pro-words**, which contrast with the **lexical** words – **nouns, verbs, adjectives** and **adverbs.** Check this in the re-written telegram, where the words in capitals are all lexical words.

You will find amusing examples of 'telegraphese' in Evelyn Waugh's novel *Scoop*, about a young man who is sent by mistake to cover a civil war in Africa for the daily newspaper *The Beast*. William Boot is not an experienced journalist, and so the telegrams he sends contain far too many words. Here is an example of a Boot telegram, with the reply that followed from *The Beast* and Boot's answer to it:

> THEY HAVE GIVEN US PERMISSION TO GO TO LAKU AND EVERYONE IS GOING BUT THERE IS NO SUCH PLACE AM I TO GO TOO SORRY TO BE A BORE BOOT

> UNPROCEED LAKUWARD STOP AGENCIES COVERING PATRIOTIC FRONT STOP REMAIN CONTACTING CUMREDS STOP NEWS EXYOU UNRECEIVED STOP DAILY HARD NEWS ESSENTIALEST STOP REMEMBER RATES SERVICE CABLES ONE ETSIX PER WORD BEAST

> NO NEWS AT PRESENT THANKS WARNING ABOUT CABLING PRICES BUT IVE PLENTY MONEY LEFT AND ANYWAY WHEN I OFFERED TO PAY WIRELESS MAN SAID IT WAS ALL RIGHT PAID OTHER END RAINING HARD HOPE ALL WELL ENGLAND WILL CABLE AGAIN IF ANY NEWS BOOT

Activity 10.7

Here is a short selection of openings from *Exercises in Style* to read. Identify the foregrounded features of the language. Try to continue some of them in a similar style, or create your own titles and styles.

4 Asides

The bus arrived bulging with passengers. *Only hope I don't miss it, oh good, there's still just room for me.* One of them *queer sort of mug he's got with that enormous neck* was wearing a soft felt hat with a sort of little plait round it instead of a ribbon *just showing off that is* and suddenly started *hey what's got into him* to vituperate his neighbour...

5 Precision

In a bus of the S-line, 10 metres long, 3 wide, 6 high, at 3km. 600 m. from its starting point, loaded with 48 people, at 12.17 p.m., a person of the masculine sex aged 27 years 3 months and 8 days, 1m. 72cm. tall and weighing 65 kg. ...

6 Anagrams

In het S sub in het hurs hour a pach of tabou swinettyx, who had a glon, hint cken and a tah mmitred with a droc instead of a borbin ...

7 Onomatopoeia

On the platform, pla pla pla, of a bus, chuff chuff chuff, which was an S (and singing still dost soar, and soaring ever singest), it was about noon, ding dang dong, ding dang dong ...

8 Cockney

So A'm stand'n' n' ahtsoider vis frog bus when A sees vis young Froggy bloke, caw bloimey, A finks, 'f'at ain't ve most funniest look'n geezer wot ever A claps eyes on ...

9 For ze Frrensh

Wurn dayee abaout meeddayee Ahee got eentoo a büss ouich ouoz goeeng een ze deerekssion off ze Porte Champerret. Eet ouoz fool, nearlee ...

10.3.2   *Style in novels and short stories*

We have seen in sections 10.1 and 10.2 that different translations or paraphrases of biblical stories produce texts so different that their only relationship lies in the abstract narrative that underlies them. The three examples taken from the ninety-nine permutations of the 'same story' in section 10.3.1 show how a game can be played with language. Queneau's 'exercises in style' are comparable to musical 'exercises' in instrumental playing, which focus on specific, limited aspects of technique.

Style is an important feature of all literature, but in some writings our attention is drawn more closely to features of style than in others.

Activity 10.8

Read the following extract from the autobiography *Cider with Rosie* by Laurie Lee (published in 1959), from which twenty-five words have been omitted. Can you say where the missing words should be, and what kind of words they are?

The sons of John Light, the five Light brothers, illuminated many a local myth, were admired for their wildness, their force of arms, and for their wit. 'We come from the oldest family in the world. We're in the Book of Genesis. The Almighty said, "Let there be Light" – and that was long before Adam ...'   5

My first encounter with Uncle Ray – prospector, dynamiter, buffalo-fighter, and builder of railways – was an occasion of suddenness. One moment he was a legend at the other end of the world, the next he was in my bed. Accustomed only to the bodies of my younger brothers and sisters, I awoke one morning to find   10
snoring beside me a huge man. I touched the legs and arms and pondered the barbs of his chin, felt the flesh of this creature, and wondered what it could be.

'It's your Uncle Ray come home,' whispered Mother. 'Get up now and let him sleep.'   15

I saw a brown face, a nose, and smelt a reek of cigars and train-oil. Here was the hero of our school days, and to look on him was no disappointment. He was shiny as iron, worn as a

rock, and lay like a chieftain sleeping. He'd come home on a
visit from building his railways, loaded with money and thirst,   20
and the days he spent at our house that time were full of wonder
and conflagration.

For one thing he was unlike any other man we'd ever seen –
or heard of, if it comes to that. With his leather-beaten face, wide
mouth, and blue eyes, he looked like some warrior stained with   25
suns and slaughter. He spoke the dialect of the railway camps in
a drawl through his nose. His body was tattooed in every quarter
– ships in full sail, flags of all nations, reptiles, and maidens. By
flexings of his flesh he could sail those ships, wave the flags in
the wind, and coil snakes round the girls.   30

Commentary

The text makes sense, but all the following words, listed in alphabetical order, occur
in the original text:

boasting (2)	Indian	round-eyed
Canadian	knotted	rust
crocodile	leisurely	satiny
cunning	magnificent	scaly
far-seeing	memorable	teeth-crammed
gaunt	muscled	thick
heroic	quivering	transcontinental
ice	resonant	wigwam

Activity 10.9

Try to place the words of the list in the text printed below, in which their places
are marked by asterisks *. Discuss the differences of meaning that are produced
by substituting alternative words.
The grammatical function of all these words is the same. What is it?

The sons of John Light, the five Light brothers, illuminated
many a local myth, were admired for their wildness, their force
of arms, and for their *, * wit. 'We come from the oldest family
in the world. We're in the Book of Genesis. The Almighty said,
"Let there be Light" - and that was long before Adam ...'   5

My first encounter with Uncle Ray – prospector, dynamiter,
buffalo-fighter, and builder of * railways – was an occasion of *
suddenness. One moment he was a legend at the other end of the
world, the next he was in my bed. Accustomed only to the *
bodies of my younger brothers and sisters, I awoke one morning   10
to find snoring beside me a huge and * man. I touched the * legs
and * arms and pondered the barbs of his chin, felt the * flesh of
this * creature, and wondered what it could be.

'It's your Uncle Ray come home,' whispered Mother. 'Get up now and let him sleep.' I saw a *-brown face, a * * nose, and   15 smelt a reek of cigars and train-oil. Here was the hero of our school-* days, and to look on him was no disappointment. He was shiny as iron, worn as a rock, and lay like a chieftain sleeping. He'd come home on a visit from building his railways, loaded with money and thirst, and the days he spent at our house that   20 time were full of wonder and conflagration.

For one thing he was unlike any other man we'd ever seen – or heard of, if it comes to that. With his leather-beaten face, wide * mouth, and * *-blue eyes, he looked like some * warrior stained with suns and * slaughter. He spoke the * dialect of the railway   25 camps in a drawl through his * nose. His body was tattooed in every quarter – ships in full sail, flags of all nations, reptiles, and * maidens. By * flexings of his * flesh he could sail those ships, wave the flags in the wind, and coil snakes round the * girls.

(The original text is printed at the end of the chapter.)

Commentary

The missing words have the grammatical function of **noun modifiers** Most of them are **adjectives**, e.g. *gaunt, magnificent, thick*, some of which are derived from verbs, either **present participles**, e.g. *boasting, quivering*, or **past participles**, e.g. *knotted*. A few are **nouns,** which can also function as noun modifiers, e.g. *crocodile, wigwam*.

The difference between the two texts, one with and one without the twenty-five noun modifiers, is one of style as much as of meaning. None of the modifiers, except perhaps *thick,* is commonplace, and this profusion of descriptive adjectives recurs in the book from time to time, and so is a consistent stylistic feature which is therefore **foregrounded**.

Not all adjectives function as noun modifiers. They also occur after linking verbs like *be* and *seem* in the predicate of a clause, and so are called **predicative adjectives**, for example,

He *was* **shiny** as iron, **worn** as a rock ...
His body *was* **tattooed** in every quarter ...

Neither are 'descriptive words' confined to adjectives. All lexical words (nouns, verbs, adjectives, adverbs and also prepositions) have a descriptive function, and Laurie Lee does not confine his creative use of words to adjectives.

The relationship between the meaning of a text and its form is the subject of **stylistics**, or to use an older term, **rhetoric**. Rhetorical figures include those familiar to you from the study of literature, like **simile**,

He was shiny as iron, worn as a rock and lay like a chieftain sleeping.

and **metaphor**, as in *felt the **crocodile** flesh of this magnificent creature.*

Activity 10.10

Read the following extract from Laurie Lee's *Cider with Rosie* and discuss his choice of words and prominent stylistic or rhetorical features.

(The author is here a child of about two years old.)

From the harbour mouth of the scullery door I learned the rocks
and reefs and the channels where safety lay. I discovered the
physical pyramid of the cottage, its stores and labyrinths, its
centres of magic, and of the green, sprouting island-garden upon
which it stood. My Mother and sisters sailed past me like   5
galleons in their busy dresses, and I learned the smells and
sounds which followed in their wakes, the surge of breath, air of
carbolic, song and grumble, and smashing of crockery.

How magnificent they appeared, full-rigged, those towering
girls, with their flying hair and billowing blouses, their white-   10
mast arms stripped for work or washing. At any moment one was
boarded by them, bussed and buttoned, or swung up high like a
wriggling fish to be hooked and held in their lacy linen.

10.3.3   Sherlock Holmes simplified

Another way of identifying the stylistic features of a text is by comparing it with a
simplified version. Some simplified editions are published as reading material for
foreign learners of English. Not only is vocabulary controlled by using only familiar,
usually short words, but grammatical structure also. Sentences are limited in length,
and syntactic complexity is avoided.

Activity 10.11 —————————————————————

(i)   Read and compare the following two versions of the opening of Sir
      Arthur Conan Doyle's short Sherlock Holmes story 'The Adventure of the
      Speckled Band'.
(ii) Identify in the simplified version what is omitted or changed in
      (a) the vocabulary, and (b) the grammatical structure.
(iii) Discuss the effect of simplification on your response to the two texts.

The Adventure of the Speckled Band

In glancing over my notes of the seventy-odd cases in which I
have during the last eight years studied the methods of my
friend, Sherlock Holmes, I find many tragic, some comic, a large
number merely strange, but none commonplace; for, working as
he did rather for the love of his art than for the acquirement of   5
wealth, he refused to associate himself with any investigation
which did not tend towards the unusual, and even the fantastic.
Of all these varied cases, however, I cannot recall any which
presented more singular features than that which was associated
with the well-known Surrey family of the Roylotts of Stoke   10
Moran. The events in question occurred in the early days of my
association with Holmes, when we were sharing rooms as

bachelors, in Baker-street. It is possible that I might have placed them upon record before, but a promise of secrecy was made at 15 the time, from which I have only been freed during the last month by the untimely death of the lady to whom the pledge was given. It is perhaps as well that the facts should now come to light, for I have reasons to know that there are widespread rumours as to the death of Dr. Grimesby Roylott which tend to 20 make the matter even more terrible than the truth.

It was early in April in the year '83 that I woke one morning to find Sherlock Holmes standing, fully dressed, by the side of my bed. He was a late riser as a rule, and, as the clock on the mantelpiece showed me that it was only a quarter past seven, I 25 blinked up at him in some surprise, and perhaps just a little resentment, for I was myself regular in my habits.

"Very sorry to knock you up, Watson," said he, "but it's the common lot this morning. Mrs Hudson has been knocked up, she retorted upon me, and I on you." 30

"What is it, then? A fire?"

"No, a client. It seems that a young lady has arrived in a considerable state of excitement, who insists upon seeing me. She is waiting now in the sitting-room. Now, when young ladies wander about the Metropolis at this hour of the morning, and 35 knock sleepy people up out of their beds, I presume that it is something very pressing which they have to communicate. Should it prove to be an interesting case, you would, I am sure, wish to follow it from the outset. I thought at any rate that I should call you, and give you the chance." 40

"My dear fellow, I would not miss it for anything." ...

(The original text, published in 1891)

1. An Early Morning Visitor for Holmes

For many years, I was a good friend of Sherlock Holmes, the famous private detective.

During this time, Holmes solved many unusual mysteries. But perhaps one of the most unusual was the mystery of the Speckled Band.

The story began in April, 1883. At that time, Holmes and I were sharing an apartment in Baker Street in London.

One morning, I woke up very early. To my surprise, Holmes was standing beside my bed. He was already dressed.

'What's happened, Holmes?' I asked. 'Is there a fire?'

'No, Watson,' replied Holmes. 'A client has just arrived. A young lady is waiting downstairs. She seems very worried and upset. I think she has something important to tell me. This could be an interesting case, Watson. That's why I woke you up.'

'I'll come at once,' I said.

(The simplified version, published in 1986)

Commentary

The simplified version's first three sentences are in complete contrast to the original's introductory paragraph of five sentences containing preparatory information about Holmes and Watson – how long they have been collaborating, the nature of Holmes's cases and his attitude towards his art of investigation, the placing of the new story in the early days of their association, the reasons for its late telling, and finally a hint of the 'terrible' nature of Roylott's death. The effect of this detail in the original is, in part, to make the story sound as if it were fact, not fiction. Such detail gives **verisimilitude** – 'the appearance of being true' – to the narrative.

All the sentences of the original are complex in structure, with **subordination** of clauses, which can be seen more clearly by setting out the text clause by clause as follows.

Sentence structure, original version (first five sentences only)

	type	ccj	scj	clause
(i)				
1	PrepCl		In	glancing over my notes of the seventy-odd cases
2	RelCl		in	which I have during the last eight years studied the methods of my friend Sherlock Holmes,
3	**MCl**			**I find many tragic, some comic, a large number merely strange, but none commonplace;**
4	NonfCl	*for,		working ...
5	AdvCl		as	he did ... rather for the love of his art than for the acquirement of wealth,
6	**MCl**	**(*for)**		**he refused to associate himself with any investigation**
7	RelCl			which did not tend towards the unusual, and even the fantastic.
(ii)				
1	**MCl**			**Of all these varied cases, however, I cannot recall any**
2	RelCl			which presented more singular features than that
3	RelCl			which was associated with the well-known Surrey family of the Roylotts of Stoke Moran.
(iii)				
1	**MCl**			**The events in question occurred in the early days of my association with Holmes,**
2	AdvCl		when	we were sharing rooms as bachelors, in Baker-street.
(iv)				
1	**MCl**			**It is possible**
2	NCl		that	**I might have placed them upon record before,**
3	**MCl**	**but**		**a promise of secrecy was made at the time,**
4	RelCl		from	which I have only been freed during the last month by the untimely death of the lady
5	RelCl			to whom the pledge was given.

(v)

1	MCl		**It is perhaps as well,**
2	NCl	that	**the facts should now come to light,**
3	MCl	for	**I have reasons to know**
4	NCl	that	there are widespread rumours as to the death of Dr. Grimesby Roylott
5	RelCl		which tend to make the matter even more terrible than the truth.

Complexity of structure does not necessarily lead to any difficulty of understanding, especially when most of the subordination is by **noun clauses** or **relative clauses** which follow their main clause. However, a long complex sentence is bound to be more difficult to read for a learner than a short, simple one. The simple structure of the simplified version is made even more obvious when set out similarly.

Sentence structure, simplified version

	type	ccj	scj	clause
(i)				
1	MCl			For many years, I was a good friend of Sherlock Holmes, the famous private detective.
(ii)				
1	MCl			During this time, Holmes solved many unusual mysteries.
(iii)				
1	MCl	But		perhaps one of the most unusual was the mystery of the Speckled Band.

A succession of simple one-clause sentences of this kind soon becomes monotonous to read. Conan Doyle created highly plausible characters in Holmes and Watson. His style is inseparable from this plausibility. In other words, the story as narrative is presented in the simplified version, but that is quite inadequate for a convincing rendering of place, character and dialogue.

10.4 Dialect in literature

Writers use non-standard language in novels and short stories to tell us that their characters speak in a regional or social dialect. If we read of a woman saying, 'I wonder if you would mind shutting the window?', we know that she is being polite, and assume that she is 'speaking without an accent'. That is, we presume she is using RP.

So it is assumed that a character in a novel or story or play is speaking RP unless we are told otherwise, and writers use certain conventions to show distinctive pronunciation, which itself is often a marker of social class, and includes a few forms of RP, like the aristocratic *huntin'*, *shootin'* and *fishin'*.

Because our accent gives away our social class or regional dialect, or both, then the same judgement is made on fictitious characters. This can be done in written English only by changing the usual spelling of words. You will seldom find that writers show dialect consistently or in great detail, and certain conventions have developed for representing dialect and accent in this way.

Activity 10.12

Here is an extract from Charles Dickens's *Pickwick Papers*. The non-standard words are printed in bold type. Describe them in relation to Standard English and RP, and suggest what the purpose of this presentation of Sam Weller's speech is.

Mr Weller proceeded to unpack the basket with the utmost dispatch. '**Weal** pie,' said Mr Weller, soliloquising, as he arranged the eatables on the grass. '**Wery** good thing is **weal** pie, when you know the lady **as** made it, and is quite sure that it **an't** kittens; and **arter** all though, where's the odds, when they're so like **weal** that the **wery** piemen themselves don't know the difference? I lodged in the same house **vith** a pieman once, sir, and a **wery** nice man he was – make pies out **o'** anything, he could. "Mr **Veller**," says he, **a squeezing** my hand **wery** hard, and **vispering** in my ear – "don't mention this here **agin** – but it's the **seasonin'** **as** does it. They're all made **o'** **them** noble animals," says he, **a pointin'** to a **wery** nice little tabby kitten, "and I **seasons 'em** for beefsteak, **weal** or kidney, **'cordin'** to the demand, just as the market changes, and appetites **wary**!"

Commentary

Sam Weller is one of Dickens's most popular characters, and speaks the London Cockney dialect of the early nineteenth century. We can list the dialectal features in groups:

1. Its most obvious characteristic is the reversal of /v/ and /w/ when they are word-initial, that is, when the consonants are the first sounds in words.

2. *An't* indicates the pronunciation which has been discussed in the Acceptability Test in chapter 1.

3. *the lady as made it the seasonin' as does it* – non-standard relative pronoun *as*, for *who*, *which* or *that*.

4. *is quite sure,* with *you* as subject, and *I seasons em* – non-standard agreement of verb with subject.

5. *arter all* – spelling shows pronunciation.

6. *out o' anything* shows pronunciation, and many speakers when talking quickly and informally would reduce *of* in this way. But it *looks* non-standard, and writers often use this way of indicating a speaker from the lower social classes. It is sometimes referred to as **eye-dialect**. Compare the spelling of *What did he say?* and *Wot did 'e say?* Both sound the same in speech. Which one is the uneducated speaker?

7. *a squeezing, a pointin'* – a form of the **present participle** which still retains a **prefix** common in Middle English.

8. *this here agin* – *this here* is still a common spoken phrase in spoken English; *agin* is a marked Cockney pronunciation.

9. *seasonin', pointin', 'cordin'* – the common pronunciation of word-final /ɪŋ/, spelt <-ing>, as /ɪn/. The apostrophe doesn't in fact mark a lost <g>, because this isn't pronounced in most English dialects today (except for example in parts of Lancashire). Notice that Dickens doesn't systematically show this in Sam's speech.

10. *them noble animals* – *them* for standard demonstrative pronoun *those*.

The effect of this representation of Sam Weller's speech is to help us to tune in to his Cockney wit and humour. It becomes a part of Sam's character.

Activity 10.13

Apply the same principles of identification and description to the non-standard spellings in the following extracts. What do they suggest about the characters? The non-standard items are printed in bold type in the first extract, but not in the others.

1   'And you are a miner!' she exclaimed in surprise.
    'Yes. I went down when I was ten.'
    'When you were ten! And wasn't it very hard?' she asked.
    'You soon get used to it. You live like **th'** mice, **an'** you pop out
    at night to see what's going on.'   5
    'It makes me feel blind,' she frowned.
    'Like a **mouldiwarp**!' he laughed. '**Yi**, an' there's some chaps
    as does go round like mouldiwarps.' He thrust his face forward
    in the blind, snout-like way of a mole, seeming to sniff and peer
    for direction. 'They **dun** though!' he protested naively. '**Tha**   10
    niver seed such a way they get in. But **tha mun** let me **ta'e thee**
    down some time, **an'** tha can see for **thysen**.'
    She looked at him, startled.
    'Shoudn't **ter** like it?' he asked tenderly. ''**Appen** not, it '**ud**
    dirty **thee**.'   15
                                    (D. H. Lawrence, *Sons and Lovers*)

2   Urmilla hardly slept for thinking of what she was going to do.
    She got up determined and went to Rita.
    'Girl, I in big trouble. Big, big trouble. If you know what Tiger
    go and do! He go and invite two Americans he does work with to
    come for Indian food tonight!'   5
    'Is wat happen to him at all? He crack? He is ah dam fool in
    truth. He bringing wite people to eat in dat hut? Tiger must be
    really going out of he head, yes. Gul, yuh making joke!'
    'Man, Rita, I tell you is true! My head hot! I don't know what to
    do. Rita, you go have to help me, girl.'   10
    'But sure, man. Wat yuh want me to do?'
    'You have to lend me plenty thing. I want glass. Plate. Cup.
    Spoon. Knife. Fork. Tablecloth -'

'Take ease, keep cool! Between de two ah we we go fix up
everything good. Don't look so frighten. Why de hell yuh fraid   15
Tiger so? Allyuh Indian people have some funny ways, oui.
Well, look. You don't worry bout nutting. Ah go help you to do
everyting.'

(Samuel Selvon, *A Brighter Sun*)

3   It was the scrub that suggested to my mind the wisdom of
Mulvaney taking a day's leave and going upon a shooting-tour. ...
    'But fwhat manner uv use is ut to me goin' out widout a
dhrink? The ground's powdher-dhry underfoot, an' ut gets unto
the throat fit to kill,' wailed Mulvaney, looking at me reproach-   5
fully. ... Can a man run on wather - an' jungle-wather too?'
    Ortheris had considered the question in all its bearings. He
spoke, chewing his pipe-stem meditatively the while: 'You better
go. You ain't like to shoot yourself - not while there's a chanst of
liquor. Me an' Learoyd'll stay at 'ome an' keep shop - 'case o'   10
anythin' turnin' up. But you go out with a gas-pipe gun an' ketch
the little peacockses or somethin'. You kin get one day's leave
easy as winkin'. Go along an' get it, an' get peacockses or
somethin'.' ...
    And Mulvaney went; cursing his allies with Irish fluency and   15
barrack-room point.

(Rudyard Kipling, 'Krishna Mulvaney', from *Life's Handicap*)

4   Grace put the room a little in order, and approaching the sick
woman said -
    'I am come, Grammer, as you wish. Do let us send for the
doctor before it gets later?'
    ''Ch woll not have him!' said Grammer Oliver decisively.
    'Then somebody to sit up with you?'
    'Can't abear it! No. I wanted to see you, Miss Grace, because
'ch have something on my mind. Dear Miss Grace, *I took that
money of the doctor, after all!*'

(Thomas Hardy, *The Woodlanders*)

PART 2   NON-LITERARY WRITING

10.5   Literary and non-literary texts

There is no clear agreed distinction between what is and is not 'literature'. The older meaning of the word *literature* itself meant simply *a body of writing about a subject* like, for example, 'the literature of motor-car maintenance' or 'the literature of chess'. But its usual meaning today refers to writing 'which has claim to consideration on the ground of beauty of form or emotional effect' (*OED* definition), and in English Literature lessons this generally means novels, short stories, poetry and plays, with certain other writings like biography (e.g. Boswell's *Life of Dr Johnson*), letters, diaries, travel books and so on regarded as *literary* by general agreement.

In Part 1 of this chapter we have examined aspects of the style of texts that are accepted as literature, and have found a number of features that may help to define the quality of *literariness*. One of these, for example, was *parallelism*, but you may have noticed that this was also a feature of some of the language of political interviews (chapter 7) which would hardly be accepted as literature. The speaker in the interview was using features of language that we could call *literary,* but these features do not define the text as *literature.* The definition of what is or is not *literature* depends upon a subjective assessment of a text's quality – what has been called 'the common pursuit of true judgement' and the subject of literary criticism.

10.5.1   *Non-literary texts*

The division of writing into 'literary' and 'non-literary' texts is not, in fact, very helpful in the study of style, because the same principles of analysis are applied to all texts. More than that, the category 'non-literary' includes such an immense range of writing that simply to list all the varieties of English writing would be a daunting task, and not very useful either. What you need to learn is not what the characteristics of all the individual varieties of English writing are one by one, but how to apply your linguistic knowledge to any text that you want to examine. That is, your knowledge of **vocabulary**, **grammar** and **discourse** helps you to identify which features of the language are **foregrounded** in any particular text.

So we shall discuss just two examples of non-literary English – a written guarantee from a manufacturer, and the text of an advertisement.

A written guarantee

Activity 10.14 ───────────────────────────

Read the guarantee and describe those features of the language that identify the text as 'legal English'.

Part of a written guarantee

If within the applicable guarantee period the appliance proves to be defective by reason of faulty design, workmanship or materials, we undertake subject to the following conditions to have the defective appliance (or any part or parts thereof) repaired or replaced free of charge.

1　The appliance shall have been purchased and used solely within the EEC countries and used solely for domestic and normal purposes and in accordance with standard operating instructions and the technical and/or Safety Standards required in the country where this appliance is used. 　　　5

2　The purchaser shall within 7 days of purchase complete the attached card and send it to us for registration. Failure to return such card could result in delay in providing the guarantee service.

3　For appliances used in the U.K., Channel Islands, Isle of Man 　10 and Republic of Ireland, the appliance should be returned with this guarantee and proof of date of purchase promptly on being found defective at the purchaser's risk and expense to the authorized dealer from whom the appliance was purchased or to the nearest authorized dealer. All enquiries must be through such 　15 dealers.

4　This guarantee shall not apply to damage caused through fire, accident, misuse, wear and tear, neglect, incorrect adjustment, modification or use in an improper manner or inconsistent with the technical and/or safety standards required in the country 　20 where this appliance is used, or to damage occurring during transit to or from the purchaser.

Commentary

Actions/processes and nominalisation

The style is *formal* and *impersonal*. The vocabulary does not contain any words, however, that belong exclusively to the 'register' of legal language, except perhaps *thereof*. It is in the way the vocabulary is used that the main defining features of this use of language lie, that is, in the grammar.

It is noticeable that a relatively high proportion of the nouns are in fact names of **processes**, things that happen. If an event has happened, or taken place, this implies that someone (a **participant** in the process) has caused it to happen, and so the event/process might have been expressed as a **verb**. For example, using the first nouns on the following list, someone or something must have *guaranteed, designed, charged, purchased, registered, failed* and so on:

guarantee	service	repair
design	proof	installation
charge	enquiries	adaptation
purchase (2)	damage (3)	modification
registration	misuse	use
failure	neglect	transit
delay	adjustment	

This also applies to some of the adjectives, for example *the **following** conditions* might have been written as *the conditions which follow*:

applicable (period)	attached
following	operating

Processes, you will remember, are actions of some kind or another, and they have a different kind of meaning when they are expressed as nouns rather than as verbs. The linguistic term **nominalisation** is used for the process of forming nouns from verbs, turning an action into a 'thing', for example:

	Verb	⇒		*Noun*
seven days after you	**purchased** it	⇒	within seven days of	**purchase**

has already been referred to in section 9.1.2.

Many words have the same form whether used as nouns or verbs, e.g. *damage/to damage, repair/to repair, use/to use*. Others are formed by suffixes, e.g. *adjust/ adjustment, install/installation* and so on.

Modal verbs and passive voice

We find a fairly rare use of the modal verb *shall* in the verb phrase *shall have been purchased and used*, where we would probably write *should* or *must*, because it expresses an obligation, something that is necessary. *Shall* is much less commonly used than *will* in expressing both future time and intention (except perhaps with the first person *I* or *we* for some speakers), and so its use here in a legal context marks it as a feature of the style.

A similar use of modals is used in advertising professional jobs, for example,

The candidate **will have** a primary expertise in the area of English pre-1660 ...

which constrasts in the use of personal pronouns and choice of modal-verb, and therefore in the impression of formality with another which appeared on the same page of advertisements,

You **should** ideally **have** experience of both teaching and
managing programmes ...

Another marked feature of the text of the guarantee is the relative frequency of verbs in the **passive** with no *by*-phrase to specify the actor (see section 9.2.2 for further discussion):

undertake to have ... repaired or replaced	attached
shall have been purchased and used	should be returned
required	being found
is used (2)	was purchased
used	caused (2)

The effect of the frequency of nominalised processes and passive clauses in the text is to distance the manufacturers from the purchaser. The reader/purchaser is explicitly named three times, and only once as the subject of a verb, *The purchaser shall ... complete*. Naming the reader as *the purchaser* is a legal formality. She or he is obliquely referred to in the third person – *she/he shall ...* – not as *you*. The manufacturers are explicitly referred to once only, as *we*, although the actions of the manufacturers are certainly *implied* in the guarantee. The style of the text is therefore clearly impersonal. The manufacturers (or their legal advisers) could have written it differently.

Activity 10.15

Read the following re-written version of the guarantee, which attempts to reduce the frequency of nominalised processes (nouns used where verbs could be) and the use of the passive voice.
  Identify the changes, and comment on the contrasts in style of the two versions of the guarantee.

If within the period during which we apply the guarantee the appliance proves to be defective because we have designed or made it faultily, or used faulty materials, we undertake to repair or replace the defective appliance, subject to the conditions which follow. We shall not charge you for this.

1   You must have purchased and used the appliance solely within the EEC countries, and used it solely for domestic and normal purposes and you must have followed the standard instructions for operating it and the technical and/or Safety Standards which the country in which you use the appliance   5 requires.

2   The purchaser shall within 7 days of having purchased the appliance complete the card which we have attached and send it to us so that we can register it. If you fail to return the card, we may have to delay serving you in providing the guarantee.   10

3   If you use the appliance in the UK, Channel Islands, Isle of Man or Republic of Ireland, you should return it promptly with this guarantee and evidence which proves when you purchased it, after you have found it defective, at your own risk and expanse, to the dealer whom we have authorised and from whom   15 you purchased the appliance. If you wish to enquire about this, you must do so through such dealers.

4   This guarantee shall not apply if fire or accident have damaged the appliance, or if you have misused, neglected, or incorrectly adjusted or repaired it, or used it for so long that you   20 have worn it out, or if you damaged it when you were installing, adapting, modifying or using it in an improper manner or inconsistent with the technical and/or safety standards which the country where you use the appliance requires, or if somone damages it when they are transporting it from the purchaser.   25

The text of an advertisement

The overall effect of press advertisements depends as much on the design layout, including graphics, different printing fonts and pictures, as on the text. This is, however, more the subject of media and communication studies than of language study, so we will confine our discussion to the written text of an advertisement published in March 1992, which is typical in its style of many others. It was a full-page advertisement; the text appeared beneath a large photograph of a motor car.

Activity 10.16

Read and discuss the advertisement, pointing out those features of language that mark its style. Look at (i) the punctuation and paragraphing in relation to the grammar and topics, (ii) its imaginary context of situation, with an implied speaker/writer and listener/reader.
Do you think that this an effective way of advertising?

One thing Europe seems to agree about

From Strasbourg to Brussels, London to Paris, Madrid to Rome, it was all smiles, hand-shakes, pleasantries all round.

The reason for this communal chuminess?

Our new Golf.

Fifty-nine top motoring writers from eighteen European countries had just voted it Car of the Year. A welcome win, for sure. Though, to be frank, not entirely unexpected.

It just goes to show that everything comes to he who improves. And improves.

And anticipates.

Already, our new Golf is designed to meet ever-tougher safety standards set for 1994.

Already, over 80% of its parts are re-cyclable.

Already, exhaust catalysers are standard across the range.

All good stuff. But what about performance? Any torquier? Mais oui.

The drag factor. Any lower? Natürlich.

The handling. Any sharper? Certo.

And the fuel consumption. Still generous? What, more generous? Claro que si.

As many a European knows, such things are common currency with every new Volkswagen.

(NB   The spelling *chuminess* and the construction *everything comes to he who improves* are in the printed text, but neither form would probably be accepted as good English. Can you explain why?)

Commentary

Punctuation, paragraphing and grammar
The text breaks several rules of writing that you will have been taught as part of 'good English'.

● **Sentences** as units of grammar belong to written English, marked with capital letters and a full stops. We have seen in chapter 5 that written sentences do not necessarily coincide with spoken tone units, and there is no spoken equivalent of a capital letter.
● **Paragraphs** similarly belong to written English, and mark changes or developments of the topic of writing.

The text is clearly divided into written sentences marked with capitals and full stops, but some of these sentences do not contain a full complement of elements which, we have been taught, make up a 'complete sentence'. They can easily be 'corrected' by changing the punctuation, or by adding some deleted words, for example,

Adding deleted elements:

S	P	C
What	**was**	the reason for this communal chuminess?
It	**was**	our new Golf

Changing the punctuation:

It just goes to show that everything comes to he who improves, and improves, and anticipates.

There are fourteen paragraphs marked by indentation, but some of them contain only two or three words,

Our new Golf.
And anticipates.

The stylistic effect of this deviant method of punctuating and paragraphing is to convey the impression of *spoken* rather than written language, because the 'sentences' in fact correspond to the tone units of a spoken reading of the text. You could test this by reading it aloud. This special use of punctuation/paragraphing is confirmed by the other features of the text which mark it as intending to convey the impression of a spoken *discourse*.

Discourse

There are several questions which imply that a speaker is responding to a person listening and actually asking them, e.g. *Any torquier? Any lower? Still generous?* The sentence *What, more generous?* seems to imply that the listener has commented on the imagined reply to *Still generous?*

Vocabulary

The vocabulary belongs to the ordinary informal talk of car enthusiasts, so the technical terms *torquier, handling, drag factor, exhaust catalysers* are not out of place.

The replies in French *(oui)*, German *(Natürlich)*, Italian *(Certo)* and Spanish *(Claro que si)*, reinforce the theme of *Europe* and the *Common Market* which runs through the text, including the names of EC capital cities and the puns on *communal* and *common currency*.

Rhetoric

You will have noticed the *parallelism* in the text:

Already,	our new Golf ...
Already,	over 80% of its parts ...
Already,	exhaust catalysers ...

	Noun phrase	*question*	*response*
But what about	... performance	Any torquier?	Mais oui
	The drag factor	Any lower?	Natürlich
	The handling	Any sharper	Certo
And	the fuel consumption	Still generous?	
What,		more generous?	Claro que si.

This is another example of qualities of *literariness* which can be found in a variety of texts that do not belong to the category of English literature.

Activity 10.17 ——————————————————————

(i) Rewrite the text of the advertisement
   (a) with conventional punctuation and paragraphing;
   (b) as a dialogue between two speakers.
(ii) Discuss the stylistic effects of the different versions of the text.
(iii) Look for advertisements in a variety of newspapers and analyse their
   written texts for evidence of similar styles of writing.

Here is the original text of the extract from Laurie Lee's *Cider with Rosie* discussed
in section 10.3.2. The noun modifiers which were omitted are printed in capitals:

The sons of John Light, the five Light brothers, illuminated
many a local myth, were admired for their wildness, their force
of arms, and for their LEISURELY, BOASTING wit. 'We come from
the oldest family in the world. We're in the Book of Genesis.
The Almighty said, "Let there be Light" – and that was long   5
before Adam...'

My first encounter with Uncle Ray – prospector, dynamiter,
buffalo-fighter, and builder of TRANSCONTINENTAL railways – was
an occasion of MEMORABLE suddenness. One moment he was a
legend at the other end of the world, the next he was in my bed.   10
Accustomed only to the SATINY bodies of my younger brothers
and sisters, I awoke one morning to find snoring beside me a
huge and SCALY man. I touched the THICK legs and KNOTTED arms
and pondered the barbs of his chin, felt the CROCODILE flesh of
this MAGNIFICENT creature, and wondered what it could be.   15

'It's your Uncle Ray come home,' whispered Mother. 'Get up
now and let him sleep.'

I saw a RUST-brown face, a GAUNT INDIAN nose, and smelt a
reek of cigars and train-oil. Here was the hero of our school-
BOASTING days, and to look on him was no disappointment. He   20
was shiny as iron, worn as a rock, and lay like a chieftain
sleeping. He'd come home on a visit from building his railways,
loaded with money and thirst, and the days he spent at our house
that time were full of wonder and conflagration.

For one thing he was unlike any other man we'd ever seen –   25
or heard of, if it comes to that. With his leather-beaten face, wide
TEETH-CRAMMED mouth, and FAR-SEEING ICE-blue eyes, he looked
like some WIGWAM warrior stained with suns and HEROIC
slaughter. He spoke the CANADIAN dialect of the railway camps
in a drawl through his RESONANT nose. His body was tattooed in   30
every quarter – ships in full sail, flags of all nations, reptiles, and
ROUND-EYED maidens. By CUNNING flexings of his MUSCLED flesh
he could sail those ships, wave the flags in the wind, and coil
snakes round the QUIVERING girls.

11. The language and sound patterns of verse

11.1 Rhythm and stress in speech

11.1.1 *Syllable and stress*

The rhythm of ordinary English speech derives from the patterns of stress in words and utterances. It is generally agreed that the stressed syllables in speech tend to occur at roughly regular intervals – the technical term is **isochrony** – especially in deliberate speech, for example (–s = unstressed syllable; +s = stressed syllable):

–s	+s	+s	–s	+s	–s	–s	+s	–s	–s	–s	+s
I	*told*	*John*	I	*was*	n't	a-	*ware*	of	all	the	*facts*
	1	2		3			4				5

This sentence can be spoken so that the stresses are equally spaced in time. The number of unstressed syllables between them does not matter – you can have none (between 1 and 2), one (between 2 and 3), two (between 3 and 4), or three (between 4 and 5). More than three tends to be unusual, but theoretically, any number is possible.

Activity 11.1 —————————————————————

Test out this theory of isochronous (equally spaced) stress by making up some short sentences, or taking some from a book, and reading them aloud. Mark the stressed syllables prominently, and note the number of unstressed syllables between them.
Can you easily speak three or more unstressed syllables between the stresses?

11.1.2 *The foot*

The stretch of sound from one stress up to, but not including, the next stress, has been called a **foot**:

|^I	|told	|John	I	|wasn't a-	|ware of all the	|facts
	1		2		3			4		5		6

This sentence has six feet. Because a foot begins with a stress, we have to think of some stresses as having no sound and refer to a **silent stress** in the first foot of the sentence, marked with ^.

Some linguists, however, do not accept the need for the concept of a foot in the spoken language, nor in the **scansion** of verse. But it is briefly mentioned because you may come across the term or want to use it.

11.2 Metre

The basis of the patterns of verse is a 'heightening' of this tendency towards a regular succession of stressed syllables, or stress-timed rhythm, which is called **metre**. The regularity of stress is **foregrounded**. Verse is usually metrical in its structure. (If its rhythm is not regular, it is called 'free verse'.)

It is useful to distinguish between the stress-patterns of ordinary speech and poetic metre by using the terms **beats** (B) and **off-beats** (o) when discussing the metre of verse, and the terms **stressed** (+s) and **unstressed** (–s) when describing syllables in speech. English metrical verse can therefore be analysed as consisting of alternate beats and off-beats. (This terminology is taken from D. Attridge, *The Rhythms of English Poetry*, 1983.)

So the rhythm of verse is a kind of **counterpoint** between the regular pattern of beats and off-beats (metre) underlying the natural pattern of stressed and unstressed syllables of the spoken language. The clash between the two often has an important effect on the rhythm and meaning. Sometimes unstressed syllables have to be **promoted** to metrical beats, or stresssed syllables **demoted** to off-beats. A metrical off-beat can consist of one, two or three unstressed syllables, called **single off-beats** (o), **double off-beats** (ŏ) and **triple off-beats** (ŏ), just as there are a variable number of unstressed syllables between the stresses in ordinary speech.

The pleasure that children get from traditional nursery rhymes is very largely derived from the rhythms, together with rhyme and the other patterns of sound which will be discussed later. Look at the example of 'Three Blind Mice' (x = unstressed syllable; ^ = silent stress; stressed syllables are in bold type):

	Three	x	x	**blind**	x	x	**mice**	x	x	^	x	x
	See	x	x	**how**	x	they	**run**	x	x	^	x	
They	**all**	x	ran	**af-**	ter	the	**far-**	x	mer's	**wife**	x	
Who	**cut**	off	their	**tails**	with	a	**car-**	x	ving	**knife**	x	
Did	**e-**	ver	you	**see**	such	a	**thing**	in	your	**life**	x	
As	**three**	x	x	**blind**	x	x	**mice**	x	x	^	x	x
metre:	**B**	ŏ		**B**	ŏ		**B**	ŏ		**B**	ŏ	

There are four beats to a line. The metre is **triple**, with a double off-beat (= two unstressed syllables) between each beat, but the first two lines have only three syllables each, so you have to stretch them to cover the rhythmic space of nine syllables altogether – three stressed and six unstressed, and then pause for the silent beat and double off-beat. Silent beats and off-beats are as important as the spoken ones in metrical verse.

Activity 11.2

Many nursery rhymes have triple rhythms. Match the syllable and stress patterns of the following rhymes to their underlying metre of off-beats.

> There was an old woman who lived in a shoe,
> She had so many children she didn't know what to do
> She gave them some broth without any bread;
> She whipped them all soundly and put them to bed.
>
> (*How can you fit* didn't know what to do *into the metre?*)
>
> Little Bo-peep has lost her sheep,
> And can't tell where to find them;
> Leave them alone and they'll come home,
> Bringing their tails behind them

Other rhymes have **duple rhythm**, that is, there is a single off-beat between each beat. Here is one that is completely regular:

I	do	not	love	thee	Doc-	tor	Fell,
o	**B**	o	**B**	o	**B**	o	**B**
The	**rea-**	son	**why**	I	**can-**	not	**tell,**
o	**B**	o	**B**	o	**B**	o	**B**
But	**this**	I	**know,**	I	**know**	full	**well,**
o	**B**	o	**B**	o	**B**	o	**B**
I	**do**	not	**love**	thee	**Doc-**	tor	**Fell.**
o	**B**	o	**B**	o	**B**	o	**B**

Because the rhythm of the lines in 'Doctor Fell' moves regularly from an off-beat to a beat, it is called a **rising rhythm**. Conversely, a rhythm regularly beginning with a beat and moving to the off-beat is called a **falling rhythm**, as in,

	Doc-	tor	**Bell**	fell	**down**	the	**well**	(And)
	B	o	**B**	o	**B**	o	**B**	(o)
And	**broke**	his	**col-**	lar	**bone.**			
o	**B**	o	**B**	o	**B**	[o	**B**	o]
	Doc-	tors	**should**	at-	**tend**	the	**sick**	(And)
	B	o	**B**	o	**B**	o	**B**	(o)
And	**leave**	the	**well**	a-	**lone.**			
o	**B**	o	**B**	o	**B**	[o	**B**	o]

It is important to establish the metre of a poem, because part of its meaning, and a great deal of the pleasure it gives, lie in the rhythm.

Activity 11.3

Read these two sentences aloud, and say where the main stresses fall.
(i)   Here was the former door where the dead feet walked in.
(ii)   She sat here in her chair, smiling into the fire.

Commentary

There is no one right way of reading them, but if the sentences are read in the rhythm of ordinary speech, do you agree that in (i) the main stresses will fall on *door*, *feet* and *walked*, (with secondary stress on *former* and *dead*), and that in (ii) the main stresses are on *sat, chair, smiling* and *fire*?

Activity 11.4

Now read the same sentences in the context of Thomas Hardy's poem 'The Self-Unseeing'. Establish the metrical pattern from the third stanza, which is quite regular, and then apply the same pattern to the first two stanzas.
Does it make you read the two sentences already discussed in a different way?
What contribution to the meaning of the poem does this revised reading make?

Here is the ancient floor,
Footworn and hollow and thin,
Here was the former door
Where the dead feet walked in.

She sat here in her chair,
Smiling into the fire;
He who played stood there,
Bowing it higher and higher.

Childlike I danced in a dream;
Blessings emblazoned that day;
Everything glowed with a gleam;
Yet we were looking away!

Commentary

The underlying metre is a four-line stanza, each line having three beats plus a silent stress, or unrealised beat at the end of each line, in falling rhythm. In stanza 3 the rhythm is always triple (/xx, or B ǒ), but it varies between duple and triple in the other two.

Read in this metre, the two sentences that were read in normal speech rhythms in Activity 11.3 scan like this:

Here	was the	**for-**	mer	**door**			
B	ǒ	**B**	o	**B**	[o	**B**	o]
Where	the dead	**feet**	walked	**in**			
B	ǒ	**B**	o	**B**	[o	**B**	o]

which is possibly acceptable. But it is very common in English verse to have two beats together, preceded by a double off-beat, and with an implied or silent off-beat (ǒ) between them:

Where the	**dead**	**feet**	walked	**in**			
ǒ	**B**	ô **B**	o	**B**	[o	**B**	o]

Similarly, you can read the second line in the regular scansion,

She	sat	**here**	in her	**chair**			
B	o	**B**	ð	**B**	[o	**B**	o]

or

She	sat	**here**	in her	**chair**			
o	**B**	ô **B**	ð	**B**	[o	**B**	o]

It seems more important to stress *she*, in reference to the dead woman, than to the less interesting fact that she *sat*. Here the underlying metre supplies the right reading.

There is much more to be said about the rhythm of English verse, but this brief outline should help to draw your attention to the importance of establishing a reading that agrees with Hardy's setting out of his verse.

11.3   The line in verse

The line is part of the grammar of verse. It establishes a way of hearing the rhythm that has no equivalent in prose, and affects the meaning also by focusing attention on particular words.

Activity 11.5 ⎯⎯⎯⎯⎯⎯⎯⎯⎯⎯⎯⎯⎯⎯⎯⎯⎯⎯⎯⎯⎯⎯⎯

Read the following short prose texts aloud, and establish a natural speech rhythm which seems best to fit them.

(i) And in the frosty season, when the sun was set, and visible for many a mile the cottage windows through the twilight blazed, I heeded not the summons – happy time it was, indeed, for all of us; to me it was a time of rapture.

(ii) As the cat climbed over the top of the jamcloset, first the right forefoot, carefully, then the hind stepped down into the pit of the empty flowerpot.

(iii) A snake came to my water-trough on a hot, hot day, and I in pyjamas for the heat, to drink there. In the deep, strange-scented shade of the great dark carob-tree I came down the steps with my pitcher and must wait, must stand and wait, for there he was at the trough before me.

(iv) Cut grass lies frail: brief is the breath mown stalks exhale. Long, long the death it dies in the white hours of young-leafed June with chestnut flowers, with hedges snowlike strewn, white lilac bowed, lost lanes of Queen Anne's lace, and that high-builded cloud moving at summer's pace.

Activity 11.6

(i) All four texts of Activity 11.5 are in fact poems, or parts of poems, printed as prose. Write them out as verse, using other linguistic features associated with verse, as well as rhythm and metre, to establish the lines. Texts (ii) and (iv) also have a stanza pattern.

(ii) Discuss any difficulties you have in establishing a pattern of lines and stanzas in each poem.

Commentary

Text (i) is from 'The Prelude', by William Wordsworth:

> And in the frosty season, when the sun
> Was set, and visible for many a mile
> The cottage windows through the twilight blazed,
> I heeded not the summons – happy time
> It was, indeed, for all of us; to me
> It was a time of rapture.

If you read the prose version of these lines, you will notice that it consists of a regular alternation of unstressed and stressed syllables:

> And |in the |frosty |season, |when the |sun was |set, and |visi|ble for |many a |mile the |cottage |windows |through the |twilight |blazed ... etc.

so that it already reads very much like rhythmically patterned verse. When it is printed in lines of verse, we recognise a ten-syllable line of alternate off-beats and beats:

> And in the frosty season, when the sun
>   o B o   B o B o   B   o B
> Was set, and visible for many a mile
>   o B   o B o B o   B o B
> The cottage windows through the twilight blazed
>   o B o   B o   B   o B o B

which are not rhymed. This pattern is known as *blank verse*, and the line has traditionally been called *iambic pentameter* (cf. section 11.1.2 on the *foot*, and section 11.5 on the *iambic pentameter*).

The difference between the prose and verse versions is marked by the more certain rhythmic regularity of the verse, and the lengthening of the final syllables of each line – *sun, mile, blazed, time* and *me*, because four of the lines are 'run-on' – that is, they end without punctuation in the middle of a clause (also called *enjambement*):

when the sun / was set	visible for many a mile / the cottage windows
happy time / it was,	to me / it was a time of rapture

and the slight pause and/or lengthening at the end of these lines is what distinguishes them from a prose reading.

Text (ii) is a poem by the American William Carlos Williams, and called simply 'Poem':

> As the cat
> climbed over
> the top of
>
> the jamcloset
> first the right
> forefoot
>
> carefully
> then the hind
> stepped down
>
> into the pit of
> the empty
> flowerpot

The punctuation lies wholly in the visual display of four three line stanzas. Williams breaks syntactic units to create his brief lines. In *into the pit of / the empty / flowerpot* the break comes between the preposition and noun phrase of a prepositional phrase, and between the adjective and noun of a noun phrase. There is no rhyme, assonance or other traditional poetic devices of language. He does not observe the convention of beginning each line with a capital letter. It is a moment of precise observation captured and then communicated through the matching precision required to read the poem line by line. We *read* it as a poem.

Text (iii) is the opening of D. H. Lawrence's 'Snake'. It is **free verse** and close to normal speech in its rhythm. It is doubtful if you can re-create Lawrence's own presentation, because it is non-metrical, like the Williams poem:

> A snake came to my water-trough
> On a hot, hot day, and I in pyjamas for the heat,
> To drink there.
> In the deep, strange-scented shade of the great dark carob-tree
> I came down the steps with my pitcher
> And must wait, must stand and wait, for there he was at the trough before me.

Lawrence's lines vary in length, and create an impression of the spoken voice, although there are other features which would seem less usual in prose – *a hot, hot day, I in pyjamas*, and the repetition of *must stand and wait*. The line between poetry and prose is not clear. We speak of 'poetic prose' when prose takes on rhythms or other figures and patterns which are more often associated with poetry.

Text (iv) is a Philip Larkin poem, 'Cut Grass', and the rhyme should have made it easy to find the metrical pattern of four four-line stanzas. The rhythm is subtly varied, and has an underlying falling triple rhythm with two beats in the line:

> Cut grass lies frail:
> Brief is the breath
> Mown stalks exhale.
> Long, long the death

It dies in the white hours
Of young-leafed June
With chestnut flowers,
With hedges snowlike strewn,

White lilac bowed,
Lost lanes of Queen Anne's lace,
And that high-builded cloud
Moving at summer's pace.

Notice that the stanzas are not complete grammatical units, so that there is a tension between metrical pattern and syntactic meaning.

11.4 Grammatical deviance in verse

The phrase **poetic licence** refers to the expectation that poets and writers take liberties with language and meaning in creating literature. This is also called **deviance**, and examples can be found in poets' use of language at all its levels – sound, vocabulary, grammar and meaning. The nineteenth-century poet Gerard Manley Hopkins said that poetic language should be 'the current language **heightened**', and the word *foregrounding* has already been used to refer to this feature of the literary use of language.

One example of grammatical deviance in verse that is very common is a rearrangement of the 'unmarked' order of the elements in a clause (SPOA, subject, followed by predicator, followed by object, followed by adverbial.) Similarly in a sentence the unmarked order is main clause followed by subordinate clause.

Activity 11.7

A. E. Housman's poem 'On Wenlock Edge' is printed below with the syntax rearranged to show clause and sentence structure in unmarked order.
(i)   Write out the poem as you think Housman wrote it. The rhyme pattern in each stanza is *abab*. Each line has four beats, in a rising duple rhythm.
(ii)   All the words of the original poem are in the rewritten version. What has happened to Housman's poem in the process of rewriting?

The wood's in trouble on Wenlock Edge;
    The Wrekin heaves his forest fleece;
The gale, it plies the saplings double,
    And the leaves snow thick on Severn.

'Twould blow like this through holt and hanger
    When the city Uricon stood:
'Tis the old wind in the old anger,
    But then it threshed another wood.

The Roman would stare at yonder heaving hill
    Then, 'twas before my time:
The blood that warms an English yeoman,
    The thoughts that hurt him, they were there.

The gale of life blew high through him
   There, like the wind through woods in riot;
The tree of man was never quiet:
   'Twas the Roman then, now 'tis I.

The gale, it plies the saplings double,
   It blows so hard, 'twill be gone soon:
The Roman and his trouble are
   Ashes under Uricon today.

11.5   Patterns of rhythm and sound in verse

The metre of a line of a traditional **sonnet** – a poem of fourteen lines – is commonly known as the **iambic pentameter**. The term *iambic* comes from the word *iambos* (shortened to *iamb* in English), which was the name in classical Greek verse for a foot consisting of one short syllable ($\cup$) followed by one long syllable (–): $\cup$ – .

In describing English verse, the term *iambic* has been used for a foot containing one *unstressed* syllable followed by one *stressed* syllable, x / (a stressed syllable is not the same as a long syllable).

The term *pentameter* means *five feet*, so *iambic pentameter* in English verse means a line of five iambs, that is, ten syllables of alternate unstressed and stressed syllables, which is the metre of thousands of lines of verse, including Shakespeare's and Milton's, sometimes without rhyme (**blank verse**) and sometimes with rhyme, typically in **couplets**.

   x / l x / l x / l x / l x /

In the terminology used in this chapter, an iambic pentameter line is in a **rising duple rhythm** (x /), of five beats to a line.

   o B l o B l o B l o B l o B

Here are some examples from English poets:

O how shall summer's honey breath hold out
Against the wreckful siege of battering days?
(Sonnet LXV, William Shakespeare, 1564–1616)

Avenge O Lord thy slaughtered saints, whose bones
Lie scattered on the Alpine mountains cold:
('On the late Massacre in Piedmont', John Milton, 1608–74)

When midnight comes a host of boys and men
Go out and track the badger to his den,
And put a sack within the hole, and lie
Till the old grunting badger passes by.
('Badger', John Clare, 1793–1864)

Season of mists and mellow fruitfulness,
   Close bosom-friend of the maturing sun;
Conspiring with him how to load and bless
   With fruit the vines that round the thatch-eaves run;
('To Autumn', John Keats, 1795–1821)

It little profits that an idle king,
By this still hearth, among these barren crags,
Matched with an agéd wife, I mete and dole
Unequal laws unto a savage race ...
('Ulysses', Alfred Tennyson, 1809–92)

Pleasure in the rhythms of verse is inseparable from pleasure in the sounds (the patterning of vowels and consonants) and the fusion of sound, rhythm and meaning is a mark of poetry. The poetry of Gerard Manley Hopkins (1844–89) is an outstanding example of this fusion. His sonnet 'God's Grandeur' is typical in its complexity of patterning. Here are the first four lines:

The world is charged with the grandeur of God.
It will flame out, like shining from shook foil;
It gathers to a greatness, like the ooze of oil
Crushed. Why do men then now not reck his rod?

Activity 11.8

The poem is written in what Hopkins called 'standard rhythm', that is, iambic pentameter (five-beat rising duple rhythm). Use this knowledge to establish the rhythmic pattern, and therefore the *five* words given meaningful prominence in each line, and read the poem aloud. You will find that lines 1 and 4 especially will read differently from normal speech.

Commentary

We know from Hopkins's letters that he wanted the first line to be read with five stresses, on *world, charged, with,* the first syllable of *grandeur,* and *God*, so although in normal speech the line would be pronounced as a four-beat line with four stresses,

The	**world**	is	**charged**	with the	**gran-**	deur of	**God**
o	**B**	o	**B**	ŏ	**B**	ŏ	**B**

we have to read it as a five-beat line:

The	**world**	is	**charged**	**with**	the	**gran-**	deur of	**God.**
o	**B**	o	**B**	ô**B**	o	**B**	ŏ	**B**
It will	**flame**		**out,**	like	**shin-**	ing from	**shook**	**foil;**
ŏ	**B**	ô	**B**	o	**B**	ŏ	**B**	ô**B**
It	**gathers to a**		**great-**	ness,	**like**	the	**ooze** of **oil**
o	**B**	ŏ	**B**	o	**B**	o	**B**	o**B**
	Crushed Why do **men**			then	**now**	not	**reck** his **rod**
ô	**B**	ŏ	**B**	o	**B**	o	**B**	o**B**

Notice how the underlying five-beat rhythm makes you stress *with* in line 1, *out* in line 2, and *like* in line 3, which you would not do if the lines were read as prose, or as four-beat lines. It affects the meaning by focusing attention on these words.

The repetition of the same or similar sounds in words leads to a 'partial correspondence' between them, or **parallelism**. Here are some examples from other Hopkins poems:

rhyme	cow - plough, things - wings	
alliteration	glory - God, asunder - starlight	*(initial consonants)*
	in - ecstasy	*(initial vowels)*
assonance	caught - morning	*(medial vowels)*
pararhyme	fickle - freckle	*(initial and final consonants)*
consonance	rose - moles	*(final consonants)*

These patterns usually apply to the stressed syllables of a line, or adjacent lines, and the sounds must be fairly close together to be effective. Notice that there can be alliteration and consonance between medial consonants of words, that is, consonants beginning or ending syllables within a word, e.g. *mystery – stressed.*

Activity 11.9

What patterns of sound are there in the four lines of 'God's Grandeur'?

Commentary

The sound pattern is complex, and includes:

rhyme	*alliteration*	*assonance*	*consonance*
God – rod	world – with	men – reck	world – charged – God
foil – oil	grandeur – God	shining – like	
men – then	flame – foil		
	shining from – shook foil		
	gathers – greatness		
	ooze – oil		
	reck – rod		

If you think that this is too ingenious, remember that you must *hear* the counterpoint of sounds, and not just look for them on the page. Hopkins deliberately created these patterns, and said,

> Poetry is speech framed for the contemplation of the mind by the way of hearing, or speech framed to be heard *for its own sake* and interest over and above its interest of meaning.

Activity 11.10

Look for the patterns of rhythm and sound in this extract from Hopkins's poem 'The Wreck of the Deutschland':

> Oh,
> We lash with the best or worst
> Word last! How a lush-kept plush-capped sloe
> Will, mouthed to flesh-burst,
> Gush! – flush the man, the being with it, sour or sweet
> Brim, in a flash, full!

12. Language and 'politically correct' usage

A new term to describe an alleged type of social behaviour and its accompanying use of language came into prominence in the late 1980s – *politically correct*. The 'correctness' of *politically correct language* implied in the use of the term is different from the meaning of 'correct English' discussed in chapter 1. It arose in advocating and presenting the ideas of **feminism** and **anti-racism** in particular and is inseparable from the political and social changes that feminists and anti-racists seek to bring about. It is therefore a very controversial term, and there is no objective way of assessing the meaning and effects of using or not using 'politically correct language' which would be acceptable to both sides in a dispute. Consequently, this chapter is different from the others in the book, because we cannot bring arguments from linguistic description to assess the truth of what is claimed to be 'politically correct' or otherwise.

The reasoning that advocates the use of politically correct language is, however, similar to that which has been implied in several chapters of this book – that the language we use defines our attitude to what we are describing, whether consciously or not. The chapter will present a variety of data for your own reading and discussion.

12.1 Language used to describe people with disabilities

The title of this section is itself an example of the use of politically correct language. According to those who work with disabled people, it would have been unacceptable to have called the section 'Language used to describe the disabled'.

Activity 12.1

Before you go on to read more of the chapter, can you suggest why it is thought to be more acceptable to use the terms *people with disabilities,* or *disabled people* rather than *the disabled*?

In December 1991 the following opening paragraph was published in a daily newspaper:

> National newspapers are presenting a partial and distorted view of people with disabilities and those who care for them, sometimes breaching the Press Complaints Commission's guidance on discrimination, according to a report published yesterday by the Spastics Society.

The report was *What the Papers Say and Don't Say about Disability*, by Steve Smith and Antoinette Jordan, who summed up their main concern in this way:

> ... if subject matter is over simplified, whether it is the intention of journalists or not, disabled people and carers will be stereotyped and portrayed in a detrimental way.

Two areas of concern are discussed in the report, (1) the 'subject agenda', or type of stories published in the press, and (2) the language or style of the papers:

> Our study showed that:–
> (1) newspapers only focus on a limited number of issues relating to disability. ...
> (2) much of the language used by newspapers is both 'pejorative' and 'prejudicial'.

Their advice to journalists, so that pejorative and prejudicial language is avoided, is summarised as follows:

> ***Don't generalise:*** –
> Of course, groups by definition have a common identity, but too often this is presented and described in an oversimplified way. For example, referring to people with disabilities as 'the disabled' or 'the handicapped' implies that there only exists one homogeneous group 'without particulars or exceptions'. The same happens when someone is called 'a spastic', 'an amputee' or 'an epileptic' etc., which has the effect of reducing the person to a medical condition.
>
> Generalisations are also made when particular life experiences are attributed to all disabled people. A common example is when people with disabilities are depicted as 'victims' or as 'suffering' from their disability. Many disabled people do not suffer from their disability, and object to being portrayed as victims. ... Individuals are treated according to these particular labels or stereotypes.
>
> ***Don't patronise:*** –
> For example, using a person's first name, whilst sometimes is a sign of intimacy, at other times is condescending, particularly when an adult is addressed in this way.

Don't marginalise:–

Disabled people are marginalised in numerous ways through the use of language. Perhaps the most blatant form of this is when different types of disability are used as insults. Expressions like 'blind stupidity', 'lame duck', 'crippled' amd 'spastic' to name but a few, are all common terms of abuse.

Disability becomes inextricably liked with the 'abnormal', which inevitably alienates and excludes. Other words with similar connotations include, 'deformed', 'defective', and 'afflicted'. As a result, people with disabilities ... are effectively reduced to a 'medical problem'.

Activity 12.2

(i) Discuss your response to the advice.
(ii) Suggest other kinds of generalisation and stereotyping which commonly occur.
(iii) How does the way we address people show our attitude to them? (e.g. using first name, surname, first name + surname, Mr/Mrs/ Miss/Ms, etc.)
(iv) Discuss some other terms for disabilities which are used as insults.

The authors provide examples of language which is **pejorative** (i.e. which depreciates or lowers the value of someone or something):

> One article/picture caption told the story of a disabled child's experience of swimming with a dolphin.

> *This little boy's dance with a dolphin is giving him more than just a few moments of joy – it is teaching him to speak.*

The image is created of a pathetic disabled child with *walls of isolation built around him*. The disability is autism which may especially encourage this kind of portrayal. The child's experience is shrouded in mystery, which marginalises disabled people.

Other articles, however, fell into the familiar 'language trap' of depicting disabled people solely as unfortunate *victims*. For example, one quality (i.e. broadsheet) item had a large picture of a small child with a very sad looking face, behind a shelf full of pills. The caption added to the melodrama,

> *Victim of care (L...C...) lost her Attendance Allowance even though her cystic fibrosis is incurable.*

One of the most notable features regarding this subject (Medical/ Scientific Research) was the use of language. Headlines were often very dramatic, and tended to categorise disabled people as *victims* waiting and hoping for miracle *cures*. For example, a Quality item was headlined,

> *Injection brings hope to dwarfs.*

The article began with,

> *Dwarfs could become a rare sight because of the successful*
> *development of a biosynthetic growth hormone.*

Distinctions were made between *normal people* and *dwarfs*. *Past studies* were said to have found that *dwarfs often lead sad and lonely lives. Few marry, and even fewer have children.* ... This presentation equates so-called 'normality' with marriage and having a family, and then assumes that this necessarily leads to happiness. In short, the journalist is falsely implying that being able-bodied encompasses the desirable and ideal, whilst having a disability will tend to lead to a life that is less fulfilled and happy.

The other main story, relating to the cuts in grants for braille services, was treated much more melodramatically, particularly in the tabloids. For example, one caption read

> *Blind kiddies suffer*

and before exploring some of the political issues behind the story, started the article by giving an account of how a child's

> *face lit up with delight, as his fingers skipped nimbly across*
> *the pages of a colourful children's book.*

This style of journalism is blatantly designed to provoke the readers' sympathy, again at the expense of portraying the child as a pathetic victim. Ultimately, the notion that a disabled child has a right to these services, regardless of whether the public feels sympathy or not, is undermined.

Final comment

Depicting disability as a medical or individual 'problem' is an incomplete way of understanding issues that relate to people with disabilities. Images will be negative and detrimental, as any so-called 'imperfection' necessarily tends to be identified with the disabled person. In turn, discrimination is more easily justified because it is the disabled person who is expected to 'fit in', putting the onus of change on the individual and not the wider society.

> *The Spastics Society, therefore, invite the press to challenge*
> *their own misconceptions, and to fundamentally change*
> *professional practice. Journalists must start from the*
> *assumption that it is not a person's disability which is the*
> *problem, but the way society, including the press industry,*
> *treats disabled people.*

Only a month later, in January 1992, there was a news report on 'a new strain of politically and socially correct words and phrases' contained in a publication on the same subject from another source:

> The Employers' Forum on Disability booklet *Disability Etiquette* aims at removing small details of language and behaviour which may seem insignificant but which can reaffirm inaccurate assumptions and cause unnecessary offence. ...
>
> The word *handicapped* should not be used because it carries connotations of *cap in hand*.

If you look up the meaning of *handicap* in the *OED*, you will find that originally it meant

> a kind of sport having an element of chance in it, in which one person challenges some article belonging to another, for which he offered something of his own in exchange. On the challenge being entertained, an umpire was chosen, and all three parties deposited forfeit-money in a cap or hat.

The word was then extended to horse-racing and other sports, but the meaning 'suffering from a mental or physical disability' is not recorded in the first edition of the *OED* (completed in 1928). The second edition published in 1991 records,

> **handicapped**, of persons, esp. children, physically or mentally defective

as being first used in 1915. The origin of the word, therefore, is from *hand in the cap*, pronounced *hand i' cap*. But neither in its original or later meanings does it have anything to do with *begging*, or *going cap in hand*.

Activity 12.3

If the word *handicap* has nothing to do with begging or going 'cap in hand' in its earlier recorded meanings, should we still avoid using it as a 'politically incorrect' word when referring to people with disabilities?

Activity 12.4

There is evidence that people are divided in their preferences for using one of the alternative acceptable terms *disabled people* or *people with disabilities*. Do you prefer one or the other? What differences in meaning and connotation are there between the two terms, if any?

The booklet *Disability Etiquette* gives a list of terms to use and not to use:

Do not say	Say
deaf and dumb	*deaf, partially deaf, deafened, hard of hearing*
victim of, crippled by, suffering from, afflicted by	*person who has, person with, person who experienced*
wheelchair-bound,	*wheelchair user,*
confined to a wheelchair	*person who uses a wheel chair*
mental handicap	*people with learning difficulties*
handicap	
spastic	
cripple	
retarded	
defective	
mentally deficient	
blind as a bat	

Activity 12.5

Discuss your response to the 'Do not say' terms and the request that we should not use them. What alternative words or phrases could you use for those that do not have a suggestion in the 'Say' column?

We can illustrate the strong feelings produced in people who agree and diagree with suggestions like these about language use. In August 1986 there was a report in a newspaper with this headline:

Cripple beaten to death at home

Activity 12.6

(i)   What is your immediate reaction to the headline?
(ii) Read the following series of 'Letters to the Editor' which were published in the paper during the following three weeks
(iii) Summarise the main arguments on both sides.
(iv) In your opinion, was the use of the word *cripple* in the headline 'offensive and demeaning' or 'honest and clear'?
(v)   Can a word 'in itself' be offensive (see letter 7)?
(iv) On which side do you find yourself after studying the letters?

1   Sir, – I wonder how a sensitive newspaper such as yours can permit the "disabled person" or "person with a disability" of your feature pages to become a "cripple" when he/she is dead. –
    Yours faithfully,
    J. O.
    The Association of Carers

2 A lame way with words

Sir, – I am puzzled and disturbed by the objection of the Association of Carers to your use of the word "cripple" in a headline. There is nothing demeaning here in the word "cripple", which succinctly identifies the particular and relevant disability from which the victim suffered.

A cumbersome expression such as the Association's "person with a disability" is so wide that it is almost meaningless; it would include a person who lacked only a sense of smell and could perhaps be understood to extend to a person whose only distinguishing characteristic lay in dyslexia. ...

I am, yours faithfully,

B. C.

St Alban's

3 When language is a handicap

Sir, – As one crippled for life in late childhood I could not agree more with B. C., who mocks the current mealy-mouthed banning of the one word in the English language which clearly and crisply defines my physical limitations.

Can we doubt that if Helen Keller were alive today she would not be listed, matter-of-factly, as deaf, dumb and blind, but rather fed into a computer as one suffering from aural, oral, orthodontal and visual handicap?

Rather than this deadspeak let's have the guts to call a spade a spade!

Yours,

A. J.

Carlisle

4

Sir, – B. C's wish for a term which defines people with disabilites within a precise and exclusive grouping is a poor and illusory justification for using unpleasant terms. Disability is neither clear cut nor confined to "the disabled".

Many methods of labelling minority groups begin with a "neutral" description. Such descriptions only acquire a cutting edge if they are frequently used in a disparaging way. The term "cripple" has such demeaning from longstanding use, and which suggest that alms and charity are the appropriate response.

The term "disabled person" is unhelpful since it suggests that we are disabled through and through. Our acceptance in society should be on the basis of what we have to offer and not on those parts of ourselves which do not function properly.

J. M.

Forum of People with Disabilities

5 Labels that add insult to disability's injury

Sir, – Language is indeed a handicap and there's no end to semantic hair-splitting. We find the World Health organisation's classification of "impairments, handicaps, and disabilities" of little help in clarifying the issue.

For many years now, like all our "with-it" colleagues, we have used "people with special needs" as a more positive term. Given our wide-ranging area of interests, the phrase has never presented any problems.

Nevertheless, I admit the phrase does evoke a bureaucratic and legal nightmare. Think of the needs of the elderly, dyslexics, people with mental illness, etc, all lumped together. Think of a secretary of state for special needs!

But it does seem to present a more positive line of thinking. Evolution lies in moving from the general to the particular: from the nonsensical "cripple" to "a person whose special need can be met by a wheelchair". Most people are affected by demeaning labels.

I shall never forget my astonishment when first hearing the word "retardates" from American professionals. Its general use to describe people with brain injuries stopped only a few years ago. I have yet to come across a more demeaning term than this.

Yours sincerely,

J. S.

Handicapped Persons Research Unit

Newcastle-upon-Tyne Polytechnic

6

Sir, – I am astounded by J. S.'s letter suggesting the use of "a person whose special need can be met by wheel chairs" in preference to "cripple." The fact is that words like "cripple" and "spastic" are being lost from polite conversation because some thoughtless people choose to use them as sneering insults.

I'm fed up with losing words from the language for this reason.

We should use "cripple" and "spastic" as honest descriptions of people and, where possible, correct those who use them as insults.

Or am I to call my diabetic father "a person whose special need can be met by insulin"? –

Yours sincerely,

J.C.

London NW 5

7 Harsh words for the disabled

Sir, – Speaking as someone who has cerebral palsy I must take issue with J. C.'s letter. It simply is not true to suggest that words like "spastic" and "cripple" have been devalued because some thoughtless people have chosen to use them in the wrong context.

The words themselves are offensive, in the same way as "lunatic asylum" and "nigger" are extremely offensive. Sometimes, however, it is necessary to be on the receiving end before one realises the full impact of such words. –

Yours faithfully,

L. W.

Solihull

8 Sir, – Some of the contributions to the debate about how disability should be defined are either misleading or dangerous.

First, the "cripple" is returning to prominent use in the English language, as our bulky file of newspaper clippings will testify. It has, however, got more to do with the definition of crime and how we perceive it than with disability.

Certain sections of the press realise that "cripple" is a far from neutral description of physical impairment. For them it ideally represents the "helpless victim" of criminal or mean acts. Combined with age and sex, this imagery becomes even more potent, (e.g. "a crippled old lady"). Despicable acts need to be reported as such. But isn't the real reason for bringing the "cripple" out of retirement to keep public opinion firmly behind the law and order society?

What of the other terms suggested? "People with special needs" is very convenient for professionals and others who earn their living meeting these so-called "special needs" (usually segregated second-rate services). But why should our education, housing, means of mobility and environmental access be so special? If my wheelchair, which enables me to get about in reasonable comfort, is "special", then so are shoes.

Starting from the false premise that disabled people are not whole human beings, the term "people with disabilities" divides us into two parts in the vain hope that what is desirable (i.e. the "person") will obscure what is undesirable (the physical impairment). This is simply resorting to escapism. Black people realised long ago that terminology (i.e. how oppressed social groups are defined) is political. Likewise, disabled people have increasingly seen the importance of defining their own situation and their own experience.

We believe it is crucial not to confuse descriptions of physical conditions (impairment) with the oppressive social conditions we experience every day of our lives (disability). J. M. [*letter* 4] says "The term 'disabled person' is unhelpful since it suggests that we are disabled through and through". So we are, but by society and the environment which surrounds us – not by any incidental physical impairment. –
Yours faithfully,
K.L.
Greater Manchester Coalition of Disabled People

12.2   Language use and racism

Racism is defined in the *OED* as,

> The theory that distinctive human characteristics and abilities are determined by race.

But to be called *a racist* in contemporary society is to be accused of a social and moral offence, which may be denied or not understood by the person being accused. It is an area of experience highly charged with emotional conflict, and one that it is difficult to debate objectively or dispassionately.

Nevertheless, it is necessary to look at some of the evidence for attitudes described as *racist*, that is, an attitude determined exclusively by the fact of another person's race, and given away by the use of *racist language*. Here is an example from a newspaper report:

Jury clear man who used word 'nigger'

A jury at the Central Criminal Court decided yesterday that a man who used the words "niggers, wogs and coons" in a speech was not inciting racial hatred. The verdict came within 10 minutes after the jury of eight woman and four man heard Judge M—, QC, say that the words "niggers, wogs and coons" were not in themselves unlawful.

J. R— aged 41, was being retried after a jury failed to agree on a verdict.

The court was told that Mr R— had told a political meeting that he could not refer to coloured immigrants, so he would call them "niggers, wogs and coons".

Judge M— told the jury in his summing-up that at school his nick-name was "nigger". The judge concluded: "In this England of ours at the moment we are allowed to have our own views still, thank goodness". He added: "And long may it last. ... You have got to look at the circumstances and you have got to allow toleration and freedom of the individual, otherwise we are all caught in the vice of dictatorship, repression and slavery."

After the verdict the judge told Mr R— "You have been rightly acquitted but in these days and times it would be well if you were careful to use moderate language. By all means propagate the views you have, but try to avoid invoking the sort of action which has been taken against you. I wish you well."

"Law is an ass"

Mr W. T, secretary of the West Indian Standing Conference, said of the acquit-tal: "I am terribly disappointed and disturbed by this decision. If the law says that calling people 'niggers, wogs and coons' is not incitement to racial violence, then the law is an ass."

(Excerpts from a judgment reported in *The Times*, January 1978 © Times Newspapers 1978)

Activity 12.7

What is your response to:

(i) The use of the phrase *niggers, wogs and coons.*

(ii) The jury's verdict (remember that the defendant was accused of inciting racial hatred).

(iii) The judge's reported summing-up and quoted statements to the defendant.

A different but related problem of the use of language is presented in this newspaper report in July 1987:

Inner city task forces get black leaders

Black community workers have been appointed to head two of the much-criticised task forces which are being expanded by the Government as part of its inner city drive. ...

The report led to the following letter:

Dear Sir,

Your headline "Inner city task forces get black leaders" on the Government's much criticized task force is very revealing. It is surely very timely to question its assumptions.

The notion of black "leaders" goes back to the view British colonialists have had that so called "tribalism" is inherent amongst black people. It assumes that we are best controlled when we have a "spokesman" or leader, who is at best self-appointed, and, more likely, imposed by others.

In fairness to the two men named in your report, I am sure they do not see themselves as leaders, but as people who have been employed to do a job for the benefit of the black community.

However, the belief that the black community is an amorphous whole, made up of childlike individuals awaiting leadership, is surely now acknowledged to be colonialist. Black people do have a common and shared experience of racism, but many of us, particularly younger black people, are no longer prepared to be "dealt" with. As we assert our rights to play an active role within all aspects of British society, we do not expect to be treated as clients.

Were I to write articles about white community leaders, your white readers would feel patronised and insulted. Perhaps you can now understand how we feel.

Yours faithfully,

L.B.

London

Activity 12.8

Explain and discuss the point of view presented in the letter.

The word *black* has different connotations for different people. Consider the following list of meanings, which have developed from its basic meaning for the colour black and the derived meaning, *of or pertaining to the negro race*, first recorded in 1852. It has since then become an acceptable word, as in the phrase *black is beautiful*, in relation to *white* as a general description of racial colour, but its other connotations make its use 'politically incorrect' for many people.

Activity 12.9

(i)   Is there a common feature in the meaning and connotations of the following words and phrases from the *OED* that contain the word *black*?
(ii) If these connotations are felt to be insulting to black people, is it right that others should respect their feelings and avoid using the words and phrases?
(iv) Look up the connotations and related meanings of *white* in a good dictionary. Are they similar to or different from those of *black*?

black

soiled, dirty
having dark purposes, malignant; deadly, baneful, disastrous, sinister
foul, iniquitous, atrocious
dismal, gloomy, sad
clouded with anger, threatening, boding ill
indicating disgace, censure etc

The word is recorded as a verb in its derived sense *to sully, defame*. It occurs as a modifying adjective in many common phrases with similar connotations. For example:

black arts	*magic, necromancy*
blackball	*to exclude from a club or society*
black book	*to be in someone's black books* means *to be out of favour*
black-browed	*frowning, scowling*
blackguard	*the vagabond or criminal class; an unprincipled scroundrel*
blackleg	*someone who works when others are on strike ('scab'); a swindler*
black list	*list of persons under suspicion, censure or punishment*
black looks	*facial expression of disapproval*
blackmail	*payment extorted by intimidation*
Black Maria	*a police van used for transporting prisoners*
black mark	*mark of censure against someone's name*
black market	*a market where goods are sold illegally*
black mood	*a mood of melancholy, depression.*
black sheep	*the member of a family who has disgrced it; scoundrel*
black spot	*a place of danger; place on a road with a high accident rate*

A problem arises over the use of other phrases with the word *black* which have no unfavourable connotations in themselves, but which, some say, should also be avoided because the connotations of *black* inevitably go with them.

Activity 12.10

Is it necessary or desirable to avoid using the following phrases?
black and blue; *black belt* (in judo); *blackberry; blackbird; blackboard; black box* (in an aircraft); *black coffee; a black eye; blackhead; a black hole* (in astronomy); *black ice; a blackout; black pudding; blacksmith; blackthorn. coal-black, jet-black, pitch-black; black in the face, black and blue.*

The following extract from a newspaper report dating from June 1991 describes the problems that the interviewee encountered working in an architect's office, and is evidence that the problem discussed in Activity 12.10 is real one.

I couldn't be racist, could I?

"Now we must learn not to use colour in a negative or pejorative way. *Nigger in the woodpile* is out, naturally; but so are phrases such as *black looks*. When the other day I used the word *blackmail*, the guy from Barbados at the next drawing-board said, 'Finna! I'm surprised at you!' so we discussed it and came up with *extortion* as an alternative."

Isn't this going too far?

"Look, that's treating it like a cross-word. It misses out your personal involvement. *Why* use expressions that cause pain, if it can be avoided? We have learned to talk about *humanity* instead of *mankind* and say *chair* instead of *chairman*; it is time to extend the same courtesy and sensitivity to racial minorities, to avoid diminishing them."

12.3 Language use and sexism

The reference to avoiding the use of *mankind* and *chairman* in the report just quoted introduces a third important area of 'politically correct' language use. The arguments over words and language which, it is said, denigrate women, or 'make them invisible' have been going on for a long time, and from the feminist point of view some progress has been made in the widespread acceptance of, for example, *chair* or *chairperson*, instead of *chairman* and in the accepted use of *Ms* instead of *Mrs* or *Miss*.

The following extracts will help to focus on some of the common problems in the argument over sexist language. Here, for example, is part of a short handbook issued by the trade union NALGO (National Association of Local Government Officers), *Watch Your Language! Non-sexist Language: A Guide for NALGO Members (1987).*

When men begin to take on jobs that have been traditionally done by women and which have feminine titles, those titles are automatically changed. No accusations of triviality are made; it is obvious – no man would take on a female title. *Matrons* become *senior* or *divisional nursing officers*; ward *sisters* become *charge nurses*. ...

How does bias happen?

Language can exclude women. The words *man, he, his* and *him* are often used in referring to human beings of either sex. ...

example	*possible alternative*
manpower	workforce; staff
manning	staffing; workforce; working; running
man-made	artificial
to a man	everyone; without exception; unanimously
man-hours	work hours ...

12.3.1 *The generic masculine*

The word *generic* means *general, not specific*. A generic word is one that can refer to both women and men. There is no singular third-person pronoun that is unmarked for **gender** (masculine, feminine or neuter) in English – we have to use *he/she/it*. A problem arises when we use **indefinite pronouns** like *anybody, somebody*, or generic nouns that might refer to either a man or a woman, like *person, applicant, member, doctor, teacher* and so on – which pronoun is to be used after the first reference?

For example, in the sentence,

> One of the most important duties of a **shop steward** is to discuss problems with **his** members.

the pronoun *his* is inappropriate for a female shop steward. The traditional answer was to declare that the masculine gender was more important because the male sex was superior to the female sex: it was called 'the most worthy gender'. In time, this concept was replaced by that of 'the most customary gender'. In 1850 an Act of Parliament was passed called *The Abbreviation Bill*, which included this clause

> Be it enacted, That in all Acts to be hereafter made Words importing the Masculine Gender shall be deemed and taken to include Females, and the Singular to include the Plural, and the Plural the Singular, unless the contrary as to Gender or Number is expressly provided.

This use of the **generic masculine** 'to include Females' is now disputed, and ways of avoiding it are recommended. One way is to use the pronoun *their* as a singular, which is similar to our use of *you* as both singular and plural. The plural third-person pronouns *they/them/their* are not marked for gender, so you could say,

> One of the most important duties of a shop steward is to discuss problems with their members.

This solution is, however, not approved by some people who insist that *they/them/their* must refer to plural referents. Alternatively, you could make the first noun plural,

> One of the most important duties of shop stewards is to discuss problems with their members.

12.3.2 *References to women*

Further advice in the NALGO booklet is self-explanatory:

> Terms which patronise or belittle women, as wives or otherwise, should never be used: e.g. *the better half; the little woman; the weaker sex; the fair sex; dumb blondes; libber*

> Don't use phrases which refer to women through their husbands: e.g. *Architect's wife Elsie Smith; Philip Grey and his wife Jean ...*

> *Girls* are female humans under 18 years of age. After that they become *women*.

Activity 12.11

Rewrite the following sentences avoiding what has been described as biased language:

Retired members and their wives.
The rights, privileges and liabilities of each member shall be personal to himself ...
The Branch Secretary shall convene meetings...he shall act...on his retirement, he shall hand over...

The NALGO recommendation, 'don't use phrases which refer to women through their husbands' is clearly illustrated by the next two newspaper extracts dating from July 1991, the first a short paragraph from an article about Steve Turner, a union official, and the second a letter to the editor from Deborah Turner:

Activity 12.12

Explain Deborah Turner's objections to the paragraph.
Are you in sympathy with her point of view?

Article extract

Married to the daughter of an air commodore, Mr Turner, a father of one daughter, has been a journalist for more than 30 years.

Part of a letter in reply

I see sexism rears its ugly head, even in your columns. I refer to the piece on my husband, Steve Turner. ...
In it Paul Myers refers to me as wife of and daughter of. I am, in fact, a person in my own right. I have a name and I have spent most of my life as a journalist. ...
By the way, my father is not an Air Commodore, he is an Air Vice-Marshal and Companion of the Bath. ...
Deborah Turner, *née* Thomas

12.3.3   *The problem of* man *and* -man

The dictionary defines two meanings of the word *man*, firstly a **generic** term for *humanity* to include both females and males, secondly a word specifying a member of the male sex. This ambiguity has led people to try to avoid using *man* when talking about women and men together, and can be illustrated in the following two extracts from a daily newspaper in November 1991. The first extract has nothing to do with the subject of sexism, but is discussing hymns as 'powerful social and political statements' in religious worship. The second extract is a letter published a day or two afterwards.

Activity 12.13

Discuss the need for 'pruning' writing of sexist language. Does the revised verse of the hymn mean the same as the original?

The power of the simple folk poem

Hymns are Christian folk poems which provide the strongest expression of the folk religion which is still deeply embedded in our so-called secular society. ...

Another hymn-writer, Fred Kaan, rejects many of the values so keenly espoused by the compilers of the 1889 *Ancient and Modern*, sanctioning a rather different world order: "All that kills abundant living,/ Let it from the earth be banned;/ Pride of status, race or schooling,/ Dogmas keeping man from man." ...

Hymn and hers: non-sexist verse

From Dr Fred Kaan

Sir: Brian Castle, in his welcome article "The power of the simple folk poem", quotes a few lines from my "Hymn on Human Rights", including the words "dogmas keeping man from man".

Having since then "pruned" my hymn texts of sexist language, I would appreciate your publishing the verse in its definitive form:

All that kills abundant living,
let it from the earth be banned;
pride of status, race or schooling,
dogmas that obscure your plan.
In our common quest for justice
may we hallow life's brief span.

We have seen examples of the use of the word *man* in ways that some people regard as sexist. A similar problem arises over its use as a suffix to a word, as in *chairman*. It is argued on one side that in being used as a suffix, *-man* is no longer specific to males, and that you can (and do) have a woman as chairman of a meeting or organisation. On the other side, it is argued that the suffix continues to retain its reference to male gender. One possible solution, if it could be enforced, would be to substitute another word as suffix, and suggestions for this have been published from time to time. Here are two fairly recent examples:

Letters to the Editor

1. February 1983

I keep waiting for somebody to mention it, but nobody does. There is in English a venerable, perfectly decent, non-sexist personal suffix. Who could construe a "chairbody" as callowly right-on, a "spokesbody" as overly secretive or the "postbody" as untraditional? Could anybody think any wrong of a "milkbody"?

Yours

B.D.

London

2. June 1988

I would like to endorse the suggestion that "bod" be used to replace "man" in the latter's generic, sexist sense.

The need for such a term has long been apparent, and "bod's" linguistic characteristics make it ideally suited to the purpose: like "man" it is monosyllabic and can be used enclitically, unlike "person" which is too long to be comfortable and needs to have a stress; it is general and so avoids the explicit circumlocutions we get with terms like "fire-fighter" and "refuse collector"; and it has the same phonetic structure as "man" and so can be easily substituted for it in traditional and established usages such as: one bod went to mow...; time and tide wait for no bod; the bod in the moon; everybod; and even if you want, bodhole cover.

In short, this use of "bod" conforms to the historic genius of the English language, and could quickly establish itself. Now is the time for all good bods to come to the aid of parity, by using it.

G.T.

Oxford

Activity 12.14

(i)   *Letter 1*
Experiment with the use of *-body* as a suffix in a number of words at present ending in *-man* (see section 12.3.5 for some examples). Is the proposal acceptable?

(ii) *Letter 2*
Explain or find out the meaning of the linguistic terms used to justify using *bod* for *man* -
(a) it is monosyllabic;
(b) it can be used enclitically;
(c) it is unlike *person*, which is too long and needs to have a stress;
(d) it is general;
(e) it has the same phonetic structure as *man*.

12.3.4 *Gender-specific nouns*

Activity 12.15 ——————————————————————

Read the following short story and solve the puzzle.

> A father and his son were seriously injured in a car accident.
> On the way to the hospital in the ambulance the father died.
> The boy was taken to the emergency operating room and the
> surgeon called. On seeing the boy, however, the surgeon said,
> "I can't operate on this boy. He's my son."

If you found this story a riddle, the reason is that you assumed that the surgeon was a man. You did so in default of other evidence. Although we all know that some women are surgeons, the majority are men. At one time all surgeons were men. This common response to the naming of a trade or profession has been called a **default assumption** – what we assume unless we are told otherwise.

Here is another example in a letter to the editor published in September 1987:

> Women students emerging from a 1987 City & Guilds exam-
> ination in dress and design complained to their tutor that they
> had not been prepared for a question requiring design for men's
> clothes.
>
> Their tutor refuted that there was such a question on the
> paper, only to be told that the question referred to required
> designs for a "young executive". The students had all assumed
> this person to be male and no-one had answered this particular
> question.
> Yours sincerely,
> **J.W.**
> Newark

12.3.5 *Male/masculine suffixes*

It is because so many trades and professions were formerly occupied by men only that the word *man* was affixed to a noun to provide a useful word for the man who did the job.

Activity 12.16 ——————————————————————

In how many of the following words with the suffix *-man* can you satisfactorily substitute *-woman* or another feminine suffix? Make a selection of those which would be acceptable, and those which would be unacceptable, and try to explain why.

-man

airman	countryman	footman	sportsman	postman
bandsman	craftsman	foreman	kinsman	salesman
barman	draughtsman	gentleman	milkman	spokesman
businessman	dustman	groundsman	ombudsman	statesman
chairman	fireman	gunman	ploughman	tradesman
clergyman	fisherman	horseman	policeman	workman

The argument that in all these words *-man* is a suffix, not a word, and therefore does not specifically refer to males is partly supported by the fact that the pronunciation of the syllable is always unstressed, and has the reduced vowel /ə/ – /mən/. These words are not compounds like:

ape-man	cowman	handyman	snowman	weatherman
caveman	freeman	husbandman	strongman	yes-man

in which *man* is pronounced /mæn/ and is stressed. But this linguistic argument is not very convincing when you consider the 'default assumptions' that most words ending in *-man* still carry – they generally refer to men, not women. The argument is not linguistic, but social and political, and language use happens to mark social and political attitudes, which are always changing and developing.

12.3.6 Female/feminine suffixes

The suffix *-man* is objected to when the word may refer to both women and men, because *-man* still carries a male/masculine meaning. But the specific use of a suffix which specifies *female* has been equally attacked.

Activity 12.17

Ils there any difference of meaning between the two following sentences? If so, can you explain it?
    The actress said, "I am a bad actress."
    The actress said, "I am a bad actor."

The contemporary objection to the use of the suffix *-ess* to mark the feminine of its masculine equivalent is that it is one of a number of '*trivialising* suffixes for women in professions' (Deborah Cameron in *Feminism and Linguistic Theory*, 1985). Seventy years ago a case was made out for the adoption of 'feminine designations' by H. W. Fowler in *A Dictionary of Modern English Usage* (1926):

> This article is intended as a counter-protest. The authoress, poetess, & paintress, & sometimes the patroness & the inspectress, take exception to the indication of sex in these designations. They regard the distinction as derogatory to them & as implying inequality between the sexes; an author is an   5
> author, that is all that concerns any reader, & it is impertinent curiosity to want to know whether the author is male or female.

These ladies neither are nor pretend to be making their objection in the interests of the language or of people in general; they object in their own interests only; this they are entitled to   10 do, but still it is lower ground, & general convenience & the needs of the King's English, if these are against them, must be reckoned of more importance than their sectional claims. Are these against them? Undoubtedly. First, any word that does the work of two or more by packing several notions into one is a   15 gain (the more civilised a language the more such words it possesses), if certain conditions are observed: it must not be cumbersome; it should for choice be correctly formed; & it must express a compound notion that is familiar enough to need a name.   20

Secondly, with the coming extension of women's vocations, feminines for vocation-words are a special need of the future; everyone knows the inconveninece of being uncertain whether a doctor is a man or a woman; hesitation in establishing the word *doctress* is amazing in a people regarded as nothing if not   25 practical. Far from needing to reduce the number of our sex-words, we should do well to indulge in real neologisms such as *teacheress, singeress, & danceress,* the want of which drives us to *cantatrice, danseuse,* & the like; *authoress & poetess & paintress* are not neologisms.   30

But are not the objectors, besides putting their own interests above those of the public, actually misjudging their own? ...

Activity 12.18

(i) Assess Fowler's argument and make your own reply either supporting or opposing him.

(ii) Use the following lists of words to illustrate your own point of view in the debate about 'ways in which English insults, excludes and trivialises women' (Deborah Cameron in the same book).
Make a selection of words and discuss their reference and connotations, e.g. are they generic (applying to both women and men) or inherently male/masculine, or female/feminine in reference? What is their 'default assumption'? And so on.

Female/feminine suffixes

actress	heiress	peeress	fishwife	charwoman
authoress	hostess	poetess	housewife	gentlewoman
baroness	laundress	priestess	midwife	horsewoman
conductress	lioness	princess		needlewoman
duchess	manageress	seamstress		sportswoman
goddess	mayoress	stewardess		townswoman
governess	mistress	waitress		washerwoman

master

master-class	form-master	master	quartermaster	stationmaster
choirmaster	headmaster	postmaster	scoutmaster	

-er/-or/-ar suffixes

ambassador	doorkeeper	householder	photographer	speaker
author	dressmaker	housekeeper	picnicker	spinster
backbencher	editor	interviewer	player	stockbroker
baker	employer	ironmonger	playgoer	streaker
banker	fielder	joy-rider	plumber	streetwalker
beekeeper	financier	juror	preacher	stripper
bookmaker	fletcher	lawyer	premier	supervisor
brewer	forecaster	lecturer	prior	surveyor
bricklayer	freethinker	liar	Quaker	tailor
broadcaster	friar	lodger	reader	taxpayer
burglar	gamekeeper	member	rescuer	teacher
busker	gangster	milliner	ringleader	teenybopper
butcher	glazier	neighbour	robber	thatcher
butler	governor	nosy-parker	sailor	treasurer
caretaker	grocer	onlooker	scholar	troublemaker
cheer-leader	hairdresser	pastor	sculptor	undertaker
commander	hijacker	pawnbroker	shopwalker	waiter
courier	hitchhiker	pensioner	skier	watchmaker
courtier	housebreaker	philosopher	soldier	wrestler

Activity 12.19

(i) Put the following words into sentences that use them to refer to either men or women, or both. Pair off as many words as you can (e.g. *dog* v. *bitch*). You will find some words that are usually only applied to one sex. Then consider the connotations of the words as favourable or unfavourable. Are the connotations similar for women and men?

(ii) What conclusions do you draw from this activity about words which are used to describe women and men?

The words are listed in alphabetical order. You will need to sort them.

bachelor	effeminate	master	spinster
bitch	to father (vb)	mistress	tomboy
buck	fox	to mother (vb)	vixen
bull	governor	old man	witch
cat	governess	old maid	wizard
cow	macho	queen	womanly
dame	manly	ram	
dog	mannish	shrew	

Booklist

The following list contains a selection of books that are mainly intended for reference by teachers and lecturers, though some are written for non-specialists and may be suitable for class-room use. Books with accompanying cassette tapes of spoken data are marked with an asterisk *.

1   Variety, change and the idea of correct English

Tony Crowley, *The Politics of Discourse*: *The Standard Language Question in British Cultural Debates* (Macmillan, 1989).

David Crystal, *Who Cares about English Usage?* (Penguin, 1984).

John Honey, *The Language Trap: Race, Class and the 'Standard English' Issue in British Schools* (National Council for Educational Standards, 1983).

John Honey, *Does Accent Matter?* (Faber, 1989).

James and Lesley Milroy, *Authority in Language: Investigating Language Prescription and Standardisation* (Routledge, 1985).

W. H. Mittins *et al.*, *Attitudes to English Usage* (Oxford University Press, 1970).

W. R. O'Donnell and L. Todd, *Variety in Contemporary English* (Allen & Unwin, 1980).

Randolph Quirk, *The Use of English*, 2nd edn (Longman, 1968).

E. H. Ryan, *Attitudes towards Language Variation* (Arnold, 1982).

Peter Trudgill, *Accent, Dialect and the School* (Arnold, 1975).

2   Dialects and Standard English – the past

Charles Barber, *Early Modern English* (Blackwell, 1976).

A. C. Baugh and T. Cable, *A History of the English Language* (Routledge, 1978).

G. L. Brook, *A History of the English Language* (Blackwell, 1963).

David Burnley, *A History of the English Language: A Source Book* (Longman, 1992).

Dennis Freeborn, *From Old English to Standard English* (Macmillan, 1992).

Geoffrey Hughes, *Words in Time* (Blackwell, 1988).

Dick Leith, *A Social History of English* (Routledge, 1983).

Simeon Potter, *Our Language* (Penguin, 1950).

3 Dialects and Standard English – the present

G. L. Brook, *English Dialects* (Blackwell, 1963).

A. Hughes and P. Trudgill , **English Accents and Dialects* (Arnold, 1979).

K. M. Petyt, *The Study of Dialect* (Blackwell).

David Sutcliffe, *British Black English* (Blackwell, 1982).

Loreto Todd, *Modern Englishes: Pidgins and Creoles* (Routledge, 1984).

Loreto Todd, *Some Day Been Dey: West African Pidgin Folk Tales* (Routledge, 1979).

P. Trudgill and J. Hanna, **International English* (Arnold, 1982).

Martin Wakelin, *Discovering English Dialects* (Shire Publications, 1979).

4 Regional accents and Received Pronunciation

Gillian Brown, *Listening to Spoken English* (Longman, 1977).

A. C. Gimson, *An Introduction to the Pronunciation of English*, 3rd edn (standard reference text) (Arnold, 1980).

Peter Roach, **English Phonetics and Phonology: A Practical Course*, 2nd edn (Cambridge University Press, 1991).

J. C. Wells, *Accents of English: 1 Introduction; 2 The British Isles; 3 Beyond the British Isles* (Cambridge University Press, 1982).

5 Spoken English and written English

D. Crystal and D. Davy, **Advanced Conversational English* (Longman, 1975).

Michael Stubbs, *Language and Literacy* (Routledge, 1980).

6 Learning to talk

M. Fletcher and P. Garman, *Language Acquisition: Studies in First Language Development* (Cambridge University Press, 1979).

Paul Fletcher, *A Child's Learning of English* (Blackwell).

J. and P. de Villiers, *Early Language* (Fontana, 1979).

Katherine Perera, *Children's Writing and Reading* (Blackwell, 1984).

7 Variety and style in spoken English – I: grammar and vocabulary

D. Crystal and D. Davy, *Investigating English Style* (Longman, 1969).

Michael Stubbs, *Discourse Analysis* (Blackwell, 1983).

Max Atkinson, *Our Masters' Voices: The Language and Body Language of Politics* (Methuen, 1984).

8 Variety and style in spoken English – II: conversation

Deirdre Burton, *Dialogue and Discourse* (Routledge, 1980).

David Langford, *Analysing Talk* (Macmillan, 1993).

Ronald Wardhaugh, *How Conversation Works* (Blackwell, 1987).

9   Variety in written English – I: reporting the news

Dwight Bolinger, *Language the Loaded Weapon: The Use and Abuse of Language Today* (Longman, 1980).

Roger Fowler *et al.*, *Language and Control* (Routledge, 1979).

Roger Fowler, *Language in the News: Discourse and Ideology in the Press* (Routledge, 1991).

G. Kress and R. Hodge, *Language as Ideology* (Routledge, 1979).

G. Lakoff and M. Johnson, *Metaphors We Live By* (University of Chicago Press, 1980).

(In chapter 9, the analysis of newspaper reporting derives from R. Fowler *et al.*, *Language and Control*, chapters 6–8.)

10   Variety in written English – II: style

David Birch, *Language, Literature and Critical Practice: Ways of Analysing Text* (Routledge, 1989).

N. F. Blake, *Non-standard Language in English Literature* (Blackwell, 1981).

N. F. Blake, *Shakespeare's Language: An Introduction* (Macmillan, 1983).

Ronald Carter (ed.), *Language and Literature* (Allen & Unwin, 1982).

Ronald Carter and Walter Nash, *Seeing Through Language: A Guide to Styles of English Writing* (Blackwell, 1990).

R. Chapman, *The Language of English Literature* (Arnold, 1982).

Roger Fowler, *Linguistic Criticism* (Oxford University Press, 1986).

G. Leech and A. Short, *Style in Fiction* (Longman, 1981).

Walter Nash, *Language in Popular Fiction* (Routledge, 1990).

Walter Nash, *Rhetoric: The Wit of Persuasion* (Blackwell).

John Stephens and Ruth Waterhouse, *Literature, Language & Change: From Chaucer to the Present* (Routledge, 1990).

Michael Toolan, *Narrative: A Critical Linguistic Introduction* (Routledge, 1988).

Katie Wales, *A Dictionary of Stylistics* (Longman, 1989).

Henry Widdowson, *Stylistics and the Teaching of Literature* (Longman, 1975).

11   The language and sound patterns of verse

Derek Attridge, *The Rhythms of English Poetry* (Longman, 1983).

Geoffrey Leech, *A Linguistic Guide to English Poetry* (Longman, 1969).

(In chapter 11, section 11.5, the distinction between spoken stress and metrical beat is taken from Derek Attridge, *The Rhythms of English Poetry*.)

12   Language and 'politically correct' usage

Deborah Cameron, *Feminism and Linguistic Theory* (Macmillan, 1985).

Jennifer Coates, *Women, Men and Language* (Longman, 1989).

D. Graddol and J. Swann, *Gender Voices* (Blackwell, 1989).

General language study and linguistics

Jean Aitchison, *Language Change: Progress or Decay?* (Fontana, 1981).
Anthony Burgess, *Language Made Plain* (Fontana, 1975).
Ronald Carter (ed.), *Linguistics and the Teacher* (Routledge, 1982).
David Crystal, *What is Linguistics?* (Arnold, 1968).
V. Fromkin and R. Rodman, *An Introduction to Language,* 3rd edn (Holt, 1983).
Richard Hudson, *Invitation to Linguistics* (Robertson, 1984).

English Grammar

Textbooks:

Dennis Freeborn, *A Course Book in English Grammar* (Macmillan, 1987).
G. Leech, M. Deuchar and R. Hoogenraad, *English Grammar for Today*
    (Macmillan, 1982).
David Young, *Introducing English Grammar* (Hutchinson, 1984).

Reference grammars

David Crystal, *Rediscover Grammar* (Longman, 1988).
R. Quirk *et al., A Comprehensive Grammar of the English Language* (standard
    reference grammar) (Longman, 1985).
R. Quirk *et al., A Grammar of Contemporary English* (Longman, 1972).

The following textbooks are based on *A Grammar of Contemporary English*:

G. Leech and J. Svartvik, *A Communicative Grammar of English* (Longman, 1975).
R. Quirk and S. Greenbaum, *University Grammar of English* (Longman, 1973).

Index